CW01011289

Journey to the
Baobab Tree
Krys Latham

Journey to the Baobab Tree Copyright
© Krys Latham 2012

ISBN 978-0-9571983-0-2
Published by Krys Latham

www.kryslatham.co.uk

Cover design by Emma Latham

*The stories of our lives are the
most precious gift we can pass on
to those who come after us.*

Part One
Witek's Story

Drowning fish

All over Poland bombs were exploding and people dying as the Germans from the west and the Russians from the east joined forces to obliterate our nation. Yet we five children, in our remote forest region in Eastern Poland, were rejoicing because the lake near our home had frozen thick enough for skating.

Not long before Christmas, on a glorious sunny day, my oldest brother Peter and I spent the morning trying to make ourselves some ice-skating blades. Skaters had been coming to our lake from villages and towns, with leather skating boots or metal blades that screwed onto lace-up winter boots. But in our family, with five children to feed on a forest keeper's wage, there were no such luxuries.

So we'd been sawing and planing wedges of pine and nailing them to oblongs of thin flat wood, the size of the soles of our feet. We drilled holes in these for string so we could attach them to our galoshes, and we had attached wire along the bottom edge so they would glide better on the ice.

Flushed with excitement, in our threadbare coats and down-at-heel rubber galoshes, we ran over the snow-covered track with our sister and two younger brothers, past the frozen marshes on one side and forest on the other, to the lake.

'No one's got skates like these!' Peter said breathlessly

as he brushed the snow off a log to sit down to tie them on. He was right there! They were most certainly unique. But when we wobbled onto the ice, ankles buckled, the strings kept getting loose, the wire fell off, and the only gliding we did was on our bottoms.

In the end, bruised and defeated, we decided to call it a day as far as skating went, and agreed to go and take our old sledge out on the hill instead.

Peter was walking away, clutching his home-made skates, looking so disappointed. He stopped for a moment, looking longingly at the vast expanse of ice, and suddenly a huge smile broke out on his face. He'd obviously had another one of his ideas.

We looked at him doubtfully as he eagerly explained.

'No really!' he nodded. 'All we need is a wheel that would float. One of those from the go-cart we're making would do, and then a long wooden pole. We'll soon be gliding faster than any of the skaters! You'll see! This time it will work!'

So we hurried home for the things we needed - our father's axe and saw too - then hurried back to the lake, pulling the little ones on the sledge behind us.

Peter led us right out into the middle of the lake, and we hacked and sawed a small round hole in the ice just a bit bigger than our wooden go-cart wheel. We fastened one end of our pole to the floating wheel, and the other end to the sledge and Antony, always the daring one, jumped on. The rest of us leaped out of the way as Peter gave the sledge a mighty shove. Antony whizzed round and round, as if on a very fast merry-go-round, screaming in exhilaration.

Now we were all clamouring to have a go, and Peter was beaming with pride and delight at the success of his latest invention. It was the best winter's afternoon we'd ever had on the lake.

Long after the town skaters had gone home, we were still there, not wanting to stop. Though finally, as the sun began to set, we unhitched the sledge from the plank and fished the wooden wheel out of the water.

But that wasn't all we fished out!

To our astonishment, fish had gathered round the hole. Not sprats, or tiddlers like those our parents used to catch at the edge of the lake on summer nights. These were big fish, carp - the kind that you needed a boat to fish for in the deepest part of the lake. Here were all these huge fish, crowding around the hole.

We peered down at them, as open-mouthed as the gasping fish.

'They're drowning!' Peter said. 'They need water that has air in it - they suffocate under the ice.'

'Oh, the poor things!'

'They really do look like they're gulping air!'

'And there's so many of them!'

'Well, what are we waiting for?' Peter took his knitted gloves off and plunged his hands into the icy water and pulled out a huge slippery carp. It was still alive but didn't struggle as wildly as you'd expect a caught carp to struggle.

'There's no fight left in them!' he said dropping it into

the sledge and giving it a quick wallop over the head with the back of the axe to put it out of its misery.

We took turns pulling the fish out, blowing on our hands blue with cold and laughing at the surprise our mother would have when we came home with a sledge overflowing with fish. We had never even *seen* fish as big as that in our lives, let alone having them to take home and eat!

Electricity had not yet reached those remote forest areas of Eastern Poland so we had no fridge or freezer, but we knew storing such a great slippery heap would be no problem. They would be frozen in water outside and stored under the snow.

We joyfully sang Christmas carols all the way home, so excited at the thought of the fish fried in butter that we would be eating with our soup that night. It was such a rare and wonderful treat. I simply can't tell you how good it tasted!

The following day our father sent Peter and me to call at the other forest keeper's cabin just down the track from ours, and also at Uzbielerz village where our grandfather lived, knocking on all the doors, telling everyone about the fish dying in the lake. And everyone who was able to - practically the whole village - hurried to the lake to make holes in the ice to pull out the fish. They would have died anyway; this way at least they wouldn't be wasted, and because of the many holes that were made in the ice, perhaps some survived that might otherwise have died.

Throughout the devastated towns and cities of Poland,

shops were empty, food scarce, and people hungry, but that winter, in our forest near the lake, the delicious smell of frying carp was everywhere and we ate better than we'd ever eaten before.

It seems to me now, on looking back, that it's as if we were being strengthened for the hard times of hunger soon to come.

Fresh lake water freezes over at minus two degrees. As our lake had frozen so thick and solid, the temperature that winter must have dropped to minus four. Little did we know that soon we would be struggling to survive in temperatures lower than minus *forty*, where even to breathe would be painful, and such good food – indeed any food at all – just a faraway dream.

Pigs in the potatoes

The summer before the war came to be known as the golden summer of '39. It seemed that the sun had never stopped shining, the first crop of hay was a good one, the wheat had grown well, and the pear and apple trees were heavily laden.

There had been rumours of war in the towns and in Uzbielerz village where our grandfather lived, but right on the edge of the forest where we lived, we were too busy - turning the hay, milking the cows, taking the sheep out to the pastures, feeding the hens, gathering marsh leaves for the pig, and churning butter and making cheese to think too much about it. Like everyone else, we were hoping it wouldn't happen.

Our father was a forest keeper, and Gajowka, the forest keeper's house we lived in came with the job. It was a just an all-on-one-floor, wooden-planked, cabin-type house, more of a shack than a bungalow. It wasn't big, and we were quite a big family, but we all squeezed in.

At the heart of the house was the kitchen with a cast-iron stove that provided heating and where the bread was baked once a week.

On bread baking day, our mother would pile the logs in for a roaring fire, and when the iron stove was red hot and the wood had burnt itself out, she'd quickly scoop the hot ashes to one side and slide the bread dough in to bake. She made enough loaves to last us all week.

Next to the kitchen was a larder to keep the bread and milk and cheese cool.

The little dining room doubled up as a bedroom for Mama and Tata, and there was a bedroom that the five of us children shared. There was no need for much storage space or furniture as we owned so little. Our few clothes were passed on from one brother to the next until they fell apart, and were then cut up and used for rags, bandages and hankies. Nothing was ever wasted.

Outside, we had a wooden toilet shed - a deep hole in the ground with a wooden seat and lid. Flushing toilets hadn't yet reached those remote forests of eastern Poland! Instead of flushing, we sprinkled sawdust. Rats scampered over our feet after dark, which didn't really bother us as we were so used to them. Spiders were as busy as the rest of us, doing their jobs, building their webs in corners, and flies buzzed around our bottoms at every visit. That's just how it was. It may seem primitive now but it was the height of luxury compared to what was to come!

All our water came from the well in the middle of the garden, which had to be boiled for drinking, and there was a pond fed by a little stream at the bottom of the garden where our mother washed our clothes.

When we had a bath, usually once a week on Saturdays, in order to be clean for church on Sunday, the big oval half-barrel would be heaved into the kitchen and water heated up in pans on the stove. We all took turns in the same water, little Albin and Tosia first, then Antony and me, then Peter, Mama, and Tata at the end.

There was no electricity or gas. We did have paraffin lamps, though to save on paraffin we often used long thin resinous pine branches from the forest, which we would light like tapers. These were hung on hooks horizontally rather than standing upright like candles.

Outside our cabin was the land that was attached to the house: a big garden, with a pear tree and a cherry tree, and a vegetable garden, where our mother grew everything we needed - carrots and beetroot, cabbages, onions, turnips, radishes and cucumbers and tomatoes as well as herbs like parsley and dill. We never dug up the onions, but just kept snipping the green tops of them; it made them last longer. The whole of this part of the garden was surrounded by a wooden fence to keep the wild boar and deer out.

Outside the fenced area was a barn where the wheat and hay were stored. There was a rough-planked stable for Kasztan, our farm horse, and a cowshed for our two cows and calf. Our potato field was right next to them. This unfortunately was not fenced off and the wild pigs from the forest would sometimes come on the rampage. Our mother would see them off with her broom. It was the only time I ever remember hearing her shout. Those hungry hogs can turn vicious when attacked and can kill a grown man, but our gentle mother, protecting her precious spuds, was more than a match for them!

In the summer, we'd all be up at cockcrow as there was always so much to be done. Turning out the cows and horse and chickens, milking, cheese and butter making, collecting eggs, watering, weeding the vegetables and potato field, gathering in the corn and the hay, sewing and spinning and weaving and knitting, making baskets from marsh reeds or thin tree roots, gathering blueberries and mushrooms and wild strawberries in the forest, storing and drying and salting and pickling food for the winter. Our father had his forest rounds to do as well, our mother the washing of clothes and sheets in the stream for our family of seven, as well as all the cooking and cleaning.

There was a meadow a walk away along the track allotted to the forest keeper, where our two cows and calf grazed and where we cut our hay. Next to the meadow was the field where our father grew wheat for our bread. Our few sheep grazed on common ground shared with Pan Andrzej, our nearest neighbour, the other forest keeper who lived some way down the track.

On Sundays, except in very bad weather (when we took the horse and cart), we walked the seven kilometres to church, barefoot, through the fields, carrying our shoes so they wouldn't wear out. Then we'd wipe our feet and put our shoes on just before we went inside. There were no roads, just dirt tracks, and not even those when it was raining. Then it was just mud.

We never had time to think if we were happy or not, but we never heard our parents speak an angry word.

We went around barefooted, and our clothes were faded and patched, but there was food enough on the table, logs for the stove, and peace in our home.

Sadly that peace was soon to come to an end.

1st September 1939
An unexpected visitor

My brother Peter had been gathering blueberries in the dappled shade of the forest, his head in the treetops as always. Even when he was busy with his chores he was always on the lookout for nests and dreaming of taming a hawk or an eagle. But that afternoon it wasn't the cry of an eagle or the hovering of a hawk that caught his attention but a strange little squeaking noise.

'Peep, pee, pee, peep…' He kept glancing round, puzzled, but didn't catch sight of her until he was out of the forest. As he came out of the darkness of the trees into the sunlit track just in front of our garden gate, a little fawn trotted out after him.

We were watering our mother's dahlias, my younger brother Antony and I, in the front garden, and stood staring in astonishment as she followed Peter right through the open gate.

'Looks like Peter's just become a mother!' Antony grinned to me as we followed them round to the back garden. Everyone came out to meet Peter's new baby, and I was sent to fetch some milk from that evening's milking. Our mother put a handful of Peter's freshly picked blueberries in the pail with it. The fawn guzzled with great gusto, and licked the pail clean.

Even our old dog Burek was wagging his tail.

'Oh Tata, couldn't we keep her? '

'We could keep her in the barn with the hay! She'd be

safe there.'

'With the calf.'

'We could tame her couldn't we? She's so tame already!'

'Look! Oh just look! Burek is making friends with her!'

It was one of those warm, late-summer evenings that you wanted never to end. But as the sun went down behind the trees, the little fawn suddenly and unexpectedly turned and trotted purposefully back into the shadows of the forest.

We ran after her, calling her back, but only the evening twittering of the birds broke the stillness of the forest.

Somewhere in the distance to the west, there was a hum in the sky, like the distant rumbling of thunder. We looked up for signs of a storm but the sky was red and clear. Mama shivered, rubbed her arms, and said it was time to go in for our supper.

It was only after we'd all eaten the good vegetable soup with bread and butter, and after Tosia had given me a friendly kick me under the table, announcing with a teasing grin that it was certainly the best butter she'd ever tasted in her whole life, (since I'd spent so long churning it that morning till my poor arms were ready to drop off – a chore I really didn't like one bit!) only then did our father reluctantly mentioned the war.

'Hitler's army invaded Poland this morning. They've been bombing the big towns since dawn.'

We had no radio, but Pan Andrzej, the other forest keeper who lived down the track, had heard it in the village.

Our mother looked at him her eyes filled with anxiety.

'Don't worry, Anna. They won't come to these remote forest regions, there's nothing worth bombing here, and everyone is saying it will be over soon. '

'Is the Polish army already fighting then?' Peter sounded surprised.

Our father nodded. 'That's what I've heard. They were mobilised within hours.'

'It will soon be over then! We'll soon send them packing!'

Tata was shaking his head. 'The Nazis have an army much, much more powerful than ours, son.'

'But we weren't defeated at the battle of the Vistula in the last war, were we? And we were outnumbered then. Why should we be defeated now?' Peter argued.

'Now, son, we are in a different league altogether. I've heard the Germans have such sophisticated weapons - huge fleets of ships and planes and tanks. Our army is still mostly on foot, lugging heavy wooden rifles.'

'But we're not alone! Or at least we won't be for long! The British have promised to come and help us defeat the Nazis, haven't they, as soon as the war starts?'

Tata nodded. 'So have the French. Britain has promised to start bombing without delay at first attack, so they should be here very soon, and France has promised to attack Germany with all her forces within two weeks of the start of the war - that's in order to give them time to get over here.'

'In that case, it should all be over within a couple of

weeks, please God!' Mama said with some relief.

There were lots of questions when our father had finished talking, but mostly not about the war. For us children, there were more important things to think about.

'Tata, do fawns eat hay, do you think?'

'I mean will a little fawn, all on its own without its mother, be safe in the forest at night with wolves and bears around? Where does she hide?'

'Do you think she'll be back tomorrow?'

'Will you be drafted into the army, Tata?' Peter finally asked.

Our father shrugged. 'If I am, I hope at least that it won't be till we've got this second crop of hay cut and stored for the winter. We're going to have to be extra busy for the next few days.' He looked out of the window at the now darkening sky, still streaked with red - a sure sign of good weather the next day. 'If the weather holds, God willing, we might get it all in before I am called up.'

The weather did hold. The sky stayed a deep blue and the sun kept beating down hot. We worked flat out from dawn to dusk in the meadow. I was allowed to help in the cutting for the first time that year - they needed all the help they could get. My father showed me how to swing the sharp scythe safely to cut the stalks in a neat row, keeping in line with the other cutters. It was heavy, dusty work. My arms ached at the end of each day, far more than from butter churning, and we were all sunburned, dusty and sweaty, but thankful that there would be good hay for Kasztan and the cows for that winter.

The little fawn came back to our garden the following afternoon, just as Tosia was finishing the milking. She came back the day after that too, and every day after that. We called her Sarenka, which just means 'little deer'. Sometimes she arrived early and stayed for a good part of the day, other times she arrived just as the milking was finished, as if she knew it was time for supper. She grew bolder each visit, licking milk from fingers, taking crusts from our hands, enjoying the petting and stroking, even butting us with her head for attention.

Burek's tail never stopped wagging at the sight of his new friend.

Sadly, another friendship had been formed not far away that was not so innocent or delightful. Hitler and Stalin, our neighbours on either side of our country, and the greatest of enemies in the past, had made a secret pact to wipe Poland off the face of the earth.

They had agreed that the west of Poland should become extra 'living space' for Germans, and the Eastern half a part of the Soviet Union.

The devils' handshake had taken place.

Poland was about to be crucified by two thieves.

Wounded!

Although Gajowka, our forest keeper's cabin, was largely cut off from the war by the surrounding forests and marshes, and we had no wireless or phone, there was always news in the village square after Mass on Sundays. There was anxious talk of the Polish forces fighting a losing battle, and soldiers and civilians being slaughtered as they tried to hold out until the promised reinforcements arrived from France and Britain.

Although no enemy planes flew over our forest regions, and no bombs were dropped at that time, I was wounded nevertheless, and I still have the scar today, but it wasn't by the Germans!

It happened like this: Peter and I had been walking home together, on the last day of the hay cutting, hungry and tired, but chatting and laughing and very pleased with ourselves, looking forward to a good supper. As always in the summer, we were barefoot, and were walking along swinging our scythes contentedly. We shaded our eyes to look up at a kestrel flying overhead, and I stumbled over a root on the rough track. As I lost my balance, I trod on the sharp scythe blade, which sliced into my foot. When I saw all the blood I collapsed on the ground clutching my foot.

Peter looking on in alarm, took out of his pocket the rag he used as a hanky and wrapped it round the cut. 'It'll be all right now!' he said unconvincingly as the blood soaked through the rag.

Our father was not far behind and help was soon at

hand. I was carried home, the foot washed clean from dust and grit (oh the pain!) and the all-purpose ointment that our mother kept on the top shelf in the pantry applied. It was the only medicine available. Mama bandaged it up tight with old, clean rags to stop the bleeding and made me lie down with my foot propped up on a pillow.

'Don't you move from there!' she ordered.

'But it doesn't hurt any more now!' I protested, sitting up, trying not to wince. It was nearly feeding time for Sarenka, the best time of the day as far I was concerned, and if I'd been on my deathbed, I wouldn't have wanted to miss that – not for anything.

But Mama wouldn't hear of it, and it was Peter who was sent to fetch the warm milk and blueberries for the fawn that evening, while I lay with my foot throbbing, blinking back tears of disappointment.

Then our mother went out to take in the washing that had been hanging out to dry, leaving the kitchen door open, with the warm evening sunshine streaming in, and suddenly there was Peter in the doorway, grinning and carrying the milk pail, and coming in right behind him was our little fawn, eyes on the milk bucket, right up to me. I held the pail and patted her while she guzzled, the pain in my foot quite forgotten.

'Sometimes, the best medicine isn't medicine at all!' Peter grinned.

Tata told us at supper that evening that in the village there had been news that the Russian army had now crossed the border into Poland from the east. They had not been challenged, since with hands on hearts, they had assured the border guards that they were coming to help liberate the Polish people. By the time it was understood what that gangster Stalin was really up to, it was too late.

Hawk in a kennel

The news of the Russian invasion seemed to upset our mother even more than the news of the German attack. Past experience of their brutality towards civilians, especially women, brought a shudder of terror to all who had lived through the previous war.

But to us children, it was all, as yet, just talk. The sun was shining, birds twittering, and Peter's best friend Jusef had called round. He and Peter went off to the forest together, into the cool shade of the fir trees and oaks, maple and silver birches, to try and spot a lynx and look for nests. 'The Russians won't get us in there!' they joked as they set off. 'The wild boar or wolves might, but not the Communists!'

Antony and I were going to look for hollow branches to make penny whistles. To shake off all this gloom and doom of war, we'd decided to make ourselves some music. Picking the wide flat grass from the grassy verges as we walked, wrapping it tightly against our thumbs, and blowing hard to make screeching noises like angry cockerels, we fell about laughing at the 'music' we were making!

Having found suitable hollow twigs, we were sitting contentedly in the sunshine on a log at the edge of the forest, taking turns whittling with a broken old penknife, when a sudden crack of gunshot didn't half make us jump. We looked at each in alarm.

'Germans?' Antony whispered, wide-eyed.

I shook my head, looking round fearfully. 'Tata said they wouldn't come out here. Too many trees for their tanks and hardly any houses, it wouldn't be worth their while.'

'What if it's the Russians, then?'

I shrugged, nervously whittling away at my penny whistle.

We listened out uneasily, and nearly jumped out of our skins as Peter and Jusef suddenly came dashing out of the forest all flushed and out of breath, Peter's bare legs all scratched and Jusef with his shirt ripped up at the front.

'Look what we found!' Peter's eyes were shining.

'We're going to keep him as a pet and tame him!' Jusef added beaming, holding out to us a huge young osprey.

'Wow! Where did you find him?'

'High up in a spruce tree!'

'In a nest!'

'You climbed up to get him?' We looked at them in awe. We all knew how high the ospreys built their nests.

Peter nodded and grinned, totally oblivious to the scratches on his arms and legs.

He was the only natural-born tree climber in the family - not that he hadn't tried to pass on his natural agility to the rest of us, but without success. Once, when we were younger, in exasperation, he had taken us a little way into the forest to pick blueberries, and had suddenly pretended to see yellow gleaming eyes in the distance. Leaping up into a tree, he'd shouted, 'Wolf! Wolf!' hoping to scare us into leaping after him. But all we'd done was stand there until until it was that he had given up.

'Not everyone was born to climb trees,' our father had said. Some people were happier with their feet planted firmly on the ground.

'There were two of them in the nest,' Peter was explaining proudly. 'Fledglings. I got right up to the nest but then they both went and fluttered out and I nearly fell out of the tree after them!'

'You could have killed yourself!'

'I just saved myself by grabbing a branch. The other one flew a fair bit away, but this one landed on a lower branch and sat there as helpless as you two that time I tried to make you climb the tree!' he grinned. 'Then as I came down after him, he panicked and fluttered away and landed practically in Jusef's arms!'

'I grabbed him all right!' Jusef grinned nodding proudly, 'But he did have a good go at tearing me to bits! Good job it's my thick shirt I've got on or he would have ripped my stomach to shreds instead!'

We looked admiringly at powerful claws of the huge bird.

'He doesn't seem all that helpless now!' I said watching the bird try to peck Jusef viciously.

'He's just a bit scared that's all. No you don't!' Jusef

25

grinned, holding him firmly at arms length. 'He'll calm down when he gets to know us.'

'While I was up in the tree we heard a gunshot.'

'We heard it too! *Was* it the Russians?'

Peter shook his head. 'As we were walking back we found the other fledgling on the track. Dead. It had been shot and its feet cut off.' Peter frowned, stroking the osprey's head gently.

'So that's what the gunshot was!'

'That stupid law!' Anthony said heatedly. 'Giving money to people for killing a hawk!'

'Well they do steal chickens. And then people go hungry.'

'And remember last year, Pan Andrzej told us about the one that got a new-born fawn!'

'You can't blame people wanting to get the reward money for killing one.'

'If one got our fawn, I'd want to shoot it!'

'Or our chickens!'

'No you wouldn't!'

'Well, maybe not, but it's a shame anyway!'

'They're birds of prey! They're *supposed* to hunt. And we go and execute them like criminals, and chop off their legs, just for doing what they were born to do!'

'Well we're going to look after this one and keep him safe from all that!'

The osprey tried to flap its huge wings, not looking in the least bit grateful.

'Where are you going to keep him?'

'In the old dog kennel by the barn'.

None of us seemed to think this was at all a strange place to keep a bird of prey.

Rat hunt

Peter tied the osprey with string to one of its legs, attached it securely to the kennel, and gave it a bowl of milk. The fawn liked milk, so we thought the hawk might too. But unlike the fawn, the hawk held its head proud and high, showing not the slightest bit of interest in the milk.

'What do you think they eat, then?' Jusef scratched his head.

'Chickens and fawns!' We all laughed.

'Rats and mice too, I think.'

'Tomorrow we'll catch him a rat,' Peter nodded.

'Well you'll have to rip it up with your teeth and chew it up for him as his mother would do!'

'Ugh!!'

'I think maybe I'll just chop it instead. Hey, or put it through Mama's little meat-mincing machine!'

'Mama won't let you put a rat in it!' said Tosia who had just come out at that moment, wiping her hands on a tea towel, to admire the hawk. 'And anyway, you'd probably break the handle if you try to turn it to crunch up rat bones in it!'

But at least there was certainly no shortage of rats

around the place at night. As soon as darkness fell, they came creeping out from under the barn and from their burrows under the ground and squeaked and scurried around the fields and garden as if they owned the place. That night Peter could hardly sleep for excitedly planning all the things he and Jusef were going to do with their osprey when they had tamed it.

He went outside to the toilet shed before dawn, and took with him Tata's axe. He planned to stun a rat on the head with it – just as our father always stunned the pig with the back of the axe before slaughtering it. After that he wasn't quite sure what he'd do, but first things first.

It wasn't as easy as he thought it would be, though. It was still dark, for a start, and he soon discovered that rats see better in the dark that he did himself. They were also quicker than he was at running for their lives.

After he had kicked over the sawdust bucket, and tried to sweep the contents back into the bucket in the dark with his hands, he'd given up. Perhaps the osprey would eat blueberries or potatoes instead.

But when I dashed out with him to the kennel at first light with a crust of bread to feed our new resident before doing the chores, we found only the string lying on the ground. The milk was still in the bowl untouched; the hawk had gone.

We looked everywhere for it, under the barn and in the cowshed, in the forest and fields, but there was no sign of the beautiful bird anywhere.

Peter went back and stood by the old kennel for a

long time in silence, looking down at the bit of string. As I watched him my heart ached for him. Had the osprey chewed through the string – or had poachers come at night and stolen it for the reward money?

Eventually, he took the dish of milk and poured it into the ̶l̶o̶n̶g̶ ̶b̶e̶f̶o̶r̶e̶ ̶b̶r̶o̶o̶k̶ ̶'No point in wasting it,' he said with a shrug. He went off alone into the forest to pick blueberries. He didn't come back for a long time.

Even though the war had not yet reached us, somehow, it was as if it's ripples of sadness were beginning to. Boyish dreams were coming to an end.

Three boys on one horse

Now on Sundays in Uzbielerz village, there were Russian soldiers in the square. Sometimes they stood at the back of the church during Sunday Mass. The little Sunday morning market stalls that used to sell fizzy cherry drinks and lemonade and yeasted buns had all gone. All the food in the village shop had been commandeered by the Soviets. Anyone who had complained had been effectively silenced. There were new graves in the cemetery, and women crying at Mass.

The Ukraine and Belarusian communists living on the borderlands were being encouraged by the Soviet communists to plunder Polish homes and harass the people into moving away.

Since our forest region of Podlasie was so close to the Russian borders, the impact of this was soon felt by us all.

As we walked home one Sunday morning in late September, through the forest and fields, barefooted as always, our shoes dangling by their laces slung over our shoulders, our mother said there couldn't be a better day for taking Kasztan to the pasture by the lake. It would fatten him up a bit before the winter. Now *there* was a chore none of us had to be asked twice to do! Peter ran to fetch the home-made rope bridle, and led our huge horse to the tree trunk we used as a mounting block. He gave Antony a leg up first, then me, then climbed on himself at the front, our brown legs and bare feet dangling, hardly reaching half way down his girth. Antony clasped me round the waist and I held on to Peter. Three boys on one horse, off to the lake on a fine, warm, sunny Sunday afternoon. A woodpecker was hammering away in the forest, butterflies fluttering, bees humming, birds twittering and Burek and Sarenka leaping and gambolling like spring lambs at our side. The leaves on the oaks and maples and birches were scarlet and yellow and gold in the sunshine. Peter tilted his head back to look up at the blue summer sky and wondered aloud if there could possibly be anything more perfect than this?

We ambled along breathing in the scent of hay and warm pine, past the storks' nest birch, with the forest to one side and the marsh lands to the other. Frogs were croaking, crickets singing and the lake water sparkling in the sunshine.

At the water's edge, we slid down and set Kasztan free to graze. He knew the routine. He went first to where the water was shallow, to drink deeply, and then wandered off a little to the rich grass by the lakeside, grazing contentedly. There was no need to tether him, we knew he wouldn't wander away too far.

We threw off our shorts and shirts and splashing and laughing waded into the water. The land there was too poor for growing crops as it was sandy, but that made for crystal clean water. We splashed and swam, not that any of us knew how to swim much, but an enthusiastically splashed doggy paddle we could do, heads held high above the water. We tried catching the little fish that swam in the clear water with cupped hands, but easier said than done. Fish are slippery and fingers not much good as nets.

Later, after drying off in the sunshine and dressing, we made cone shaped baskets from the bark of the silver birch trees that grew there, and gathered into them the tiny sweet wild strawberries that grew at the edges of the forest in abundance. There were hazelnuts too, those that the squirrels hadn't taken, ready for the picking. We tasted the fruit as we picked, but saved most of it for Mama to make jam to store for the winter months when there was nothing growing. The hazelnuts we didn't eat at all. These would be for Christmas Eve. Our mother would roast and grind them in her hand grinder to make traditional Christmas nut cake layered with brandy butter-cream.

We came home, all clean, glowing and happy with birch baskets overflowing, and a contented horse full of good grass, to find Mama and Tata talking seriously together out on the home-made wooden bench in the garden.

'Mama! Look at the heaps of berries we found and hazelnuts too!'

Our mother gave us a smile, but her eyes were anxious. Tata was flushed.

'What's the matter?' Peter asked in concern. 'Has something happened?'

'We've had a visit from the Byelorussians!' said Tosia, coming out from the open kitchen door, her blue-grey eyes flashing in anger. 'They shouted at Tata! They said he was a *Kulak*! A landowner! A *capitalist*, they called him! And all his hay and land they said belonged to everyone now - now that the Communists were ruling the land!'

We looked at her wide-eyed.

'But we don't even *own* the land! It belongs to the government!'

'Yes but the hay *is* ours! We cut it and dried it and gathered it in!'

'They said that everything now belonged to 'the people'.'

'What people?'

'They mean themselves! They just want our land for themselves. That's what their Communism means, it just means they can steal what they like and keep it for themselves! They call themselves 'the people' but we're people too!' Tosia was bursting with indignation.

'I've heard they're working with the NKVD,*' Tata said quietly. 'Helping to harass the locals away, so they can move in.'

'You mean steal our *homes*?'

'If they can get away with it, I suppose!'

'They kicked down the cross on Kicia's grave!' Tosia shook her head in disgust.

Everyone was silent.

Peter shook his head. 'You know, the Ukraines and Byelorussians were *welcoming* the Soviets into Poland, waving red star flags!' he said. 'Josef told me – he saw them!'

'That's because they're hoping to get these Polish border lands back for themselves!' Tata said. 'It's just what they've been waiting for.'

'But that's stealing! They can't get away with that! Surely there must be a law that will stop them!'

It seemed that there wasn't.

* *The Soviet Secret Police, later better known as the KGB*

Trouble in the neighbourhood

That night there was terrible trouble in the neighbourhood, and there was no law to stop it.

Our neighbour Pan Andrzej's barn was burnt to the ground with his whole winter's supply of hay and stored vegetables. The smell of the smoke and the blaze lighting up the sky woke us.

Tata and Peter were up and running over straight away, barefoot with trousers and shirts thrown on over pyjamas, to see if they could help, but it was too late.

They hadn't seen it start, Pan Andrzej told them later, but a petrol can had been left on the ground near the barn. The arsonists hadn't even bothered to hide it. It was as if they wanted them to know it had been no accident.

'Was it the Russians?' we asked when they returned home, tired, dirty, dispirited and coughing from the smoke.

Tata shook his head. 'Pan Andrzej says the Byelorussians have been harassing them for days, calling him and Jusef enemies of the people. That's the phrase they spit out at everyone.'

'But Pan Andrzej is just a forest keeper like you, Tata! He doesn't own his house anymore than we do ours!' Peter put in. 'It's all owned by the government, so how on earth could he possibly be an enemy of the state? – He *works for* the *state*! And it's hardly a rich man's house! It's just a rough old bungalow shack even smaller than ours.'

'And even if he did own it – since when is owning your own home a crime?' said Tosia angrily.

'Since the Communists invaded!' Tata said quietly, with a sad shake of his head. 'It seems they make up their own laws as and when it suits them.'

Too dangerous to stay

The following morning, our father received his call-up to the army.

He gave Mama an anxious look. 'I don't want you to stay here alone without me,' he said, 'it's getting too dangerous now.'

Since Pan Andrzej's barn had been burned, there had been thefts and harassment in other forest homes. 'Who knows what they will do if they know you are here without protection!'

Our mother nodded. They had been talking long into the night, knowing that the call-up was coming.

'How long will you be away, Tata?'

'Not long, God willing.'

'But what's the point of you going at all?' Peter wanted to know. 'Jusef said the Polish army is defeated already.'

Tata shrugged. 'They haven't disbanded yet, but I don't think they are still fighting. I don't think I'll be away long, but while I'm gone, it will be safer if you go and stay with Dziadziu in the village. It's further from the borders.'

He read the call-up letter again. 'They don't give much notice. I'll have to be leaving early tomorrow morning. Peter, will you be able to move our things without me?'

Peter nodded, sitting up straighter. 'What about the cows and the pig?'

'Move the cows first, and as much hay as the cart will hold.'

'Shall we take everything from the house?'

'Everything you can, son. Take everything you can.' he shook his head bitterly, 'If you don't, *they* will!'

The next morning as dawn was breaking, our father set off to walk through the forest to the town where he had to sign up. It would take him most of the day to walk there. Mama had heated up soup from the evening before for his breakfast and wrapped him a sandwich with some boiled eggs and tomatoes to take with him in his faded old forest-keeper's canvas knapsack that he wore over his shoulder. He kissed and hugged each of us tight, told us to help and look after our mother and each other, and waved as he walked away along the forest track.

'God go with you!' Mama called after him, then she was crying, and went to busy herself with packing for the move.

There was suddenly so much to do.

After the animals had been fed and watered, we started loading up the wagon. Mama, Tosia, Antony and little Albin were going to walk to our grandfather's village, taking the shortcut through the fields and forest. Peter and I would take the longer way along the dirt track between the forest and the marshes, as that was the only way the horse and cart could go without getting stuck in the trees.

We loaded up the sacks of wheat and the barrel of our home-grown pickled cabbage. Everyone helped, even little Albin, carrying baskets of pears and onions, jars of plum and gooseberry and blueberry and wild strawberry jams that Mama had made, and the mushrooms we had picked and dried and threaded onto long thread to hang in the loft for the winter.

'Mama! Mama!' Antony was suddenly shouting from the back garden. 'Come quick! Pigs at the potatoes!'

Mama grabbed her broom and came rushing out, shouting angry threats at them. We followed her, yelling and screaming at the top of our voices too. The pigs were bigger than we were, grunting and guzzling, but they scarpered off back into he woods.

'They don't like people shouting!' Peter grinned triumphantly, then added with a rueful shake of his head, 'I just wish it were as easy to shoo away the Communists!'

'The hogs, at least, have left us a few potatoes, and they had the grace to run away when we screamed.'

'And they don't burn barns down!' Antony added.

'We'll come back and dig up what's left of the potatoes in a day or two, ' Peter assured our mother. 'We can dig a new winter storage pit for them at Dziadziu's'.

I looked with regret at the fine deep pit by the side of the house which we had only just finished digging, and which, when covered with a lid of wood and straw, would have kept our spuds and carrots and beetroot cold and fresh all winter and protected from the frosts and snows. And now we were going to have to start all over again at Dzidziu's.

The storks from the silver birch nest nearby were circling overhead. 'Look!' cried Antony, 'It must be time for them to be flying off to Africa for the winter soon.'

We all watched the huge birds flying back to the silver birch where they returned each year, (and woe betide any other storks who tried to move in to their nest before they were back - there would be such a rumpus and a fight and the storks who'd built the nest always won).

'One day, I'm going to be like them,' Antony mused, I'm going to fly off to Africa and other far away lands where the winters are hot and where oranges grow! See the whole world!

Little Albin ran around flapping his arms like wings and squawking like a hen.

Peter laughed, 'Maybe you will, Antosh, maybe you will. Who knows?' He himself had no desire to travel far. He would be a farmer and grow fields full of yellow sunflowers and orchards full of apples and pears and plums and a garden full of green beans and tomatoes. He would keep bees for honey and hens for eggs, and ducks on a pond with ducklings every spring cheeping and pecking and chasing flies all over the place, and maybe an eagle and a kestrel or two as well, and why not?

I was smiling at Antony's dreams too. Like Peter, I had never really yearned for that kind of adventure. In those days, in that region, even to visit another region of Poland was to travel far. People generally stayed where they'd been planted. I would have liked to have been a forest keeper like our father, and adopt all the orphaned fawns.

But the sun was high in the sky now and there was no more time for daydreaming. Back to the packing and lifting and loading up the cart, and locking everything up securely before we all set off. There had never been any need to lock up before, but now, since the fire at Jusef's, things had changed. Jusef and his father had been forced to sell their livestock and had moved away to the town to stay with Pan Andrzej's brother. Pan Andzej had hoped it would be safer there for Jusef. But there was nowhere safe anymore in Poland. And Peter had lost his best friend.

It was our first loss of that war. Sadly, there were more to come.

Gleaming yellow eyes in the dark

Kasztan plodded slowly along the track back to Dziadziu's village - the marshlands on one side and the forest on the other. It was just wide enough for a horse and cart to go along, but not wide enough to turn round – not unless you wanted to risk getting the wheels stuck in the bog. It was a long slow journey.

Mama and the others had already arrived when we got there, and Dziadziu Ignatius was waiting to welcome us at the open door, with hugs and pats on the back. Feather quilts and bedding were unloaded, and somehow squeezed in. Arms were aching from all the extra work, and just when we felt so tired that all we wanted to do was collapse on the mattresses, Peter and I then had to go back to get the cows, and later we'd have to go yet again to take as much of the hay as we could. It was going to be a long, long day.

Neither of us said a word of complaint. We knew it had to be done, but every muscle in my body was complaining! And to top it all, when we got back to Gajowka, after our quick lunch of bread and cheese, the cows were not at all keen on taking a walk at a time they would normally be lazing and grazing in the shady meadow.

'Come on, Krasnula!' Peter shouted at her, waving a stick. 'Move it!'

Once we'd got her going, we knew her calf would follow and laid back Lala wouldn't want to be left alone.

Krasnula ambled lazily along as if on a picnic, stopping every minute to have a little rest and chomp at the grass. 'Move!' Peter shouted at them. 'Picnic time tomorrow, not today!' The cow looked at him and mooed.

'I didn't say *'Moo'* you silly cow!' Peter laughed, 'I said *move!*'

At last we got the cows into the meadow behind Dziadziu's house, and it was time to take the cart back to collect as many bales of hay that the cart would hold.

We'd also packed the hens, squawking and protesting into sacks, those we could catch anyway. Some roosted in the forest bushes and were hiding away already. They would have to be left behind for now. The afternoon was over, our backs aching. We were covered with dust and sweat and hay seeds. But instead of setting back straight away in order to get home well before dusk, we both lingered in the garden looking out towards the forest. It was time for supper, and we were hungry, yet neither of us had eaten the apple Mama had given us to take with us. We drank some water from the well and rinsed the sweat and dust off our faces, and brought the bucket for Kasztan to drink. Then we sat on the wooden step looking out towards the forest.

'We really should be getting back now, ' Peter said, reluctantly, not making a move.

I nodded. A few minutes went by, then a few more, and the sun was setting lower.

Peter shook his head. 'I don't think she's going to turn up.'

'Perhaps she's already been before we came back.'

We called to her, but there was no eager squeaking in reply. Only the hammering of a woodpecker in the distance and then the cawing of rooks, then the silence of a still, warm, early autumn evening.

With heavy hearts and weary limbs, we climbed up onto the cart. The sun was low now, and we still had the long journey to make back to the village, and we knew it would be dark before we got back.

Before we were half way there, both of us dozing off, Kasztan plodding on, not needing to be guided as he knew the way, and anyway there was no choice but to stay on the narrow track, an owl suddenly screeched in a tree close by, startling Peter from his sleep. He opened his eyes, looking around with a yawn, then suddenly sat bolt upright staring into the distance.

'What's the matter?' I asked in alarm, wide awake now too, seeing the fear in his eyes.

Peter shook his head. 'I saw something gleaming - over there!'

'Are you sure?'

'Oh yes!' he nodded.

'And there's more than one.'

I saw the yellow glints too. 'Let's turn back!'

'We can't!'

The track was so narrow it barely let the cart through, there was no way we could turn round without the danger of getting stuck in the marshy bogs.

'Even if we could it's too late! We've got to get back to Dziadziu's before night. We can't stay in Gajowka on our own. No way would that be safe.'

There was no choice except to keep going towards the gleaming yellow eyes.

'We should have brought Tata's rifle with us,' I said, beginning to feel really scared now. Grown men would have been scared, and we would be no match at all for a hungry pack of wolves.

'We have to shout and sing out loud!' Peter said. 'They hate the sound of people's voices!'

So, very much wide awake now and with pounding hearts, we began to sing. As loudly as we could, voices trembling, we belting out the words like crazy. We sang the hymns we knew from church, shouting ourselves hoarse. If we hadn't been so scared no doubt we'd have laughed at how ridiculous we sounded.

As we got closer to the gleaming eyes, we sang even louder, till our voices were packing in, and we finally realised what the gleaming was.

We could smell it! We could even see it now. Smoke!

Not a pack of hungry wolves, but sparks from a bonfire that someone had lit in the evening! Oh how we leaned back in relief. Oh how we breathed again and slapped each other on the back in joy. How we laughed at ourselves till we cried.

Leave my little brother alone!

At Dziadziu's, straight after supper, we collapsed onto the mattress we were sharing without even washing our faces. Even before Mama and Tosia and little Albin had gone to bed we were dead to the world. Dead beat.

An hour later, Mama was suddenly shaking Peter awake.

'Peter! The cows have gone!' she said. 'They managed to push the gate open and must have wandered off some time ago!'

Peter rolled off the mattress, hardly able to open his eyes, but with not a word of complaint, he was straight away putting his shirt back on.

'Can't you wait till the morning?' I asked, seeing how exhausted he looked.

Peter shook his head. 'The wolves are out at night,' he said. 'Not just distant gleamings,' he managed to grin in spite of his tiredness. 'Maybe we're already too late!'

Mama had already lit the paraffin lamp, and they hurried out into the dark, the lamp swinging it's yellow light between them.

I was anxiously awake early the next morning, but they still weren't back. All night they had silently searched the forest, not daring to call to the cows for fear of attracting wolves. There had been no sign of them anywhere all night, but at the first light of dawn, Peter had found hoof prints and they'd followed them.

'They weren't used to their new meadow,' Peter shook his head, telling us about it when they finally returned. Maybe it was all too strange for them.'

They'd found bloodstains, then the hoofprints led to the lake, near our house in Gajowka, then to a neighbours' farm.

Pan Stasio, a neighbour of Dziadziu's had found them, and had put them in his meadow, with his own cows to keep them safe until they were claimed.

The sun was already warm by the time they came back. Sadly, they had lost our calf, but at least the two cows were safe.

After Peter and Mama had had a short sleep and a late breakfast, we began work on securing the meadow gate and fencing. We worked without talking much, tired still and subdued and sad about the little calf.

We knew we'd have to make another journey to Gajowka the following day to fetch more hay and the vegetables stored in the barn loft. The potatoes would have to be dug up too before the wild pigs took the lot, but first we'd need to dig the new storage pit by Dziadziu's porch.

A shock awaited us when we finally did go back for the hay and the vegetables. We found our padlock broken, and the barn door securely locked with a padlock and chain that didn't belong to us.

'It's those Communists stealing our hay!' Peter was so angry he kicked at the door with a heel of his bare foot. Then cried out in pain and jumped around on one foot clutching the other in agony. He banged at it with his fist. 'Thieves!' he shouted. 'They've not just stolen the hay, but the whole barn! Dirty rotten thieves!' How would we be able to feed the cows and Kasztan throughout the cold months to come without our precious store of winter hay?

We arrived back to the village that afternoon, tired, angry and uncertain as to what to tell our mother about the barn. We didn't want to upset her. She had enough to worry about already.

Our little brother Albin was collecting eggs from the hens in the back garden. As we walked by, the cockerel was crowing angrily at him, pecking and flapping his wings, trying to see him off. Peter gave the bird a warning kick. 'Leave my little brother alone, you bully!' he grumbled.

He was also worried about what had happened to Sarenka – being so tame she would be an easy target for poachers, and was wondering whether to make another journey back one evening soon to look out for her, but he dreaded what he might find there next time, and another dark ride through the forest was not something he wanted to risk.

A sudden screaming from the chicken coop interrupted his musings and made him dash back outside. Little Albin was running towards us with his hand to his cheek, face bleeding from a nasty scratch just a centimetre away from his eye.

'The rooster scratched me!'

It was the last straw! Peter went storming off to the chicken coop. I ran after him. 'Peter! He's only trying to protect the hens! He's a good cockerel! '

'And I'm only trying to protect our brother! He could have blinded him! Next time – *if* we let there be a next time - he could blind him!'

He grabbed the cockerel by the legs, held him upside down, and with one swift, strong pull, wrung his neck.

The hens were all hiding their heads under the barn with their bottoms sticking out.

That night there was chicken soup. It was eaten in weary silence.

I ate with a lump in my throat, and Peter too, I think. He looked so pale. Tired, no doubt, of trying to look after everything and everyone. Our hearts were aching for the lost calf, and for the good but vicious cockerel that we were now eating, and for how our father would feel when he got back to find our barn and the rest of our hay had been taken over by the thieving communists. I could see there was so much hurt and bitterness churning up inside my brother. He needed our father back. 'Please God,' I prayed silently, 'Please, please, God, bring him back home soon'

An unexpected swim!

The sunny weather could not last for much longer, and with our father still away, Peter decided one warm, still evening that we should go to the lake for some fishing. He wanted to look after the family as well as our father would have done, and Tata always made a few fishing expeditions in the summer and autumn, saying the oils in the fish would build us up for the winter.

Our parents would always go fishing at night, when the fish came into the warmer shallower water at the edge of the lake. They would both wade in, Mama staying close to the shore and Tata wading in deeper. Then they would walk very slowly with the net spread out in the water between them, fish getting caught in it as they dragged it along. It was never a great catch, and the fish were always small - sprats mainly - but dipped in flour and fried in butter they were a good supplement to our fairly frugal diet.

Mama expressed some doubts about our going out into the water at night though, warning us that it could get unexpectedly deep in places, even by the shore. She knew we weren't strong swimmers.

'We'll stay in the shallow part,' Peter assured her. 'Where we swim when we go with Kasztan. We'll take care and we'll be fine.

It was a cloudy night with no moon.

The lake looked so different at night – black and deep. I

was regretting coming even before I'd dipped a toe in and I could see even Peter was hesitating a bit. It all seemed a lot more daunting now than when we'd talked about it in the kitchen at home, but we had promised Mama some fish, and could hardly go home without them.

Thankfully, the water felt warmer than it looked.

Slowly, silently, we let the net out in the shallow end where we always swam, and dragged it along. An owl flew over us, its huge wings almost touching our heads. We stood still watching it disappear into the dark forest. There were fewer fish than we'd hoped for, so Peter kept moving slowly towards the deeper water, till his shoulders were submerged. I watched him worriedly, as I was already waist deep and had no wish to go any deeper. I was getting cold too. Then suddenly Peter disappeared under the water.

I looked around in panic. There was no sign of him.

'Peter!' I screamed, dropping the net, and I, who hated water in my ears and always kept my head well above the water, now dived desperately to find my brother. At that same moment, Peter re-emerged gasping and spluttering, shaking the water from his hair and eyes, treading water as he was out of his depth and panicked himself now because I had disappeared!

Having given ourselves such a fright, with hearts pounding, and shaking lake water from our mouths, noses and eyes, we doggy paddled back to the shore dragging the tangled net behind us, not caring anymore now about being silent and not scaring the fish. We'd had enough of fishing!

We thought all the fish would have been frightened off by all the noise and commotion we'd made, but as we dragged the net out and untangled it, we were surprised to find a fair number of fish in it. It wasn't a huge catch, but enough for a good meal, and we were able to return home with our heads held high.

Our mother thanked us for the fish with relief in her eyes, and if she noticed our wet hair, and raised her brows, she made no comment.

The following day, Tosia washed the fish and Mama dipped them in flour and fried them in butter, and everyone ate eagerly, bones and heads and all. Every bit was eaten, except for the tails.

Each night, with our grandfather Ignatius, we prayed for our father's safe return, and listened anxiously to any news of the war in the village. The Polish army was beaten. With two super-powers attacking from both sides, and the allies not turning up as they'd promised, defeat had been inevitable.

Our mother's anxiety for our father increased daily, as reports of prisoners of war being deported or murdered reached us. On the eastern borders, most of our soldiers and officers had been imprisoned or shot.

But then, suddenly and unexpectedly, even before the weather turned really cold, Tata was home! Looking thinner and quieter, but smiling with arms open wide to greet us. There were such hugs and tears of happiness.

'Has the war ended then, Tata?'

He shook his head. 'No. But our army has been disbanded.' He shook his head. 'What there is left of it.'

'And the allies?'

'If they had come, this war would have ended by now, 'he shrugged wearily. 'As it is, I fear it is only just beginning.'

Killing the pig

Peter and our father went back to Gajowka, our forest keeper's cabin, with an axe.

Tata chopped off the chain with one strong angry blow, and they loaded the cart up to overflowing with our hay. Then Tata locked it with his own padlock. 'We will come back again soon to take the rest,' he said.

Peter looked at him, his eyes full of anxiety. 'While you were away, we heard that they burnt down a whole house while the family was asleep inside.' he said quietly. 'And they ...,' he shook his head, 'They badly hurt some women. Young girls too - in the forest. Just a few kilometres from here.'

Tata's eyes were dark with disgust, but he replied calmly, 'I don't think they would dare come anywhere near us in Uzbielerz. It's further away from them there. And there are more houses and people to witness their actions. They're after these easy, remote places nearest the border.'

While there was still some warmth in the sun, Peter

and Antony and I made trips to the marshes with sacks to gather piles of huge marsh leaves for the pigs, to fatten them up before the winter. It was a pleasant chore, as there was always something interesting to watch – in the springtime we spent more time catching and cuddling the downy wild ducklings than collecting the leaves.

Sadly, though, earlier that year, we had witnessed men from the big towns coming with boats to the marshes to shoot the ducks. It wasn't just for food, as the local poachers did – these men didn't look hungry or poor - but for sport. To kill such lovely creatures for fun was incomprehensible to us.

At home, we passed the huge marsh leaves through the big hand-turned chopping machine, mixing them with straw and a bit of hay. The pigs chomped and guzzled this mixture with even more greed than the wild hogs did Mama's potatoes!

And every day now we went out to gather wood from the forest. Tata and Peter chopped logs to store outside, under the lean-to porch for keeping the stove burning throughout the winter. I wanted to help, but remembering the episode with the scythe that summer, my father thought it best to wait another year before letting me anywhere near the axe!

As the cold winds started blowing in from the east, and the damp scent of ferns and mushrooms filled the forests, it was time to slaughter the pig that we had reared that year.

Tata and Peter and Dziadziu, and Pan Stasio, a neighbour, gathered for the slaughter. Tosia ran away to the bedroom and put the pillow over her head as she always did. She hated to hear the squealing. But it only squealed and screamed while it was being caught, then our father stunned it with a sharp swift blow on the head with the blunt edge of the axe, and while it was knocked out, they quickly slaughtered it with a sharp knife, catching the blood carefully in a bucket.

Then the hard work began. We all helped in pulling out all the hair from its hide. This was really hard work as it was long hair and stiff, but it was well worth the trouble as we knew that later Tata would sell it for a good price to a shop that would make hairbrushes out of it.

A huge bonfire was made to burn off any remaining hair, so the skin was smooth and clean. The acrid smell of smoke and burning hair filled the yard.

Then the cutting and chopping began. Every bit of the pig was always used, not one bit would be wasted. Mama made her own sausages with a hand turned sausage machine, using the guts for skins. These would be smoked and hung in the loft of the barn. The rest would be salted to preserve it for the winter.

It was always a special occasion, pig-slaughtering day, as it meant we would eat fresh pork that night. Mama would make a good goulash with plenty of the meat in and everyone would have a generous helping. It was a rare treat for us all. The neighbour who helped would also be given a good share of the meat to take back to his family.

Jusef and Pan Andrzej had always helped in the past, joining in the work and sharing the meal with us, until the burning of their barn and stores had forced them to move away to live with Jusef's uncle in Bialystok. Everyone felt their especially absence keenly that day, especially Peter, who was quiet at dinner that night.

But it didn't take away our appetites! We all ate appreciatively knowing this was the best meal we would have for a long time.

The rest of the meat would have to last the whole winter and the following spring and summer. Little did we know that it wouldn't in fact last more than a few weeks. It was soon to be taken away from us by jackals and hyenas.

Calm before the storm

We had been out with our father to choose and fell a Christmas tree, and we got it home just before the snows came.

The scent of pine filled the house, mixed with the sweet scent of spicy Christmas biscuits baking in the stove.

Mama and Tosia and Albin had been baking, and Antony and I were making coloured chains by threading short hollow lengths of straw onto cotton thread, with little squashed balls of coloured paper in between. Peter, because he was the eldest and tallest, had the privilege of clipping little candles onto the edges of the branches.

That Christmas Eve, while all over the rest of Poland, there were food shortages and great mourning for those who had been brutalised, traumatised and murdered, here in Uzbielerz village, surrounded by the silent forests, with only an owl hooting and a dog barking occasionally, it was as still and quiet as that night in Bethlehem long ago, when the Son of God was born into the world.

Because everyone kept livestock and grew and gathered their own wheat and fruit and vegetables, there was still food enough to eat, and because of the frozen lake, thanks be to God, more fish than we had ever eaten before. We would have gladly shared with those who had less, but there was no way we could travel to the war zones, even if the snow hadn't started to fall so thick and fast.

Though the snow would make it unlikely for anyone to venture out that night, we still set an extra place at the table, as we always did on Christmas Eve. It was so that any visitor would find a welcome, so that no unexpected traveller would be turned away as the Holy Family had been turned away from the inns in Bethlehem. No matter how tight a squeeze it was around the table, there was always an extra place set. 'A guest in the house means God in the house,' Mama would repeat, as all Polish people did in those days and still do today - hospitality being more than just a way of life – but something sacred.

Tosia had been helping Mama for several days prepare the special Christmas Eve supper, making the mushroom filling for the stuffed uszka (tiny ravioli called 'little ears') to put in the beetroot soup. There was plentiful fried carp, salted pickled herrings, potato salad and pierogi stuffed with cheese and potato, and also with mushrooms and saukraut and cabbage. There was fruit compote made from plums, apples and pears dried from the garden and flavoured with vanilla pod. To follow, there was Mama's wonderful poppy seed cake and baked cheesecake. And finally, a beautiful nut torte made with the hazelnuts we'd gathered by the lakeside that autumn, with butter icing. Twelve dishes in memory of the twelve apostles. No meat dishes were ever served on this holy night, in memory of the privations endured by Mary and Joseph on their journey to Bethlehem.

Mama had laid a bit of hay under the clean white table cloth, as she always did, as a reminder that the Holy Child had been born in poverty in a stable and laid in a manger. The blessed wafer of unleavened bread had been placed on a white plate, to remind us that Jesus, who came to become living bread for the world, had been born in Bethlehem – which means 'house of bread'.

Albin and Antony were glued to the window, wiping away with their sleeves the condensation from their breath, looking out for the first star to appear so they could start the supper. All Polish children would be doing the same, remembering the star that had shone over the stable in Bethlehem that the wise men from the East had followed to worship the new-born King.

Albin was sure he'd spotted one.

'Unless I can see it too it doesn't count,' Antony told him doubtfully, peering out squinting into the darkening winter sky.

'It was there! It's gone behind that cloud!'

'Then we'll have to wait a bit till it comes out from behind the cloud. It won't be long.'

But at last the first star was definitely twinkling.

Our father and Peter lit the candles on the Christmas tree. It looked so beautiful with the flickering flames lighting up the coloured straw and paper chains and the sugar sprinkled biscuits and the silver star at the top. Tata led us in singing 'Dzisiaj w Bethlejem' 'Today in Bethlehem' and 'Shepherds hurried joyfully to the stable,'

The Christmas readings from the Bible that Dziadziu read out were especially moving because of the war throughout our defeated land; 'The people that lived in darkness has seen a great light - on those who live in a land of deep shadow, a light has shone...'

'The maiden will conceive and give birth to a son and they will call him Emmanuel a name which means God is with us... '

Then the wafer that had been blessed by the priest after Mass on Sunday, was broken and shared, everyone taking a bit of the wafer and sharing blessings and wishes with everyone else.

We thanked God for the food, asking his blessing on it, and prayed for all soldiers and fellow country men and women and children who had died or were dying in the war, for all those who were suffering and mourning, and for those who did not have food that evening.

At last, at last, at last! Mama served the steaming hot dark red beetroot soup and the mushroom uszka, and the lovely Christmas vigil meal began.

'Mama, that was the best Wigilia ever!' Peter thanked her appreciatively when we had finished every last bit of it, every last crumb. Everyone agreed wholeheartedly. It was the custom in those days in Poland to kiss the hand that cooked the food, and that evening everyone of us eagerly wanted to pay our mother that sign of gratitude and respect. Tosia received a few pats on the back too.

After the supper, we sang carols together until it was time for midnight Mass. And much, much later, when we children were in bed, we were lulled to sleep by our Grandfather Ignatius softly singing his evening prayers and psalms.

'Tomorrow we'll start baking nice and early.'

January was the coldest month ever, and February brought icy winds from Siberia with more snow.

Bread baking day was always something to look forward to when it was so cold outside, as the logs would be piled into the stove to make a roaring hot fire. When the flames died down, while the stove was still red hot, our mother would push the hot ash to one side and slide in the loaves to bake. The whole house would soon be filled with the scent of baking bread.

Our mother baked once a week, making enough to last the whole week. She mixed and kneaded in a huge wooden bowl - a bit like a half-barrel but more shallow - about a metre in diameter. There was no yeast available, so she would make a fermented sourdough starter some days before and knead it into the flour the day before baking, leaving the dough to prove overnight, then kneading it again the following morning before leaving it to rise by the stove before baking it.

It was good, stone-ground, whole-wheat bread made from our own wheat grown in our field and milled by the local miller.

Towards the end of the week it was always a bit stale and hard, but dipped or crumbled into soup or milk it was still very good.

'Tomorrow we'll start baking nice and early,' Mama

said to Tosia, after kneading the dough in the large wooden bread bowl, covering it with a damp tea towel and leaving it near the stove overnight.

Peter and I had piled up a good supply of logs, in the log basket by the stove, ready for the morning.

But it is never certain in this life what the next day will bring, and the bread was never baked.

That night, at four in the morning, the Soviet Secret Police paid us a visit.

A night a hundred thousand families would never forget

Long before dawn, on that bitterly cold February night, when the snow lay too deep even for the wild pigs to venture out of the forest, and we were all snuggled together in our beds, we were woken from a deep sleep by a sudden pounding on the front door. Burek our dog was barking.

'Utwierajcie! Open up!'

Again, the loud insistent hammering at the door, then an unexpected sharp rapping at our bedroom window, which made us all jump. Peter leapt out of bed like a startled deer and headed for the kitchen, with the rest of us close on his heels.

Our mother was already there, in her long cotton nightgown, standing with her hands joined in front of her face, looking anxiously towards the door, while our father was lighting the paraffin lamp.

'You're not going to open it, are you, Tata?' my brother Peter whispered anxiously. 'What if it's the partisans?'

We all knew only too well what had happened to poor Pan Stefan the week before. A group from the Polish resistance hiding in the forest had called at his farm asking for food.

'And the way they demanded, it was not easy to refuse!' That's what he'd told his neighbours with a rueful shake of his head the following day. 'Ah, but they were fellow Poles after all, and they were hungry.'

And so he had given them bread and milk.

Two days later the NKVD came to his house and arrested him. For 'helping the resistance' they tied him by the feet with a rope to the back of one of their lorries and dragged him along behind it till he was dead.

My father made the Sign of the Cross and was walking towards the door. We watched him slide the bolts and open it, standing squarely in the doorway, as if to protect us. A flurry of snow greeted him, blowing in on his tousled fair hair and faded pyjamas.

Even in the darkness outside we could make out Russian soldiers from their boots and heavy long coats, and fixed bayonets. Unceremoniously they pushed their way in and forced our father to stand against the kitchen wall.

As they searched him Antony turned to me with a shake of his head and whispered, 'As if he could be hiding anything under his pyjamas!'

Mama looked at us, eyes full of anxiety and put a finger warningly to her lips.

The soldiers were now searching the house. As it was all on one floor, we could see them turning mattresses over, opening cupboards and drawers. One of them was leading our grandfather, half dressed, out from his little box room, ordering him also to stand against the wall.

The NKVD officer with the soldiers addressed my father in Russian.

My father shook his head in bewilderment. 'I don't understand,' he said.

'Where are your weapons?' the officer repeated in Polish.

'I have no weapons'.

'No guns? - Niet karabiny?'

'Just the rifle - for protection against wolves,' Tata explained lifting his chin towards the hooks over the door where it hung. 'It doesn't belong to me. It's a government rifle. I am a forest keeper,' he shrugged, 'It's part of my job.'

One of the soldiers walked across and pulled the rifle off its hooks.

'You will not pack the rifle!'

'Pack?' Tata was looking as if he hadn't heard him right. The officer glanced impatiently at a printed document he was holding. 'Your name *is* Boleslaw Gryg?'

'Yes.'

'And your wife is Anna Gryg, formerly Jaskielewicz?'

Tata glanced across at Mama and nodded.

'And you have five children - Peter, Tosia, Witold, Antony and Albin?'

'Yes.'

'And Ignacius Gryg?'

Tata looked at Dziadziu, our grandfather, standing in dignified silence against the wall beside him. 'My father.'

'You are all to be relocated. You must pack quickly. You may take two bundles or boxes each.'

Mama put her hand over her mouth.

Tata stared at him. 'Wait! There must be some mistake...' he began.

The officer lifted a hand to silence him, though glancing at our mother's pale, panic-stricken face, his face softened a little, 'It will be all right,' he said in a placating tone. 'Everything will all right. Things will be good for you, if you do as you are commanded.' He glanced at his watch, and began to issue orders.

We were to be packed and ready to leave in one hour. We were to take no knives, jewellery or watches. We were to hurry; there was a sledge waiting outside.

'But capitalists have shoes!'

"But this is our home!' Tata was flushed. 'My father and I built it with our own hands!' He shook his head in disbelief. 'My father was legally allocated this land by the government after the war. We have all the papers to prove it!' he protested.

The officer looked at him with barely disguised

contempt. He unfolded a second document and read out loud, slowly, in Polish, our deportation order.

Barefoot, still in our pyjamas, shivering as the last glowing embers in the stove died down, we listened to the order that sentenced us to being 'relocated' to the 'great and glorious Soviet Union.

As he was reading, Antony and I exchanged a glance at the word 'capitalists'. We had all heard the whispers in the village that every peasant who owned a few hens or a pig, every householder who had built a wooden shack – everyone – bakers, cobblers, those who worked the land, and their wives and children - was suddenly, in the eyes of the Communists, a Capitalist, and therefore an enemy of the people, and a criminal.

'But Capitalists have shoes!' I whispered to Antony, looking down at our weather-beaten feet. 'Even in the summer, I know they have shoes! We should tell them we have no shoes!'

Antony nodded, and flushed but bold, took a step forward, clearing his throat to speak, but he never got a chance. The NKVD officer was now demanding to know where our father kept his money.

Everyone watched as our father walked across the room, still in his thin faded pyjamas and barefooted, his fists clenched. He reached up for the tin behind the little saucepan on the top shelf above the stove. He opened the lid in silence and tipped out the contents: a few coins and notes.

Surely now they would see their mistake, surely

capitalists had more than a few zlotys in a tin can. Perhaps they would understand now and go away and leave us in peace.

The officer went away, but the soldiers stayed, settling themselves comfortably in our kitchen without being invited to sit, taking over the wooden benches my father and grandfather had made with their own hands. They slouched, their feet stretched out as if they owned the place, the smoke from their cigarettes making us cough, and the snow from their boots melting into puddles on Mama's clean kitchen floor.

Who were they, these strangers with rifles and bayonets who had invaded our home in the middle of the night and were ordering us to pack and leave? How could they just come and take over our home in this way?

I could hear Burek whining outside.

One of the soldiers, the youngest one, seeing our mother gathering our clothes into a pile in our bedroom but not knowing what to put them in since we had no suitcases or trunk, came over and said to her quietly, kindly, 'Pack your things into bedspreads or sheets if you do not have suitcases,' he looked round at the very simply furnished room. Then he said to Peter, 'You're going to a forest, so take an axe and a saw. They'll be useful to you. He glanced across to the kitchen to the other soldiers who were talking together and sitting in a haze of their cigarette smoke. 'Dress warmly, and take all the bundles you can carry.' He added with feeling. 'You will need them.'

'Take food,' one of the other soldiers later called out. 'It will be a long journey.

'Take bread. Take as much food as you can.'

But we had no bread, except for less than half a small stale loaf. The bread dough had been rising all night, the logs piled up ready for the stove. I wanted to whisper to Antony to explain to them that we had no bread, that we couldn't go away yet as this was bread-baking day. We needed to pile the logs into the stove, but our mother once again put her finger to her lips to warn us to keep quiet.

Now she was hurriedly putting the salt pork from the barrel in the pantry into a sack. The pig had been slaughtered only weeks before, and most of the best meat was in the barrel, stored in salt to last the whole year. At least we'd have that. My sister Tosia, who was helping pack the food, came hurrying out of the pantry with some apples and dried mushrooms and the stale crust of bread. She stumbled as she stepped nervously over the feet of one of the soldiers and the bread fell to the floor by one of the soldiers. She stood hesitating, cheeks flushed, not knowing what to do.

The officer kicked the crust away impatiently with his wet boot.

I saw my father wince at this and I knew what he was going to do. Leaving the wall where he had been ordered to stand, still in his pyjamas, he was walking across towards the now dirty crust of bread.

We all knew what he was going to do.

No Tata! Don't do it! My heart sank. Don't Tata! I willed

him silently. Please God, don't let him do it! I prayed with all my heart for him. Didn't he know these were the same men who tortured Pan Stefan to death?

But our father stooped to pick up the crust of bread and then put it to his lips to kiss it reverently before placing it on the table.

There was a tense silence in the room.

In those days in that part of Poland, no bread was ever thrown away. If a piece were dropped, it would be picked up and treated with the same reverence our father had just shown. Bread wasn't just food for us, it was the symbol of life, and the symbol of God who gives us life and became Living Bread for our souls.

The soldier who had kicked the crust cleared his throat and spat on the floor, giving my father a look of contempt.

We children dressed quickly, in the half dark with the bedroom doors left open as commanded.

'Do capitalists have darned socks?' Antoni whispered to me, holding up the evidence with a shake of his head.

'And patched pants?' I whispered back, also holding up the evidence. In spite of everything we grinned at each other. We were children, and although we knew something terrible was happening, we could not even begin to understand or imagine what the future now might hold.

We were all packed and ready within the hour, as ordered. Everyone was taken outside, even our grandfather. It was still dark as they loaded us onto a horse-drawn sledge that we recognised as Pan Andrzej's and Jusef's. The village was silent and sleeping.

A cockerel crowed in the darkness.

Peter's eyes filled with anxiety. 'Tata! What about the chickens?' he whispered.

'Who will let them out and feed them and gather the eggs?'

'How long are we going away for?'

'Who will milk the cows?'

'What about Burek?' Who will feed him and look after him?'

'And the sheep and lambs! We can't just leave them all!'

'What about our wheat in the loft?'

'And the vegetables in the pit?'

As we five children huddled together with our anxious questions clutching our bundles on our knees, the horses were whipped on and the sledge started along the village road heading out towards the town.

Burek ran after the sledge barking. One of the soldiers guarding us looked round in irritation.

'Go back, Burek!' I shouted to him, scared he'd be shot. 'Go home!'

But he continued to run after us for a long time, until eventually he could run no more. He collapsed in the snow and howled as if his heart were breaking.

It was as if he knew he'd never see us again. And my last words to him were shouted ones for him to go away. That was when I wept for him. We all did.

All over Eastern Poland in that one terrible night,

two hundred thousand families - even new born babies, children, sick people from the hospitals and those too old for travelling, were ordered to dress and pack hurriedly, and deported to hell.

Worse than a prison cell

At the station, we had to carry our bundles through the now slushy snow from the sledge to the platform. A huge, black, steam-powered locomotive, with a seemingly endless train of rough wooden wagons that snaked into the distance as far as the eye could see, awaited us. Soldiers with rifles and bayonets were ordering pale, anxious, stunned-looking families into the wagons with pushes and shouts. Babies were being carried along with bundles and bags, children were crying.

All along the length of the train, soldiers stood on guard. Already many of the wagons were closed and locked like prison cells on a railway track.

The two heavy sacks of food that Tata and Mama had been carrying on their backs, they were ordered to put into a separate store wagon. They stood by the store-wagon, hesitating.

'It will be safe there,' the commanding soldier told them impatiently. 'It has your name on it.'

Mama and Tata watched so anxiously where the soldier carelessly threw the sacks, it made my heart ache for them.

They were ordered to move away and we were assigned to one of the trucks near the front of the train, past where the platform ended.

As there was no platform, and the wagons were high, climbing up was not easy for Dziadiu and Mama. Peter and Tata climbed up first and held their hands out to pull the rest of us up. The smell inside the wagon made us gasp and cover our mouths. It was far, far worse than our toilet shed at home on a bad day.

There were rough wooden slatted planks about a foot off the ground on either side of the wagon to serve as bunks and another set of the same about a meter higher up. A steel barrel stove stood in the middle. At the top at either corner were small, oblong ventilation holes, but these were boarded up with planks nailed over them.

Tata found a place in the corner of one of the lower bunks. Even though the stove was lit, it was damp and cold on the bunks – so cold that when Antony leaned back for a while against the wall of the truck, his damp hair froze to the wood.

More than fifty people were eventually squeezed into that one small, claustrophobic wagon, crushed in like herrings in a tin. Then without any shout of warning, the sliding doors were slammed shut and locked from the outside. It was worse than a prison cell. In a prison cell there would have been more room. Although it was now morning, we were once again in the dark. As I fought back feelings of panic and claustrophobia I felt Peter's reassuring arm tight around me, and Dziadziu quietly began to pray the Rosary.

Many of the last ones in had to sit on the filthy floor. Tata gave his place on the wooden slats to a young mother with a baby in her arms, who had been pushed in right at the end. He himself then had to sit on the wet floor - the coldest part of the wagon.

There was such a mess and confusion of bundles and boxes and people shivering and in a state of shock, children whimpering.

'They should kick in the planks that are covering the ventilation holes!' Peter said out loud, peering up in the dark. Suddenly there was a thudding and banging and ripping of wood and one of the ventilation holes had been kicked open. Obviously others had felt the same need. There was a tense moment while everyone waited in silence wondering if there would be repercussions for doing this. But there was no shouting or shots fired, so soon the other ventilation hole was forced open too, allowing some fresh cold air in and a small chink of light for those on the top bunks. Those of us below remained in the dark.

For two long days we sat in the stationary, dark wagon, while the other wagons were filled with families.

The sliding doors were unlocked once each day to let prisoners out to go to the toilets under guard. But in between times little children wet and soiled themselves and there was nowhere to wash their soiled clothing. The smell in the wagon grew so disgusting, it was hard to breathe.

Mama shared out the food she had been allowed to bring into the wagon, offering some to the young mother with the baby who had nothing with her. We learned that her name was Marta, her baby's name Stefan. She had been taken away from the hospital where she had given birth just two days before. She did not know what had happened to her husband.

The following day, there was much noise and shouting on the platform. When the sliding doors were opened, we could see a great crowd of local people had gathered on the platform. Word had got round as to what was going on. Local people were desperately running up and down. Names were being shouted, people calling out, crying, screaming, trying to find their loved ones before they were taken away.

After the toilet visits were over, and all the deportees back in the wagons, suddenly Tata raised his head, and stood up off the floor of the wagon. We'd heard it too. Our names were being cried out! And it wasn't by the NKVD. It was someone from the crowds along the platform.

'Anna! Bolek! Anna Gryg! Boleslaw Gryg! Piotrus! Tosia!! Witek! Antony!' I recognised the voice. It was Aunty Serafina, our father's sister!

She had come with many others from the villages and the surrounding towns, searching for their families.

'Anna! Bolek!'

'Serafina!' Tata, all flushed, shouted to her at the top of his voice, pushing his way to the still open doors.

'Serafina! I'm here! Serafina! We're all here!'

She heard him calling and turned and waved in relief, and thankfulness.

'Oh Bolek!' She ran over flushed and out of breath. She handed him up some loaves of bread, and a bag of pears and looked at him with such compassion and pity. The guard inspected the bread and fruit first, and would not allow Tata to leave the train.

'Where are they taking you?'

'What about Burek? Burek is all alone!' I shouted to her, trying to push my way to the door.

But in all the noise she didn't hear.

'Tata! Tell her he ran after us and got too tired to walk! Tell her to go and look for him!'

'God go with you!' Aunty Serafina shouted, choked with tears, as soldiers approached, ordering the crowds away from the train. Doors were being slammed all along the platform.

'Write to us and let us know where you are!' she cried before our doors too were slammed shut and locked. Antony desperately pushed his way in the darkness and climbing up to the top slats to the ventilation hole, shouted at the top of his voice to Aunty Serafina to find Burek.

'Perhaps she heard me!' he said as he came back to join us.

Peter hugged him. 'For one who never could shin up a tree, you did pretty well climbing up there so fast just now!'

Are we nearly there?

Antony wiped his tears with the back of his hand and on the sleeve of his coat, as the steam engine hissed and groaned into motion, and the slow journey across thousands upon thousand of miles began.

At first, everyone sat in numbed silence. As the hours chugged by in monotony and discomfort, little Albin asked Mama, 'Are we nearly there?'

Someone peering from the ventilation hole on the top slats called down that we were now leaving the Polish borders. Someone on the lower slats began to sing the Polish national anthem - 'Jeszcze Polska nie zginela' (Poland has not yet been destroyed while we are alive), and soon the whole wagon was filled with rich, strong Polish voices, singing. Both men and women wept as they sang. Then someone began to pray, "I believe in God, the Father Almighty, creator of heaven and earth…' and others in the wagon joined in.

'Give us this day our daily bread and forgive us our trespasses as we forgive those who trespass against us….' The familiar words calmed us. 'Hail Mary, full of Grace, the Lord is with you, blessed are you among all women, and blessed the fruit of your womb, Jesus,' soon more voices joined the rhythmic meditation prayers, 'Holy Mary, Mother of God, pray for us sinners, now and at the hour of our death, Amen.' Even the littlest children joined in mumbling the bits they knew, and were soon asleep.

Finally, exhausted from having had so little sleep, and

numb with cold, curled up on the freezing damp floors and wooden slats, with no room to stretch out, most of the occupants of that wagon slept.

Before the end of that first day of travelling, people needed the toilet. But the train showed no signs of stopping. The smell of sweaty, unwashed people and children who had wet and soiled themselves was getting stronger and more nauseous; the small amount of water a few had with them could not be used for washing as it was desperately needed for drinking. But there was no shortage of axes, and our father, with the help of another father of a family, soon hacked a small hole in the floor by the wall. A blanket was held in front of it when someone needed to go. When I had to go, Peter went with me to hold me steady as the train lurched along, but even then it wasn't easy. You had to aim at the hole while swaying from side to side. Looking at the stinking mess on the floor around the hole, it was obvious that others had missed the mark before me, and then what was being expelled was blown straight back into the wagon, showering a bare bottom, shoes and socks and clothes with what should have gone out through the hole. The wooden floor around the hole was so soaked and soiled, it stank so much it turned your stomach over. There was no toilet paper, no leaves to wipe our bottoms, and nowhere to wash hands. We were to find out later that toilet paper was considered an unnecessary luxury for the common masses by the Soviets.

After a few more people visited, the waste began to

freeze in the hole so that it soon got completely frozen over and clogged up. Then Tata and the other men had to ram it with the blunt end of the axe, to make it possible for the next person to go.

The following day, the train stopped on a siding in the middle of vast fields of deep snow. The sliding doors were unlocked letting in the brightness of the snow-covered landscape, and people, stiff after so long without moving, blinking and shielding their eyes from the unaccustomed light, were allowed out to relieve themselves.

Modest girls and women looked in horror at the soldiers standing on guard, watching their every move. When they tried to go further away from the soldiers for some privacy, they were herded back with bayonets to where the soldiers could watch them. Women covered themselves with their coats or skirts as best they could. It made our hearts ache to see our mother and our modest, fair-haired thirteen-year old sister having to crouch in the snow in front of the guards. I hated them for watching.

The snow all around the siding was soon soiled and stained.

We were soon to find out that there were no toilets wherever we stopped. No toilets in the railway stations, no toilets in the Soviet Union anywhere. It seemed that in the whole of the vast, 'glorious' Soviet Union, there was no attempt at providing any form of sanitation or hygiene for citizens by the communist regime. Toilets, as well as toilet paper, were regarded as a capitalist luxury, and were scorned. Everywhere the train stopped, there were fields covered in frozen human waste. So many parts of 'the mighty Soviet Union' had become a great and stinking latrine.

A christening party?

Inside the filthy wagon, the blankets and all our clothes were soon infested with fleas and lice that crawled out from the wooden slats and walls at night. Everyone was covered in itchy bites and scratches that oozed and were soon infected as there was no way of keeping clean.

Marta, the young mother sitting near us, kept trying to breast-feed her tiny baby, but although he suckled, he kept stopping to cry.

'Has your baby been baptised, child?' Dziadziu asked her quietly, with compassion. She shook her head, tears welling up in her eyes. She understood what that gentle question meant.

'It is always a good idea to baptise a child as soon as possible after birth,' Dziadziu told her quietly, 'Especially in difficult circumstances.'

The young mother nodded tearfully.

'You know that in an emergency, when there is no priest, anyone can baptise a baby? I have a little water. I know what to do. I had to do it once for...' He shook his head sadly. 'I had to do it before in an emergency. Would you like me to do this for your little one?'

Mama put her arm around the young mother, to support her, as she sat weeping throughout the short baptism. Everyone in the wagon listened respectfully, the men and boys with their caps off, heads bowed, as Dziadziu prayed the Our Father, and the I Believe in God, then poured the precious few drops of water over the baby's head saying, 'Stefan, I baptise you in the name of the Father and of the Son and of the Holy Spirit, Amen. May God hold you close to his heart.' There was not a dry eye in the wagon. Many were openly weeping for the little child and his mother. The baby now slept.

'He is a brand new little saint now.' Dziadziu told her with a smile. 'His soul so light that he will fly straight to heaven like a bright shooting star if God calls him from the misery of this sad world.'

'A christening party?' someone whispered with a smile, making even the young mother smile.

People who had, till then, sat too numb in their individual shock and misery to speak, now began to open up and quietly share with each other the stories of their lives, and how they came to be on this train 'to glory!'

Day after long weary day the train rumbled or crawled along, sometimes stopping for a day or more at a siding, with no explanation. Sometimes the doors of the wagons were opened for a while, other times they were left locked.

Once every other day or so, the train would grind to a creaking halt at some small, out of the way, deserted station, with the name of the station always well covered over.

'They don't want the ordinary Russian people to witness what their Communist regime is doing to so many human beings,' someone commented with feeling.

'And they don't want us to know where they are taking us, so we're disorientated, so we can't escape!' someone else put in.

But at least at every station there was a boiled-water tap. Kipiatok was the Russian word for boiled water. It was a word we all soon knew. We all called out for it at each stop, begging the soldiers for water. But sometimes the taps weren't working because the boiler was broken or had run out of fuel. Everyone was thirsty all the time. Even when a bucket of water was available, it was never enough for fifty people to quench their thirst. It was barely enough for a few small sips each.

On some stops we were given a bucket of watery buckwheat or cabbage soup, again to share between the whole wagon of people.

'Considering the Communists have taken from every family and every person here - our homes, our land with everything in and on them including cows and horses poultry, carts, wheat and all our crops – this watery gruel seems such a very generous recompense!' was one of the milder sarcastic comments made.

On one of the toilet stops, where there was no boiled water tap, my brother Peter noticed others running to the train's engine with pots or kettles. As we were near the front of the train, he quickly took Mama's kettle and jumping out, ran to do the same, begging like the others for some of the boiled engine water. The engine driver, a Polish man, filled his kettle. It tasted so strongly of coal and oil it made you feel nauseous, but at least it was boiled for sure so wouldn't be carrying disease. It kept us alive, but only just, and then not all of us.

'In the Soviet Union, everything belongs to everyone!'

Marta and her baby were curled up on the bunk, with Mama's blanket over them. The baby had cried in the night, then whimpered, then grown silent and still. His young mother held him tightly close to her heart, not wanting to let go. Everyone in the wagon remained silent, out of respect for the child and his weeping mother. Many wept with her.

Dziadziu talked to her in a whisper for a long time, until finally, weeping, she allowed him to gently take the baby from her. A white pillow-case was offered, and the body of baby, wrapped inside it.

Everyone joined in the sorrowful mysteries of the Rosary, praying for the child's young mother.

When the train stopped soon after, and the doors were opened, Dziadziu, with tears in his eyes, took the little pillowcase bundle, though Marta now clung to it shaking her head and weeping.

A passing guard saw what was happening. He wasn't a bad man. He took the baby from them gently, with compassion in his eyes. Marta wept as if someone were tearing her heart in two. Even the men in the wagon were moved to tears.

Later, as the wagon doors were abruptly slammed shut again, Antony managed to climb up and squeeze onto the top bunk to look through the ventilation hole. He came back down subdued. 'There are others who have died,' he said. 'Many others,' he shook his head. He had seen their bodies being carried away by the soldiers.

'It won't be easy to dig graves through the ice and snow.' Peter whispered so the young mother would not hear.

'They poured water over them.' Antony replied quietly. 'Like Mama did our fish we caught in the lake. It froze even as they were pouring. After that they took them where I couldn't see anymore.'

After over a week of this travelling, on one of the stops, Mama and Antony went to look in the store wagon for our sacks of salt pork and other food they had packed. She was searched anxiously through the sacks and bundles that were now piled one on top of another, each one was labelled, but she couldn't find our sacks among them.

'I'm sure they were put in here!' she said, shaking her head anxiously.

A young soldier came by, the same one that had taken

the baby away, and seeing Mama's anxious face, said to her, as he passed by, 'Take whatever you need. In the Soviet Union, everything belongs to everyone.'

Mama looked after him, bewildered.

'What does he mean?' Antony asked. 'How can everything belong to everyone? That was *our* salt pork and our food. These bundles are all labelled with names! They don't belong to *everyone!*'

'Shhh!' Mama warned him to keep his voice down, worriedly.

'But they aren't communal!' Antony continued in an angry whisper. How can they be? Every one of these bundles belongs to *someone*! To people like us!

Mama squeezed his shoulder to calm him down.

'But it's not fair! That pork was from our pig – it belonged to us!'

Mama pressed her lips together nervously, blinking hard, searching through the other bundles in the store wagon.

'Then let's take someone else's bundle, like the soldier said!' Antony urged her.

'Antony, we are not Communists!' she replied quietly, shaking her head. 'Let's not start acting as they do.'

That sack of salted meat was supposed to have fed our large family for the whole year – it was from our own pig that we had fattened for over a year and slaughtered ourselves, and now someone else was eating it!

I was so indignant and angry when I heard about it that it made me feel sick. To think that someone could just take the precious food that belonged to us, and that the soldiers let them take it.

'I heard them say to you it would be safe in there!' Antony cried. 'That's what they said when you put the sacks in there!'

'It may well have been the soldiers themselves who took it,' Tata said. 'Since they had no qualms about taking all the food from all the shops in Poland, to feed themselves, leaving nothing for the Polish people.'

And so the long cold journey continued, but now our food supplies had been taken, and hunger, as well as dehydration began to take its toll.

Through a crack in the wood, that we had made bigger with a penknife, Peter and I took turns in peering out. We passed by a huge town with lots of lights on in the dark. Someone looking out from a ventilation hole said they thought it must be Moscow. But mainly it was vast fields of snow and sometimes forests blanketed in snow.

At each siding stop, the corpses of the dead were carried away, and there were many. In every wagon, people wept for their loved ones who had died, and were not even given the dignity of a burial in this frozen foreign land.

Then one day, after four long weeks of incarceration, the train stopped at a small station, and for the first time, we could hear voices on the platform. Doors of wagons were being unlocked and opened, commands being called out in Russian and people talking.

Blinking at the unaccustomed brightness as our

door too was opened, we saw large, pony-drawn sleighs standing a little distance away. And beyond them, forest. Everywhere we looked there was dark, dense snow-covered forest.

'People are being ordered off the wagons and they're taking their things with them!' cried Antony who had squeezed to the open door and was leaning out to see what was happening.

Straight away everyone in the wagon began to move at once, gathering blankets, bowls and spoons, pots and bundles together. Stiff and weak and faint with hunger, but hurrying, almost in a panic, as if frightened that they would be left behind. We stumbled out, so unused to movement, and so faint from lack of water and nutrition that we could hardly walk, clutching our bundles tightly. Sharp, icy wind tore at our hands and faces, freezing the breath in our mouths and noses. It literally took our breath away - such a painful cold we had never experienced in Poland, not even in the harshest winter.

Numb, unsteady on our feet, half starved and frozen, we were ordered onto the sledges, as names were called out. But how good it was at least to be out of the prison of the dark, stinking cattle truck, and even though the cold hurt our lungs, how good it was to breathe air that was not stale and foul-smelling.

But where on earth were we? Everywhere you looked was nothing but forests. Was this Siberia? We all knew that all deportees were dumped in Siberia – and it was certainly cold enough for that, but this wasn't at all how we had imagined it. Everyone was looking around bemused, wondering, people asking each other where we were.

'If you do not work, you do not eat!'

After a long, long, freezing ride along snow-covered forest track, we stopped at last at a large forest clearing. We could see a settlement of small, rough wooden huts on top of a hill, with a larger hut that was used as a schoolroom.

The administrator of that settlement was waiting for our arrival.

'You are in Kizielsk,' he informed us briskly, first in Russian then in Polish. 'Kizielsk, Molotowskaja Oblas, Cizel Rion, Poczta Ivaka, Posiolek Szczepanowka. This is where you will start your new life. Here, if you work, you eat. If you do not work you do not eat.'

We stood in silence, listening to the list of rules and regulations.

'Well, it's got to be better than being locked up in a stinking cattle truck!' Antony whispered to me, though, in fact, for our first night at least, it wasn't so very different – about a hundred very hungry and cold deportees packed into one small school room to sleep on the bare cold floor. Once again we were as tight as herrings, the windows closed against the bitterly cold wind. Once again, the overwhelming smell of seriously soiled and unwashed people in such close proximity making you feel sick.

But in the morning, as the winter sun streamed in through the large window, it brought hope to our hearts, though after four weeks in the darkness of the wagons, to be suddenly in bright morning sunlight was more than our eyes could cope with at first.

That first day, we were allowed to rest. There was an oil-drum stove in the room fuelled by wood.

'There are logs outside for the stove,' said the administrator. 'You may bring them in as needed.'

Most people sat too exhausted and weak to move. But not Antony. Although the four weeks of constant hunger had reduced him almost to skin and bones, he was determined to help keep us all warm. Putting on our father's outdoor trousers and boots which were so big on him that he had to stuff the trouser into the boots so as not to trip up, he went out to brave the arctic cold and bring in the logs. Peter and I followed to help. Just to be able to go outside into the fresh air (even though it was painfully cold) felt so good. So good just to be able to open a door ourselves and step outside and even though faint with hunger, to stretch our legs and to look out at the snow-laden forests all around.

But getting the logs in was easier said than done. We found them buried under a deep pile of snow that was frozen solid. But with an axe and some bashing with bits of planks lying close by, though we were exhausted by such unaccustomed activity in our weakened state, we managed to dig out some of the logs and brought them in.

Everyone looked up anxiously and warily when the administrator came in later, to see what would happen next.

That afternoon, we learned we were in the dense forest region of the Urals, and we were here to work. If we did not work, we would not eat. If we did not eat we would die. There were no wire fences around us but it was made very clear to us that no one had ever escaped. No one had even attempted to. Where on earth was there to run to? The administrator laughed. To Poland? The Russians were there now and it was thousands of frozen deep-snow-covered miles away. We were told we would be allowed to go into the forest to forage for food but not as far as Ivaki town which was about thirteen kilometres away. It was another settlement, but a larger one than the one we had been brought to, with maybe a hundred people, a couple of NKVD offices and a post office.

When we were registered, the administrator asked for those who were skilled carpenters to step forward; they were needed for work in Ivaki town. Our father, although he and our grandfather had built their house in Uzbielerz, did not think of stepping forward as he was a forest keeper by profession not a carpenter.

All other men, my father and Peter included, were registered for work outdoors in the forest. We later realised that there were men who had never hammered a nail and didn't own a decent saw who had stepped forward to say they were carpenters. They had been cunning enough to realise the carpentry work in the town would be easier than living and working in the extreme conditions of the forests. In fact, all the 'carpentry' work consisted of was making rough crates and building huts of wood – just plain work. Our father and Peter could have done it with their eyes closed.

'Red Army' attack at night

The settlement in Kisielsk was on two hills and divided into two. On one of the hills were the small, rough, wooden huts to house the families of the forest workers, on the other hill the school and the house of the administrator of the settlement. His hut was the same as all the other dwellings, but he didn't have to share it with fifteen other people and it was called the Head Office. There was also a small bakery where the bread was baked each day. It was rationed by weight and was therefore always under-baked, because gluey, under-baked bread contained more water and was therefore heavier, so less had to be given away.

Between the two hills was a stream, and also a well – which was simply a spring with low walls around it. And what a blessing it was! Summer or winter, amazingly, that spring never dried up and never froze - not even in the worst of the Siberian winter when temperatures often dipped to minus fifty degrees when even to breath outside was dangerous.

Everyone from the settlement would go to that spring for water. We would carry the water on our shoulders in wooden buckets at each end of a four to six foot long piece of wood. In the winter it was treacherously slippery and much of the water sloshed out of the buckets when we lost our balance.

There were some small half-built wooden huts by a snow packed track on top of the hill. These huts we learned, had been built by previous deportees, most of whom had not survived the brutal winters, the lack of food and the hard physical labour.

For such a small settlement there was a very big cemetery on the outskirts. The few previous deportees who had survived had been moved to live in Ivaki town to make room for the new batch of imported slave-labourers.

Each small wooden hut was partitioned into two by a thin screen, to give some privacy, though the screen did not reach to the ceiling, so there was no soundproofing at all.

'Boleslaw and Anna Gryg and family!' the administrator finally called our names and ordered us to follow him, slipping and stumbling along the icy track to what was to be our new home - one small, dark room in one half of one of the rough-planked huts. There were already seven people in the other half of the hut, the Ziewkowicz family who had five boys.

Each half of the hut had a flimsy steel-drum stove which served as a heater and cooker. There were some rough wooden planks along the walls to serve as beds, and a small, stained wooden table and bench. There was no space for anything else.

Mama allotted a small bunk behind the stove where it was warmest for Grandfather Ignacy. It was cramped and dark, but there he would have some warmth and a little privacy. We children would squeeze together on the planks along the wall, Mama and Tata on the narrowest and coldest bunk by the door.

Before darkness fell, we all went to stand outside, gratefully breathing in the freezing cold fresh air, and we watched the sun going down behind the dense forest. Oh how good it was to look out at a view again, to see the sky turning red with the setting sun, and though weak with hunger and shivering from the cold, we were grateful to still be alive, and to still be together.

Mentally and physically exhausted after the gruelling journey, and having been warned that the following day work would begin at dawn, we desperately needed sleep. That night, however, we were to learn, that sleep was not something that came easily to anyone in those rough wooden huts.

That first night in the hut, as soon as we had laid down to sleep on the rough planks, with our few blankets, filthy and flea infested from the cattle truck, we were soon woken by excruciating pain. We were being eaten alive by disgusting beetles crawling out of the wood from all directions. Round, flat, reddish-brown beetles sucking our blood with every nasty deep and very painful bite. They crawled out of every crack in the bunks and walls and roof to feed off the fresh blood of the new inhabitants of the hut. As if we had any blood to spare, I thought angrily as I was bitten again and again, by those bugs from hell.

The first few nights were spent wearily killing them, but when you crushed one the stench was so disgusting it made you retch.

'Bloody demons!' Peter swore at them.

But no matter how many were killed, it made no difference to their numbers. They just kept multiplying. The whole hut was riddled with them. There were hundreds of them crawling over the beds every night, inflicting torture upon everyone of us without mercy.

Because of these disturbed nights, we were constantly in a state of exhaustion.

Interestingly, we later found out from the communist school, that if you locked a bedbug in a box, say, an empty matchbox, with nothing in it, no food or water , it could survive in that empty box for seven to eight years, so long as it had just once had a drink of blood. It was an enemy that did not die easily.

Night blindness

There was a small pile of logs outside the huts for our first night, and when all the new arrivals were assembled the following morning at the administrator's orders, it was explained to us by an NKVD officer from Ivaki town that it was possible to buy more wood if we wished. He explained that it was possible to take out a loan from them to pay for wood, which would then be repaid from wages earned.

Peter took out of his pocket the few Polish zloty he had taken from our kitchen table at home, and held them tight in his hand, nodding to me hopefully. Our father, we knew, did not believe in taking loans. He had always hated the idea of living beyond ones means and being in debt. But perhaps Peter's money would be enough to buy some logs.

But one of the Polish men was asking the officer how much they cost and was told the price in roubles.

'And in Polish zloty?' the man asked.

The NKVD officer shook his head. 'Polish zloty are no good here. You are in the Soviet Union now. Only Russian roubles.'

Peter quietly put the money back in his pocket.

My heart sank. I glanced at our father. Neither he nor Grandfather Ignatius had ever taken out a loan in their lives. They had both always hated the idea of spending more than you had, always saying it was best to buy only what one could afford.

I could see the uncertainty in my father's eyes, saw him glance at all of us looking at him anxiously to see what he would say. He shook his head regretfully, then for the first time in his life went forward with everyone else to ask for a loan for wood - from the very people who had stolen his home and livelihood and all he owned.

'There was no choice,' he explained to us later. 'Without wood for the stove how could we survive?'

He'd had to take the loan not only for logs, but also to buy bread for us to live on as well until they began to earn some money. For this big family, even to have a small slice each, a lot of bread was needed.

Tata and Peter were both taken away to work some kilometres away in the forest chopping and sawing trees. We were told they would not be back, except for brief visits, but would live in the forest clearings where they worked. There was a steam-powered tractor with huge sledges attached for transporting the logs, and those sledges also transported the workers to their work areas in the forest. They loaded Tata and Peter and all the other men and women and young people sixteen and over. Everyone was expected to work. Peter was the youngest of the workers.

The forest was divided up into large square areas each of which had rough, temporary barracks for the workers to sleep in and eat. Peter was on the 48th area and Tata the 49th.

If they wanted to come back to the hut to see their family, they had to walk. It was a seven kilometre trudge through the snow in the dark forest.

Peter made the long walk back to the hut whenever he could, to give our mother the extra bread he had earned. They had to work 'a norm' in order to get their ration of bread. That meant you had to cut or saw down a certain number of trees each day. To accomplish this norm meant exhausting, unrelenting, heavy work from dawn till dusk. Peter was young and had a good sharp saw. As he got used to the work his strength increased, he occasionally managed to do more than the norm, and was rewarded with extra bread. This he would carefully hide under the sack that served for his bed, and bring it to Mama on his visits back to the hut.

'We are in theory free to come away whenever we want,' Peter told us, 'But unless you do the norm, you don't get your ration of bread. So if you can't do the norm, you're a prisoner there.'

Whenever Peter made the journey back to Mama in the evenings, in the dark, he always prayed he would not meet a bear or a pack of wolves. It was not unusual for even grown men to disappear in the forest never to be seen again; wolves and bears were as hungry as every other creature in that starving land, and there was little chance of surviving an encounter with either.

He always carried with him his large flexible saw, carrying it wrapped around his waist. Although it was too big to carry easily, he didn't dare leave it behind because it was a good saw with strong teeth and others were jealous of it. Things were stolen out of desperation. It was a matter of survival.

Each time he came back to us on the settlement, he spent some time carefully sharpening his saw with a stone.

'It's nice and sharp and shiny now! It looks lovely!' Albin remarked appreciatively, watching him work.

'The sharper it is, Al, the more trees I can saw,' Peter explained to him with a rueful smile. 'And the more bread I can bring home for Mama to feed us all.' He was then just barely sixteen years old.

Our father worked to the limits of his strength each day too. The communists, refusing to keep Sundays holy and hating anything to do with God, arranged the work days of the deportees so that it was impossible for them to keep Sundays holy. Instead of a seven day week, they made the weeks nine or ten days long. With such a heavy workload, and having given Peter the best saw, our father simply did not have the strength for the two long hours of walking to get back to us on his one day off, so he suffered loneliness and grief as well as exhaustion and malnutrition. Like many others in Siberia, he soon developed night blindness, caused by a lack of oils and vitamins in his diet. This meant he couldn't see in the dark, which now made it impossible for him to make the walk in the dark through the woods.

Strange new boots

When Peter made the long trek through the forest to come and see us, our mother always wept with relief to see he was still alive.

She always made sure that he had the largest piece of bread and the biggest helping of our water-and-flour soup.

'You work so hard,' she said urging him to eat it. 'You need it more than we do.'

'The food is a bit better for the workers in the forest, Mama,' he would say to try and ease her anxieties. 'Look, you can see, the bread they give us is not as gluey and undercooked as yours is. They feed us a bit better so we can saw down more trees!'

'But you're so thin!' She'd say looking at his pale, gaunt face and caved in cheeks with such anxiety for him in her eyes.

'We have women workers with us, now,' he said, explaining why he was no longer able to work over the norm and had not been able to bring us some extra bread. 'They had them working in their own square kilometre of the forest at first – number 47, but they couldn't manage anywhere near the norm, so they weren't given any bread. They were collapsing with weakness and after one of them died, they put them with us, so we have to help them.' He shrugged. 'It slows us down a lot. We can't do more than the norm now and even that now takes longer than before.'

'But that's not fair!' Antony cried in indignation.

'What do you do at night?' I asked him, changing the subject, because to start talking of fairness would spoil our short time with our elder brother and only bring bitterness.

'Sleep!' Peter smiled ruefully. 'We don't finish work till it's dark, then we eat the watery soup and bread, then we collapse on the bunk and sleep. And then we get our blood sucked by the demons from hell, like everyone else!'

'Don't they keep you awake?'

'Antony,' he smiled, 'I am so dead beat that rats could be eating my toes and I wouldn't wake up!'

'But aren't you wet after working outside all day in the snow?' Mama asked anxiously, looking at his worn out, thin rubber boots that were not high enough to stop the deep snow falling in over the top. 'Are you getting chilblains?'

Frostbite was a constant worry, because of the danger of gangrene and death that often followed, since there was no health service and no medicines for deportees. Life was cheap in that land. People could easily be replaced.

'Mama, don't worry! My feet are fine!' he reassured her, and then grinned. 'We have new boots every day!'

She looked at him in astonishment, as we all did. What was he talking about? We knew only too well from experience that the Communists did not give anything away for free. Not even the smallest crust of bread. Where on earth was my brother getting brand new boots from every day? To obtain even one pair of the warm felt Valonki boots was unthinkable - it would have meant bartering all the clothes we possessed between us on the baraholki market, and going stark naked for the rest of that Siberian winter!

'So where are these boots then?' our mother asked, anxious now that he had foolishly left them behind to get stolen. 'You have *new boots* and you have left them behind at the work barracks!'

'Don't worry, Mama!' Peter was still smiling. 'No one will steal them! *Everyone* has a new pair of boots every morning!'

Now we were all looking at him as if he'd gone crazy. Many cracked up under those extreme conditions.

He shook his head and laughed. 'Since we don't have socks, you know, we wrap rags around our feet each morning in the barracks, then, would you believe it, we go outside and pour water over the rags.' he explained. 'It freezes solid straight away, before it's had time to soak in, and it makes a solid ice boot around the rags. Everyone does it!' he shrugged. 'OK, felt Valonki they are *not!*' he grinned, 'But it works! The Russian deportees who've been here longest showed us how to do it.'

'And does that keep your feet dry all day?' Mama was astounded.

'Yes. And when we're sawing and chopping we stay warm from the hard work!' he reassured her. 'We take the rags off at night, shake off the ice and hang them over the stove to dry and next morning we make ourselves some brand new ice boots!'

He saw Mama looking anxious again so he added cheerfully, 'But, you know, this last week in the barracks we stayed up a bit once, in the evening. There was a man who had brought his accordion with him and he played some tunes for us.' He looked wistful. 'It really was so lovely to hear. Some people even danced a bit.'

'Did you dance?' Antony asked him.

'Peter shook his head with an embarrassed smile, 'No, not me!'

I knew how he felt. It was the same shyness we had all inherited to some extent.

'I didn't feel like dancing anyway,' he added, with a shrug, glancing across to Dziadziu, who was lying on his bunk, suffering badly from malnutrition and cold. I knew what he meant. How could he dance, when our Grandfather was coughing and wasting away and there was nothing any of us could do to help? How could he dance when Tata was growing old and grey and blind before his time and working harder than his body could take?

Deportees who didn't have a family to feed had just enough bread to eat and could stop and rest. But not Tata and Peter. They had to practically break their backs in order to earn enough bread to just keep themselves and their loved ones alive.

'But I really liked the tunes.' Peter smiled to us, his eyes lighting up. 'One day, I'd like to learn to play like that.'

Mysterious illness

Our mother did all she could to find extra food for our grandfather, who was growing weaker day. Several times she made the two hour walk to the little town settlement to barter some of our clothes for some extra food. She was able to obtain a few potatoes sometimes, or half a cabbage. The local people had no other way of obtaining clothing, as there were no clothes shops. Like toilets and toilet paper, even basic clothing was considered a capitalist luxury, not necessary for the common people. In that impoverished land, therefore, clothes and food were both more precious than gold.

She brought her precious few bartered goods home, clutching them to her as if she were carrying the greatest treasure. She made soup to nourish and warm our grandfather. It was still mainly water soup though and there was never enough. Even with the soup, and with the stove lit, our grandfather was constantly shivering.

Our father and Peter had managed to pay off the loan for the wood, and had also managed to buy more logs, so at least the stove was kept burning. But it wasn't just our grandfather's health that was deteriorating.

Roman, one of the younger Ziewkowicz boys from the other half of our hut, used to come into our side of the hut sometimes, to visit. One evening, Antony and I heard a thud outside our door and ran out to see what it was.

It was Roman - collapsed unconscious outside our door. He was lying on the earth floor looking deathly white.

'Is he dead?' Antony whispered to me, as we crouched by his side.

'I nervously felt for his pulse in his neck. I'd seen this done so often on the journey in the cattle trucks when so many people had died. I wasn't quite sure where to touch, but knew that this was the way you could tell if someone was alive or dead.

Antony, far more simply, held his hand up to Roman's nose. 'He's breathing. He's still breathing!'

We patted Roman's cheek, and we both leaned back with a sigh of relief as his eyelids fluttered open and he groaned and rubbed his head where he had bumped it when he'd fallen

'What happened?' he asked groggily.

'You tell us!' Antony replied. 'We thought you were dead!'

'Have you had something to eat today?'

Roman nodded, wincing as he moved his head. 'A slice of bread and Kipiatok. But I'm not hungry. I feel sick.'

That evening, when I went out of the hut to fetch some more wood from the porch area I came back feeling dizzy with my head spinning. Antony too was feeling sick.

'Maybe we're all slowly dying from starvation,' Antony whispered to me that night as we lay close together for warmth on our hard bunk. My heart sank. There was no doubt that we were starving - our stomachs caved in and constantly gnawing with hunger pains. You could see all our bones. What if Peter came home one night and found us all dead in the hut?

It wouldn't have been anything unusual out there. Two young children had died the previous week, just collapsed and died in their hut.

Antony was so determined that this would not happen to us, that the following morning he got up when it was still dark, to go and queue early for bread. If you didn't get to the baker's early, you could wait for several hours and then they would run out of bread before it was your turn and you'd come home with nothing. The ration book was of no use when the bread ran out.

The thought of Peter coming home to find us all dead was so frightening, he decided to have less sleep in order to be one of the first in the queue, and be sure of getting bread.

So out he went in the darkness. He stood waiting. It was too cold to sit on the ground. You just had to keep stamping your feet and standing and standing and standing. The queue behind him got longer and longer. By the time it was dawn, everyone was out waiting for the baker's hut to open. He glanced behind him and knew there would never be enough bread for all these people. The ones at the back of the queue would have to go back to their huts empty-handed. Mama would be so pleased to get the bread early today he thought happily in spite of desperately aching feet and feeling frozen and faint.

But as soon as the doors of the bakery were opened, suddenly the long, orderly queue turned into a surge of pushing people - a tidal wave of starving humanity, all aware that there would not be enough bread for them all. And Antony, eight years old and so thin now - so very light - that a puff of Siberian wind could have carried him off like a dandelion seed, was trampled on in the rush. He was shoved to the outside of the queue by stronger, bigger people – elbowed hard, kicked and pushed, bruised, and trodden on.

With tears of pain and anger and frustration, he tried to push his way back, only to be shoved angrily away, as if he were the one pushing in. No one let him back in. Finally the doors of the bakery were closed. All the bread was gone.

Antony stared in disbelief at the closed doors with such bitterness, anger and frustration that he felt he couldn't bear it. Mama would be wondering why he had not come home. She would be waiting for the bread. Dziadziu Ignatius would be waiting for his breakfast. He knew that he would now have to wait until the next batch of bread was baked. Then the doors would open again. So, faint with hunger, his feet numb with cold, but not wanting to go home to Mama empty handed, not wanting us all to die of starvation he now sat on the frozen, trampled dirty snow and waited.

After two hours, blue with cold, his feet so numb he could hardly walk, he stood up as the shop was opened again, this time he was determined to hold his ground, but, once again, he didn't stand a chance. Once more the surge of starving humanity trampled the skinny little boy and shoved him out of the queue and away from the bread. He screamed at them to let him through. He fought like a wild animals, kicking and beating them with his fists. It did no good. Hot tears ran down his face that was now blue with cold.

When the shop closed its doors for the day, he finally had to go back empty handed to the miserable hut. He would never ever forget that most horrible of days. That morning we had more watery soup, with no bread. Once again we were both feeling so faint and sick that when we lay down for the night, our hearts pounding in fear, we were wondering if we would still be alive in the morning.

The following day, our Mother went to queue. She who in Poland had defended our potatoes from wild pigs would now defend her place in the queue with every bit of strength she possessed if her children's lives depended on it. She came back to the hut later, not only with some bread, but also with news. While waiting in the queue, she had heard talk about the two children who had died the previous week. It was the fumes from the stoves that were poisoning people, she had been told – a deadly gas was being emitted from the resinous wood burning in the stoves, and where there was not enough ventilation in the hut, could be lethal. The two children had died from the fumes in their hut since their poor mother had not opened the small window in order to protect them from the cold.

Antony and I looked at each other in such immense relief, I with a lump in my throat, so grateful to have found the reason and the remedy for this sickness. After that our mother always kept the little window always opened a bit, no matter how cold it was, for some fresh air to come in and the poisonous gas to escape.

'Be careful what you say, brother!'

All of us children had to go to school in order to receive a bread ration.

Communist propaganda was foremost on the curriculum, as was the refutation of religion and the existence of God. Stalin, it was made clear to us, was now 'our father' and greater than any God. Each morning began with Communist songs and rousing shouts of 'Long live Father Stalin!'

But there were other things that were good there, like singing and learning Russian, and the school had a wood -burning stove in each class and big airy windows, which were wonderful to gaze out of during lessons.

I enjoyed going to school and liked most of the lessons. We had a good teacher who was kind and fair and I picked up Russian quickly, worked hard, and took time over my homework and pride in my learning. It took my mind off hunger and bedbug bites, fleas and the many anxieties and fears that constantly plagued me. In spite of being quiet and shy, I soon became the star pupil of the class. This, in the Soviet Union, was considered a great achievement, and a tremendous honour. I was called to the front of the class and our teacher explained to me that I had now achieved the distinction of being an 'atlicznik' – a student of excellence. With great solemnity I was awarded a small red triangular scarf, which was placed on my shoulder as a sign of this great honour. The little ceremony finished with everyone enthusiastically clapping and arousing communist song.

My younger brother, Antony however, was not quite as academically inclined or as conscientious about his work, and was always ready with an excuse not to take long on his homework.

His whole nature rebelled against the communist propaganda which his teacher unfortunately revelled in, and he spent much time in school gazing out of the windows feeling rebellious.

'Antony! Stop day dreaming and concentrate!' his teacher had to frequently remind him. But there was one thing he really did like and that was when his teacher Nikolai Nikolajevicz, would sing to the class, which he did quite often. He said it made up for having to put up with all the rest. Having been starved of anything beautiful for so long, my brother sat totally entranced as his otherwise very stern teacher stood in front of the class and delighted them with his rich strong baritone voice.

One afternoon, that first Siberian winter, Antony's class were given a poem to learn, about the great and glorious Soviet Union.

Antony did not like this poem. How could he like it? - he explained to me as we made our way back to the hut together after school that afternoon. The Soviet Union and its God-hating, people-murdering, filthy, thieving

105

communism, had stolen everything from us and was slowly killing both our grandfather and our father. No, he would not recite a poem about what a paradise it all was, when it wasn't! How could he say that *hell* was paradise. It was all just a filthy brainwashing lie! It wasn't fair!

'But Antony – you'll be in big trouble, and you *like* Nikolai Nikolajovicz.!' I tried reasoning with him. He couldn't accept that nothing was fair in that hellish land. Nothing was fair about Communism, but if we couldn't come to some acceptance of our present situation we would end up dying of rage and bitterness. 'You like your teacher, don't you? And you don't have to *believe* the poem. Just memorise it and then forget it!'

'I *do* like him but I don't like this stupid verse!' It's all such a pack of lies!'

I nodded in sympathy.

'*You* remember what Dziadiu used to read out to us when we were still in Poland?' Antony went on angrily, 'You know, about filling our minds with all that is good, and beautiful and noble and praiseworthy?'

I remembered it well. – 'Be careful what you put into your mind because it goes into your heart and becomes part of you,' was what he used to say.

'Well, I'm not putting the stinking Soviet Union in my heart for anyone!' Antony said determinedly.

Famous last words!

That afternoon, while I worked at my homework, Antony stubbornly refused to even look at his. He went out instead to gather sticks to store for the stove, determined to do something useful instead of wasting his time, he said.

The following day, however, he walked more slowly to school than usual.

'Just don't go telling your reason for not doing your homework,' I warned him, 'or you'll get Mama into trouble. People have been sent away to the salt mines for having rebellious children. That would kill her! She'd never survive that! And who would look after Dziadziu, if she were gone? And us? And Tata would die of a broken heart! Be careful what you say, brother!'

At the very first lesson that morning, in Antony's class, everyone had to stand up in turn and recite that dratted verse. And everyone recited it – some very well, some a little hesitantly – but every child had memorised it more or less.

Antony was sitting near the back of the room by the window, not daring to gaze out now, his heart thudding as it came nearer to his turn. Finally Nikolai called out his name.

Flushed and nervous, he stood up and admitted that he hadn't learnt it.

'Why not?' Nikolai asked.

Antony, feeling sick with fear by then and anxious that Mama would get sent away to the salt mines, said it was because he felt ill. This was certainly true at that moment, his stomach was churning away.

Nikolai, perhaps seeing how flushed he was, gave him a look of concern and sent him home to bed. Once out of the school building, with the prospect of a day of freedom ahead, Antony's sickness suddenly left him, and he skipped all the way home, so relieved to have got away with it. Or so he thought.

He spent the day whistling in the forest, collecting sticks for the stove.

I came home from school and asked him why I'd seen him skipping away from school that morning.

'Nothing to worry about, brother!' Antony grinned. 'I felt sick and he sent me home, that's all!'

'But you were running up the hill! You didn't look sick. Sick kids don't run fast up hills!

Antony shrugged. 'I felt fine once I left school!'

'But if I saw you, what if Nikolai Nikolajevicz did too?'

The next day, as soon as the school doors opened, Nikolai Nikolajevicz called Antony over to the front of the class. 'Did you learn the verse?' he asked quietly, giving him a long look.

Flushed, Antony shook his head..

'Then you will stay behind after class until you have learnt it.'

So there was Antony, after all the other children had left the school, sitting with the propaganda poem in front of him, while I was waiting outside for him anxiously. He glanced out and saw me and waved me away with a resigned shrug.

He would have to fill his mind with lies, or stay there, it seemed, forever.

He chose the lesser of the two evils.

'Don't mess with such things!'

The Russian deportees in the settlement were very superstitious, especially the women, and also greatly attracted to fortune telling and all kinds of divination.

Our grandfather used to say that when people stop believing in God, they don't then just believe in nothing; they believe in everything, no matter how foolish. When we first began to see how much fortune telling and divination was encouraged by the communists – even in the schools, our grandfather had explained that these things were forbidden by God because they were harmful to our souls.

'But what if they really work, and we could find out the future?' Antony once asked him.

'Child, if there is any power in these things, you can be sure it comes from evil not good spirits.

'But couldn't it come from spirits that are just neither good nor bad?' Antony had persisted.

'There's no such thing as a neutral spirit, child. In the invisible realm there are only two kinds of spirits - those who belonged to God and are obedient to him, and the disobedient ones that come from the realms of darkness.'

Antony had accepted our grandfather's words at that time, but later - in that first Siberian winter, when all the men, except for the sick and infirm, were away working in the forest, there was very little for a boy to be occupied with. Antony, young and foolish, and up for anything as usual, was eventually cajoled by some of the local girls and women into joining in their Ouija board séances. They needed him, they insisted, because it was best to have both men and women present for it to work really well. So five or six of these local girls and women, together with our nine year old Antony, would sit around a small table. On top of it they had a piece of paper with a circle drawn on it and all the letters of the alphabet written outside and around the circle. Right in the middle they had a glass or a saucer. They would each put two fingers lightly on the glass or saucer – only just touching it, and they would call upon the spirits.

When he excitedly he told me about it, I was uneasy. 'Antony, this is scary stuff!'

'But they need me because you can't have just women present and all the other men are away!'

They would sit in a huddle and call upon the spirits of deceased relatives and other people they had known. Antony was convinced that spirits came to spell out replies to their questions – usually just a yes or no.

'But, Antosh, what did Dziadziu tell us? If God says don't do such things then it can't be good spirits that come! Do you really want to mess with evil spirits?

'But Witek! It really does work! None of us pushes the saucer!'

'If that's true, that makes it even scarier!'

But Antony was in no mood to listen. Soon however, these meetings were put to an end by the administrator. It wasn't because the communists had anything against divination - on the contrary, they encouraged anything that was against

God's commandments - but because gatherings of any kind were forbidden. Those in charge of the settlements lived in constant fear of rebellion and uprisings.

For once I was glad of the administrator's intervention.

Very soon after the séances stopped. Antony became suddenly very ill. He started to complain that he could smell a horrible smell and then developed such a high fever that we did not think he would survive. With that fever came the most dark and terrifying nightmares, leaving him soaked in sweat and screaming in horror, with hallucinations so terrifying that even now, seventy years later, he says he would rather die than live through such nightmares again. He can still recall the disgusting smell and shudders to remember it.

'Unfortunately, no leeches here!'

Spring came with thaws and floods of melting snow.

Everywhere and everything was wet. The wooden hut was saturated; the roof was leaking, the earth floor sodden and muddy and the blankets damp. Our few clothes were wet through and couldn't be dried as the stove never really got hot enough. Our feet were constantly wet, muddy and cold.

Every morning when our mother woke she prayed for

God's mercy and for the strength to get through the day. These were particularly difficult times especially for her. Her husband had been taken away from her, and she was suffering because she knew he must be suffering to be away from us. She worked so hard and looked so tired, so pale and thin and worn out. She wasn't an educated person, yet she managed to feed her children, and her father-in-law. Her great determination to provide and care for us all must have given her the motivation to keep going.

When the floods dried up, and the first of the spring sunshine warmed the earth, she started to dig the ground around the hut, using a sharpened bit of wood that she had asked Peter to make her as a trowel. She was determined to grow potatoes, like the Russian deportees on the settlement who had been there for longer than we had. She had bartered her one spare blouse for half a sack of seed potatoes and she sowed these with great care.

'Things will improve when the potatoes grow,' she told Dziadziu cheerfully, hiding her weariness. Her dress that once fitted her so well, now hung about her like a stained and dirty shapeless tent. Her skin was grey, her cheeks caved in. To see her like this made my heart ache with pain. It made me want to cry out at the unfairness of it all. Why did our hardworking, uncomplaining, gentle mother have to suffer like this?

I wasn't the only one whose heart ached for her.

One day, when I came back from collecting wood in the forest, I found Antony lying curled up on the bunk, weeping like his heart was breaking.

Our mother was outside tending her potato patch.

'Antosh, what's the matter?' I asked in alarm, sitting on the edge of the bunk. Are you in pain?'

He shook his head.

'What is it then?'

'Mama is selling her other dress – a Russian woman is coming to buy it tomorrow, so that for those measly few roubles she'll get, we can buy bread.

'But we have to eat Antony! A dress will be no good to Mama if we are all dead and she is too!'

Antony shook his head so wistfully. 'But it's her best dress! It's like we'll never leave this place now, never go back home to Poland!' Tears spilled down his cheeks again. 'Tata used to tell her how beautiful she used to look in it…. Now she looks so…' and he was crying again, and couldn't finish, but I knew what he meant, and I suffered with him.

Now our mother's face and hands were covered in scars from bedbug bites and scratches, even her scalp. She suffered too from constant reinfestations of lice, as we all did. There were always dark bags under her eyes and her hair was so dull now and limp and thin and dirty. Her hands that did so much work were rough and grimy, as there was no soap for washing. And now her blue dress, which our father used to love her wearing, was going to be worn by some stranger.

And as if things weren't bad enough for her, they got even worse. She suffered on and off with a terrible toothache. It must have been an abscess, as she was often

113

in such awful pain. For a while it would ease off then come back again with a vengeance. She would lie groaning on her wooden-plank bed at night when she thought everyone was asleep.

There were no dentists in that land for deportees though. There *was* a dentist in the Ivaki settlement, but you had to pay to see her, and we didn't have enough money for bread to keep us alive, never mind to pay for a dentist.

Here there was no leech pond to suck out the infected blood, as there had been in Poland. This was the way the peasants at home dealt with abscesses. You took a leech carefully from the pond and put it inside a hollow twig, letting just the sucker end stick out, then you placed it on the infected gum, and it sucked out the blood – and the infection. It wasn't pleasant, but it did seem to work.

Here, however there were not even any leeches.

When our father came back to the hut for one of his rare day visits, when he had a whole day off, Mama was in too much pain to hide it from him. Tata went out saying he would be back soon. He came back with a pair of pliers he had borrowed, and sent us children outside.

Our sister Tosia put her hands over her ears just as she used to put a pillow over her head in Poland when the pig was being slaughtered. We were expecting to hear screams. But there was just a groan and we ran back in to find our mother sitting holding a rag to her mouth, and Tata holding the infected tooth in the pliers.

'It wasn't as hard as I thought it would be,' he said shaking his head, 'The tooth was much looser than you'd expect.'

'Good!' Antony said, so happy and relieved that the worst of Mama's pain was over, but I could see that Tata wasn't looking so pleased, and I understood why.

Roman, the boy our age from the other half of the hut had lost his teeth. He'd been chewing on stale bread and they just fell out. Four of them anyway- all from the front. It was caused by scurvy.

Tata warned us all from then on to dip our bread into soup or hot water before eating it. 'Or you will lose your teeth too! Don't chew on anything hard.'

The thought of looking like Roman, who now looked like an old man, appalled me. And Peter too, on his last visit to the hut, had mentioned his teeth were loose. My tall, handsome brother! These were not baby teeth we had now. If these fell out, that would be it, for life! No more would grow. We would all look like toothless old men even before we grew up. What girl would ever marry us if we looked like that?

'Oh please God, don't let us loose our teeth!' I prayed fervently that night. But how could it be prevented? We needed fresh fruit or vegetables for vitamins, and there was no way of obtaining these. It became a constant preoccupation and anxiety. I decided there was nothing else to do but to pray very hard.

But where to pray?

There was no church to go and kneel in, as befitted such desperate prayer, and praying was forbidden in public places. Our grandfather still sang his psalms to God when his coughing permitted, in the evenings. Even when our mother pleaded with him to pray more quietly for fear of his being arrested or worse, he would just smile at her and shrug. 'Dear daughter, what can they do? They will either ignore me, or they will kill me. If they kill me for praying, I will be taken straight up to heaven. That way, what happiness they will have obtained for me! Either way I'll be at peace, Anna, so don't you worry. There are worse things than dying, you know.

'What could be worse than dying?' I'd asked him.

'Living without God, as they do.'

I went a little way out into the woods to think about what Dziadziu had said. But how could any of us live *with* God now, when there was no church, no Mass on Sundays, not even a crucifix on the wall as we had at home in Poland. It was all forbidden.

I stood still, listening to the silence of the forest and a sense of peace came over me. I whispered my prayer.

A butterfly came by. One small, white butterfly, settling for a moment on a leafless shrub in front of me. The snows had not long gone, so it seemed too early in the season for butterflies. I watched it with delight.

There was no church here, but now it seemed to me that the whole forest was praying; every tree pointing its branches up like arms lifted up towards heaven.

I felt my prayer had been heard, though for the life of me I couldn't see how it could be answered.

One blessed egg

Easter came with heavy rain, and warmer air.

In Poland, on Easter Saturday night, we would always go to church in the dark. The Easter fire would be flickering in the church porch, lighting up the night and symbolising Jesus, the light of the world.

Here in the forests of the Urals, even though there was no church to go to, at least our father and Peter had come back from their workers' camps so we could all be together. That night, we all sat close around the stove, with Dziadziu holding a thin, resinous branch as a candle.

By the light of this candle, he read out to us from his precious prayer book the Easter prayers and readings.

'On this most holy night, when Our Lord Jesus Christ passed from death to life, the Church invites all her children throughout the world, to come together in vigil and prayer.'

It was comforting to think of churches full of people all over the world praying exactly the same prayer. '...all time belongs to him, and all the ages,' Dziadziu continued to read, '...This is the night when Jesus Christ broke the chains of death, and rose triumphant from the grave.'

Dziadiu lit our smaller thin branches of wood from his and the flames flickered in the dark hut, lighting up our faces.

'This Easter candle, a pillar of fire that glows to the honour of God, let it mingle with the lights of heaven, and continue bravely burning to dispel the darkness of this

117

night! Christ, that Morning Star who came back from the dead has shed his peaceful light on all mankind.'

After the prayers and hymns, our father proudly showed us the great treasure he had managed to obtain and had brought back with him from the 49th - one medium sized hen's egg. He had exchanged it for some of his bread rations from one of the Russian forest workers. One brown egg. We stared at it in awe. It was the first egg we had seen since leaving Poland.

We would eat it the following morning, he said, for our Easter Sunday breakfast!

(It is a great Polish tradition to share a blessed egg, a symbol of new life, at Easter, as well as blessed bread, a symbol of the Living Bread, and other foods that would be taken to the church in a decorated basket to be blessed by the priest.)

The following morning, Mama boiled it with the greatest of care. She saved the water it had been boiled in. Our grandfather prayed a prayer of blessing on it.

'One egg for eight people!' Peter shook his head with a rueful smile.

'No Peter,' Tata shook his head and smiled too, 'We must invite our neighbours to share it with us.'

So we invited Roman and his family to share the blessed egg – all seven of them. Mama peeled it so carefully while everyone watched in silence. She didn't let the tiniest part of the white remain with the shell. And the shell she put carefully to one side too. Later she would crush it and add it to the soup. It contained precious calcium. It would be good for our bones, she said.

Our father cut the egg with a sharp penknife he had borrowed specially for the cutting of the egg. First in half, then in quarters, then he carefully cut each quarter in half, then each eighth in half until there were sixteen tiny pieces of egg equally divided. We prayed the Lord's Prayer together, and wishing each other God's blessings, and the courage to keep surviving, we shared the egg!

That was our Easter celebration that year. So poor, and yet it seemed that Joy was with us that day. He was truly risen and living in our hearts – even in that inhuman land.

Rebellion in the Camp

In Poland, May is celebrated as the month of Mary. The Mother of Jesus is held in great esteem by the Polish people, and we had always honoured her especially in this most beautiful of all months.

Every evening in May, whole families would gather in the fields or in churches to pray the rosary and say or sing together the litany to Our Lady. And here, too, even in the middle of such a dark and Godless land, it seemed no one had any intention of letting our atheistic oppressors stop us from honouring the Mother of God.

'More than ever now we need her prayers and protection!'

Every evening, Polish deportees were meeting in small groups, going to a different hut each night to avoid being discovered. But in our hut there was a meeting every night, so that our grandfather could join in.

Someone must have reported it to the authorities, (there were spies everywhere, keen to earn an extra slice of bread for information given) because the commandant of the settlement came quietly one evening to the hut and stood there in the doorway as people were sitting or kneeling praying the Litany.

'...Queen of all the angels and saints pray for us,

Mother of Jesus our Saviour, pray for us.

Queen of peace, pray for us...'

He stood in silence, watching.

One by one, people became aware of his presence and fell silent.

He looked at the small picture of the Madonna and child, a copy of the Polish icon of Our Lady of Czestochowa with the cuts across her cheek, which the Russians had slashed when they had attacked Poland in the previous war.

He said slowly and clearly, 'I do not wish for such meetings to take place. All meetings are forbidden. It is forbidden to meet together in this way.'

He stood to one side and waited pointedly for the group to disperse.

After everyone else had gone, and he had gone, there was silence for a while. Then Dziadziu quietly finished the Litany to Our Lady.

'We're prisoners in an open jail,' he spoke to us children

120

after he'd finished praying. 'But, you know, and don't forget this children, our hearts are still free. They can stop us meeting with others to pray, but not even the NKVD, not even the great and mighty Stalin himself can stop us praying to God and honouring the Blessed Mother of Our Lord in our hearts.'

A fatal remedy

As the cold, wet, short spring turned into summer, suddenly, everything in the forest seemed to burst into life. Buds, dormant for so long, were opening up to the sunshine. Green shoots sprang from the warmed earth, and nettles appeared from nowhere - new shoots everywhere.

Nettles! Those nasty stinging nettles that we used to pull out of the garden when weeding at home, now became our saving grace.

Our mother sent us out daily wearing our winter mittens to pick these precious young shoots. We brought them home and Mama put them in the water with some salt to make nettle soup.

Will they sting our mouths as we eat?' Antony asked looking at the first pot of soup hungrily.

'Even if they do, I'm still going to eat it!' I told him. But they didn't sting

Mama also made tea with the leaves. Actually, the only difference between the soup and the tea was that one had salt in and the other didn't! But we suddenly felt rich indeed! And very blessed!

After just a few days, our teeth began to feel less wobbly for the nettles were rich in vitamin C! Antony and I literally jumped for joy at this. Such tremendous relief filled our hearts. When Peter and Tata came back to the hut on a day visit, Mama presented them with nettle soup as if she were offering the greatest of delicacies. They too were overwhelmed with gratitude for this simple but health-preserving weed.

It didn't fill us up. Far from it. The hunger kept gnawing at our stomachs, but it strengthened us a little, and our gums and teeth grew stronger.

Our mother tried rubbing some nettle juice over our arms at night to see if it might deter the bedbugs from biting. It didn't. But she wasn't going to give up.

As the weather turned hotter, she decided it was time to wage a fresh war on those gruesome and disgusting creatures.

When school finished for the summer, one hot sunny morning, we took outside the sacks we slept on, and the few blankets and bedspreads we still had, and all the rough wooden planks, and Mama boiled a huge pot of water to pour over the planks. They would surely not survive that! she said with satisfaction. And to make extra sure, after scalding them with one huge potful, she boiled up another and poured it steaming hot over the planks a second time, turning them over to soak every bit of the wood with the boiling water. She used nearly all of our supply of precious wood for the stove. But she said it was well worth it – because surely that would finish off the disgusting vermin once and for all!

We then beat the blankets hard, whacking and shaking them with all our strength, to beat out every nasty crawling little bug. And stamped on the ground to kill them. The stench was appalling, but at least it was outside!

As the blankets aired and the planks (and the blood of the squashed beetles) dried in the sunshine, we were so happy at the thought of a good night's sleep.

At the end of the day, back into the hut went the bed planks. And once it was dark, back onto the 'beds' went the hopeful humans. And for a few hours there were no more bites.

Before dawn however, the bedbugs still living in the walls and roof of the hut began to migrate like a terrible army towards the beds. It was as if they knew there was fresh clean wood to move into. Fresh clean wood with human bodies and human blood! It seemed they could smell people from a distance.

And before the night was over, we were, once again, being viciously attacked.

Those beetles multiplied so quickly it was truly incredible.

Would there ever be an end to the nightly torture?

When the summer was at its hottest, sweltering and humid, sleep at night became almost impossible because the bedbugs and lice thrived even more than ever in that climate.

Everyone was drained and exhausted, bitten all over.

A quiet, elderly Polish man from a nearby hut, whose wife had died that winter, came to Mama one morning and gave her a small sack of flour and some buckwheat groats.

'I won't be needing these anymore,' he told her. 'I will not be here much longer'.

He looked so weary and downtrodden, bowed low, but he just shook his head when Mama asked if he was all right and if we could help in any way.

She thanked him from the bottom of her heart for the provisions.

'May God bless you and repay you!' she said.

Two days later, we heard that he had poured petrol over his clothes and bedding to kill the bedbugs, as he simply couldn't stand them anymore. The petrol killed the bugs. But the toxic fumes also killed him.

Mama wept for him. 'God have mercy on his soul.' she prayed, 'And God give us the strength to carry on.'

Climb a tree barefoot and come down with boots on!

On one of his days back with us in the hut, towards the end of the short summer, Peter came back to the hut with a new survival skill that he passed on to us. He taught us how to make simple, rough boots from birch bark. He had been shown how to do it by one of the other workers in the forest barracks - a Russian deportee who had been working in the forest for nearly three years.

'It's not all that different from the way we used to make birch bark baskets in Poland!' Peter told us excitedly, so pleased at the thought of being able to make boots for everyone for the coming winter. 'You have to tear off the bark in long wide strips and then wrap them round to shape them into boots!'

Once you knew what you were doing, you could make a pair in an hour or so, though it took him a lot longer than that at first as he was teaching us too. There was no shortage of trees, and although chopping the trees was forbidden, there were no rules about taking the bark.

We watched and helped Peter, and at the end of that day, we were all proud owners of a brand new lightweight pair of birch bark boots, Mama and little Albin too. They were not as expertly made as some that Peter had seen, but they would be a great help in the cold months to come. Although they were very light, they were tough and hardwearing and very popular with the local people who, like us, could never afford the warm but very expensive valonki felt boots. Some of those who had lived there for a long time, had five or six pairs of these birch bark boots each. They'd certainly be a lot better than going barefoot when the snows came.

We had been warned that the summers here were very short, turning quite suddenly and always, somehow, unexpectedly, into the depths of winter.

'What the Russians do, 'Peter told us, 'is they wrap their feet in strips of cloth or rags first, to act as socks, and then they put these birch bark boots on top. I've seen them do it – and even in the deep snow they seem to keep you dry footed and they say you can walk for weeks in them before they wear out.'

'You know, one of the Russians who works alongside me in 48th, told me that they are so popular here that there's even a local saying – that you can climb up a tree barefoot and come down with boots on!'

A bright new dawn

By 1940, one and a half million Polish civilians were imprisoned in sub-human conditions in the Soviet Union. Many thousands of them did not survive the first winter.

Our grandfather, Dziadziu Ignatius, in spite of the nettle soup, was still getting weaker. He was not able to get up off his plank bed by the stove. He no longer had the strength to walk.

When he could no longer read his beloved psalms and prayers, I would sit in the evenings and read to him. Every evening after school, when homework was done, I would open his little Bible and read to the emaciated old man who had once been our strong and hardworking Dziadziu, who had made our sledge, and cut wheels out of wood for us to make a go-cart, now lying on a louse-infested sack.

During the day he had the blankets from our bunks over him as well as his own, but even in the heat of the short Siberian summer, he was constantly shivering. But he was not afraid of dying. He had often spoken to me, during those times when I had been reading to him, of heaven. 'Don't be sad when it's time for me to move on, child,' he'd told me. We're a bit like caterpillars, you know – they're never meant to stay caterpillars for ever – it's just a growing stage before they die from being a caterpillar and then are born to a glorious new life as butterflies. We were created to fly too you know. We were never meant to stay for ever in this world. We're on our way to joy.'

One warm evening that first summer of exile, it was clear that Dziadziu was dying. We knew the signs; people died here every day. We were almost used to it, but when it was someone you loved dearly, it made your heart ache to breaking.

We gathered round his bunk to say the sorrowful mysteries of the Rosary - our mother, Tosia, Antony and

Albin and I, kneeling on the dirt floor by the small rough wooden bed.

Dziadziu was no longer fully conscious, but he called out for Peter several times.

'Peter will be on his way home now, Tata,' our mother reassured him, holding his hand in both of hers. He will be home soon. He said he'd be here tonight. He is probably walking through the forest right now. He'll be with you soon.'

But before Peter came home, our grandfather's soul had slipped peacefully away from the misery of this earth to the bright new dawn of eternity. He died so softly we hardly knew he was gone. It was the 8th August 1940. He was seventy-seven years old.

Mama made the sign of the cross on his forehead and kissed his cheek.

One by one we all kissed him goodbye, his boney pale face was wet with our tears.

Mama then said to Antony and me, 'Peter will be on his way home now, but you must go now to the 49th and fetch your father. Tell him what has happened to his father. It will be dark by then so you will have to lead him through the forest.'

So that night, we made the long, long dark walk through the forest, with subdued and heavy hearts.

We found our father lying on his hard narrow bunk, and he knew straight away when he saw us that something was wrong. He hugged us and wept openly with us on hearing the news, grieved that he had not been at his father's side when he'd died.

We then took our father by the hand and lead him through the night, and in this way brought him to the hut to say a belated goodbye to his father.

The following morning, Peter, Antony and I went out early to dig the grave. The cemetery was on the other side of the settlement, a long walk away. We found a shady, peaceful place under a tree and started to dig, Peter doing most of the digging, with Antony and me keeping him company and taking over for a bit when he needed to rest. The only spade we had managed to borrow was old, loose and blunt, and the digging was hard, as the ground was full of roots and stones. We were scared the spade would break and we would be blamed and end up having to pay for it. There was no money even for the most basic survival, never mind paying for a spade. There were lots of thick, tangled tree roots that had to be hacked away with an axe in order to make a pit big enough.

'Perhaps a nice shady spot under a tree was not such a brilliant idea!' Peter said ruefully, wiping the sweat and dust off his brow. We continued, taking turns until we had dug about three feet, then, as I pushed in the spade, I struck something hard. We stood staring down in dismay! It was a coffin. We had unknowingly been digging towards an existing grave!'

Drained of energy, totally exhausted, we weren't sure what to do. In the end, not being able to face the thought of starting all over again, we continued to dig in a slightly different direction, avoiding the coffin.

When the grave was long and deep enough, we gathered evergreen fir branches to cover the earth and make it look nice for the following day and went back to the hut.

The next morning, the day of the funeral, all the deportees from all the huts gathered by our hut, ready to walk in procession with us to the grave, in order to pray and to pay their last respects to Grandfather Ignatius. He had been loved and respected by all. It was a gloomy, dark, cloudy day.

Mama asked Antony to walk ahead of the funeral procession carrying Dziadziu's precious crucifix. Behind him came what should have been the coffin, but even if there had been time to make one, there was no money to buy the wood. All the trees in the forests belonged to the government and you had to pay dearly for any wood you needed for your own use. People caught stealing were shot. Our grandfather was simply wrapped in a sheet and carried on a stretcher, with four men from the settlement helping our father and Peter to carry him on their shoulders.

They walked slowly, Mama with Tosia, then me with little Albin, following the pallbearers, and after us walked all of the other deportees from the settlement. For Catholics, to pray for the souls of the dead is an act of mercy, an act of charitable kindness as well as a way of showing love and respect to a well-loved neighbour. Even some of the men from the forest camps had come to mourn and pray and stand in solidarity with Mama and Tata in their grief.

The sky was reflecting more and more the gloom of the day. Heavy grey clouds gathered as if heaven too was in mourning, and the wind picked up.

When we were about halfway there, and there was still another fifteen minutes walk, the sky turned black and the skies opened and torrential rain came bucketing down. It was such a downpour that it took your breath away and drenched everyone to the skin within seconds.

Catching a chill when you are already weak from starvation was a serious matter in that place where there were no medicines, no doctors. Fevers could kill.

So, with deep regret, most of the dripping funeral procession had to turn back and hurry to the shelter of their huts, to change out of the soaking clothes and escape the wind and rain.

Even the pallbearers had to leave as soon as they reached the grave.

So, in the end, it was just our family who remained standing there.

We covered our grandfather with dripping evergreen branches before filling the grave. Tata had made a wooden cross with Ignacy Gryg and the dates of his birth and death carved on it.

Soaked to the skin and with such aching hearts, we prayed the prayers for the dead from Dziadziu's prayer book, asking the saints to accompany him to heaven; God's angels to lead him to paradise.

We believed that our dear grandfather was now in his true and eternal home in heaven with our grandmother;

that he was now experiencing a joy that we could not even begin to imagine here on earth, but still we wept.

'I know he's at peace now,' Antony said. 'But it's still so sad for us who are here without him.'

'Heaven is very close to earth, child,' Mama gave him a hug as we walked away. 'So perhaps he is not so very far away from us. Who knows? Perhaps he is nearer to us now than he was before.'

Birds or angels?

They say that sadness and joy come in waves, like the tides of the sea, one following the other.

After the sadness of Dziadziu's passing, and the torrential rain that had fallen that day, the forest seemed to suddenly explode a second time at the end of summer with colour and new fruitfulness.

The prickly undergrowth and bushes, that had been flowering throughout the short, hot summer, now began to produce wild raspberries.

My heart soared with joy as Antony and Tosia and I went out picking them every day. It was, for us, manna from heaven.

'It reminds me of being back home in Podlesie!' Antony cried, as we picked, our fingers and lips stained with juice.

There was never enough of them to fill us up, or even to

half fill a small basket, but, as our mother used to say, they provided much needed vitamins.

Going into the forest always was always risky because of the ever present danger of meeting a bear. We had to look ahead and tread quietly, as they could be aggressive. Our excitement at picking the wild raspberries, however, made us a little less careful than usual. We ventured deeper into the forest than we would normally dare. One morning, as we approached a sunny clearing in the forest, we stopped dead in our tracks. In front of us, in the clearing just a few paces away, stood an enormous grizzly bear. The sheer size of him took my breath away. He was standing upright picking tiny wild raspberries with his massive paws and delicately putting them in his mouth. He had his back to us, thank God, and was so absorbed in eating that we managed to creep away backwards, feeling our way with bare feet so as not to stand on a twig. When he was out of sight, we turned and ran faster than we'd ever run before, not even stopping to pick up the precious raspberries that we dropped as we ran.

That Autumn, nature provided another source of food - Kozaki forest mushrooms. They sprang up in clumps overnight in the forests, and you could smell them in the air. They had reddish tops and were quite thick and dense with a good root.

We children went out picking them every morning at dawn. Even when the frosts came, we still went out barefoot and shivering to search for this precious forest food.

As the sun rose and warmed up the earth and moss

on the forest floor, where the dappled sunlight reached in between the trees, we would stand on the warmed moss to warm our cold wet feet.

The mushrooms grew in clusters, but you had to know where to find them and this wasn't always easy.

I kept my eyes on the ground searching for them, but Antony soon began to look up and around.

'Mushrooms don't grow on bushes, Antosh!' I grinned at him. 'It's *under* the bushes you should be looking, not over them!'

But Antony just shrugged and continued looking round. When a bird fluttered away from a little clearing in the distance, he headed for it purposefully. I followed, curious, and sure enough, in the place where the bird had been, we found a huge cluster of mushrooms!

From then on, I too stopped looking for mushrooms in the normal way, on the ground, and looked out for birds too. Whenever we saw a bird flying off, we hurried to the spot and it was always a place where mushrooms grew in abundance.

'You know, I said a prayer, asking God to help us find lots of them,' Antony said, shaking his head, half in disbelief, half in awe. 'Do you think He's helping us?'

We were never to find out. Perhaps it was simply that those birds ate the mushrooms too. Perhaps there were more worms or insects where the mushrooms grew, but from that time on, we always looked out for birds –and they were always a very good indicator of where there was a huge clump - sometimes ten or even twenty big ones.

We would proudly carry the precious stash back to Mama, who was impressed with our mushroom gathering skills. No one else brought back so many.

There was no oil or butter or fat of any kind to cook them in, but Mama would slice them and put them in a pot with a bit of water, add a bit of salt and cook them like that. If we had a slice of bread she would crumble it in with the mushrooms, if a couple of small potatoes, they would be thrown into the pot too. And that was our breakfast.

For lunch it was nettle soup with mushrooms in it. For people who were starving, this was life-saving food.

In the evening it was mushroom and nettle soup again, because there wasn't anything else, and, while there were still berries about, a few wild raspberries for dessert.

Our mother also sliced up many of the mushrooms and laid them out in the sun to dry, on rags or any planks of wood we could find. We soon found that the best place to dry them was the roof of the hut, as there were fewer insects that crawled over them there. Also, as there was a little more breeze up there, they would dry in just a couple of days. Then we would thread them to hang up and store for the winter .We treated them with the greatest care, knowing they would help to keep us alive through the coming winter. Every single mushroom was used, whether it was wormy of not, (and many of them were). Not a single one was discarded. 'If there are worms, so much he better, because then we'll have a tiny bit of meat!' Antony joked. Though when it later came to eating soup made with the dried wormy mushrooms – it wasn't quite so funny to see horrible worm grease floating on top of the soup. It looked disgusting and made my stomach turn over but I learnt to close my eyes and eat it anyway. We all did.

We dried nettles too. We went out gathering great bunches of them on dry, sunny afternoons, and dried them too on the hut roof. Our mother was determined to do everything she could to prepare for the coming winter.

Ginger boy, ginger goat!

One morning as we were eating our boiled mushrooms and nettles for breakfast, our mother announced that she was going to get a goat.

'A goat?' We looked at her in astonishment.

She nodded. 'You children need milk and so does Peter when he comes back here from his hard work!'

'But Mama – they must be very expensive?'

'I have sold a few things,' Mama said quietly.

Antony and I went with Mama that afternoon in great excitement to fetch the goat. She had already agreed the price with Mr Lechtovicz, a Russian exile who lived in a hut not far away. Many of the local people had a goat. About one hut in three had a nanny tethered outside their hut or in a grassy clearing.

A goat was tethered outside Mr Lechtovicz's hut. A beautiful, fine large gingery-brown one, with big horns, and a bright ginger beard - the most attractive shade of ginger - Antony thought as looked at it admiringly. He said he could just imagine her tethered outside our hut. Oh what a luxury! Soon we would have lots of milk to drink!

Behind the hut, however, was another goat. This one was scrawny and plain – a dirty white. It's head was drooping wearily and it looked old and tired.

When our mother came out of Mr Lechtovicz's hut with Mr Lechtovicz and his son, Antony and I stared at the boy in amazement. Mr Lechtovicz's son had such a mop of ginger hair exactly the same shade as the ginger goat! The boy and goat matched each other perfectly!

To our great disappointment, though, it was the thin old scrawny goat that he untethered, handing the rope to Mama. My heart sank as our mother took the rope. She nodded and thanked him politely, her face expressionless, and we walked away in silence.

'Well,' Antony shrugged, when we were out of sight and earshot of Mr Lechtovicz and son. 'I don't suppose he'd want to sell that ginger one, since it matched his family so well!' and we had to laugh in spite of our keen disappointment.

The poor scrawny old goat had already been milked that morning, so we fed it grass we gathered from the clearings in the forest and waited eagerly for the following morning when our mother would milk her for the first time. For the first time in two years, we would have milk!

We gave her an extra good feed and walked her out to a grassy clearing to graze. But the following morning when Mama did the milking, all that she gave was barely half a small jug of milk. Hardly enough for a little sip each.

Mama looked at the jug with such disappointment in her eyes, though she said nothing. She added the milk to the mushroom soup. It was so delicious to have even that small addition to the usual recipe! But there was so little of it, and we were still hungry, as always.

'But it will do us good, all the same,' Mama said – 'Even if there isn't much of it. It will do your bones good.'

'Well, since that's all we have left of us,' Antony grinned, 'It's just as well!'

'Mr Lechtovicz cheated us, didn't he, Mama?'

She shrugged. 'God will be his judge not me. Let's just be grateful for what we have. A little bit of milk is better than no milk at all!'

'And anyway, doesn't she suit our family better than the ginger one?' Antony was grinning again, 'Since we are all scrawny, poor and dirty too, and not a ginger hair between us!'

We looked after our poor old goat as best we could. Antony and I took her out each morning to the best patch of grass we could find and tethered her so she could graze in peace. Peter had sawn a little wheel out of wood, which we would stick into the ground with a sharp stick, and she would walk around tethered to that, without getting tangled, and was able to graze all the way round it.

138

'But what is she going to eat in the winter when the snows come?' we wondered.

Mama went to ask Mr Lechtovicz and came back with the information that goats could eat dried leaves all through the winter.

So, Antony and Albin and I set to collecting huge bunches of birch tree branches and dried them on the roof of the hut and on the ground outside. We tied them in bundles just like Mr Lechtovicz had shown Mama he'd done. We also cut some grass and dried that too, so that she would have a bit of variety.

We stored the leafy bundles and grass in the simple lean-to porch outside the hut. We worked out that about seventy bundles would last her through the winter.

'You know, all the branches hanging here might also help to keep the hut a little warmer,' Mama said.

Silent Night

Before we had time to adjust to colder temperatures, the Siberian winter was upon us once more, with early snows, and freezing winds, making life, once again, a constant struggle.

There was hardly ever any daylight, since nights in the Urals seemed to never end. It began to grow dark in the early afternoon, and stayed dark until nearly the middle of the following morning. Temperatures plummeted to minus thirty degrees, then minus forty, and by Christmas, reached minus fifty or fifty-five degrees. When it was this cold, the air itself was thick and frozen, and breathing was painful. Your whole body shivered violently, incessantly. Even the workers in the forest were ordered not to go out in such temperatures. The exertion of chopping and sawing trees in such extremely low temperatures would have damaged their lungs and could be fatal. To go out at all, it was necessary to cover up completely from head to toe – even your nose and ears. Frostbite was an ever present danger which was dreaded by everyone as in those conditions could lead to gangrene.

During the winter, night blindness wasn't the only problem that affected the vision of so many deportees. Now, in the few daylight hours that there were, the vast expanse of dazzling snow blinded your eyes too.

It was hard to look forward to Christmas in such conditions. There was never enough wood for the stove to keep it warm, and most of our winter clothes were either bartered for food, outgrown, or worn threadbare.

Our father with Peter walked the ten kilometres in the dark through the forest, so we could be together for Christmas Eve. It was too cold even for the workers to be sent out to the forest. The long walk reduced our father to exhaustion and both of them to coughing with pain in their lungs.

It was our first Christmas without Dziadziu, and we were all subdued.

We had no Christmas tree as chopping down trees for

one's own use was not allowed. There wouldn't have been room for one in our tiny cramped part of the hut anyway.

Little Albin and Antony tried to look out for the first star of Christmas, but the little window was too frozen to peer out of, and anyway darkness had already fallen in the middle of the afternoon.

Before eating, we broke a piece of bread and shared it as we had always shared the blessed wafer in Poland, wishing each other blessings, health and the strength to endure each day's hardships.

It gave me a lump in my throat, wishing health and endurance, while our father was looking so very thin and exhausted. All of us so emaciated, weak and dirty, huddled together for warmth. I had trouble swallowing my little piece of the shared bread.

I looked at Peter, so subdued that night, and my eyes brimmed with tears. Where was my cheerful handsome brother who used to climb up to the tree tops to peep into birds' nests, the dreamer who had brought home the fledgling hawk to tame; the laughing inventor who'd had us sledging on ice? Our grandfather had already been taken from us, how much longer before the rest of us would be joining him in eternity? Dying no longer seemed such a terrible thing.

That year it was our father who read the Christmas readings from Dziadziu's little Bible:

'The people that walked in darkness have seen a great light, on those who live in a land of deep shadow, a light has shone, For there is a child born for us...'

141

The words spoke to me as they had never done before, and for a while my heart was filled with peace.

For the Christmas Eve supper, there was bread and nettles boiled with water and some goat's milk, and boiled mushrooms. We bowed our heads and thanked God for it gratefully and for all his graces. There was no Christmas tree lit up with candles, no church scented with incense and fresh hay, no organ and fiddle playing in the choir, but when I went out to the porch to fetch more wood for the stove, it seemed the night itself was full of glory. The clouds had dispersed, and a bright full moon was surrounded by a golden halo. The snow was sparkling in the moonlight. Somewhere in the distance an owl hooted.

When I came back in with the wood, Tata started singing softly , 'Cicha Noc - Silent Night, Holy Night,' Everyone joined in; our neighbours too, behind the thin partition. And in many huts in the forest settlement that night, people were singing of a baby born two thousand years before, into poverty and suffering.

'He's not heavy!'

Soon into the New Year, my youngest brother Albin fell ill. Even a cold in those conditions could be fatal. This was far more serious than a cold. He developed a dangerously high fever and was taken to the hospital in Kiedzilo – a town about twenty or thirty kilometres from the settlement.

Our mother stayed with him, but it was too far for the rest of us to visit. They said it was probably meningitis. As his immune system was so weak, they did not expect him to live. There were very few medicines in the hospital, even less food, and hospitalisation for any illness or injury was not something many survived.

The whole family prayed for little Albin incessantly, and against all the odds, to our great joy, he slowly began to recover. He stayed on at the hospital for some time and when he was discharged he was still too weak to walk. They said there was nothing else that they could do for him, and that they could no longer spare the bed.

There were no ambulances or buses. Tata and Peter were away working in the forests, so in order to bring him back to the hut – over twenty kilometres away, our mother had to carry him twelve kilometres on her back in the deep snow, she herself barely alive.

Albin was eight years old then. Being so skeletally thin, he wasn't heavy, but still, to carry an eight-year-old boy on your back for seemingly endless kilometres in deep snow when you are nothing but a weary sack of bones yourself, shows what a mother can do when it is her child's life she is struggling for.

Whenever a lorry or sledge came by she begged them to take them to Ivaki town, which was the big town closest to our forest clearing, but no one offered. Perhaps, understandably, they were afraid of contagious disease. Finally she succeeded in begging a lift to Ivaki on a sleigh, but until then she continued to carry him on her back, never stopping to put him down.

From Ivaki they got a lift on another sledge and that sledge brought them back to the settlement.

Albin was just a skeleton; too weak to even stand up properly. To walk he had to lean on the table or wall.

I watched my little brother struggling for life, and saw the pain in my mother's eyes as she nursed him. I wondered again how much longer we could hold out. Would the same fate that took most of the last batch of deportees also take us?

Every night we prayed for God's mercy.

'Things will be good for you.'

Summer came again to that frozen land, as a brief but desperately needed respite, and before it ended, a miracle happened.

We had all been summoned together by the commandant of the settlement. Even the workers in the forest camps had been ordered to return to the huts to hear what he had to say. It was the last day of August 1941. There was a tense, uneasy silence in the gathering.

The commandant cleared his throat. As he began to speak, we all stared at him uneasily, in disbelief.

Was he really telling us that Stalin, had agreed to an amnesty for all Polish deportees? Because the Soviet

Union needed our help now in fighting the Nazis?

'…..Therefore,' the commandant finished his speech, 'As of today, you are all free citizens!'

For a moment, everyone in the forest clearing stood staring at the commandant without moving. Then suddenly everyone was speaking at once. *What was he saying? Stalin, who had stolen everything from us, murdered our loved ones, was now wanting us to join forces with him?*

Were we free to go back to Poland? Could we trust what we were being told? Was it just another cunning communist trick?

Some spoke in anger, some in excitement. We looked at each other stunned. Were we truly free? Could we go back to our homes in Poland? People were shaking their heads. Was this the same man speaking now of freedom, who had declared when we first arrived, 'From here there is no escaping. Here you will stay and here you will die?'

We were to later find out that, on the 22nd of June that year, the Devils' Handshake had come to an end. Hitler had broken his alliance with the Russians. Not satisfied with having taken the western half of Poland, he now wanted the eastern half too, and not satisfied with all of Poland, he was now also hell bent on taking Russia, and the rest of the world.

The Soviets were being defeated and desperately needed more soldiers to help them fight against their former allies.

At a meeting on 12th August 1941, General Sikorski had boldly pointed out to Stalin that there were thousands of courageous Polish men wasting away in work camps all over Siberia. Good soldiers. Lots of them. They would be a lot more use to him in helping defeat the Germans than they were felling trees in the forests. He knew the Polish had a well-earned reputation for being fierce and brave soldiers. 'Set them free to form an army for you on Soviet soil,' Sikorski had urged Stalin, so they could help fight against their now mutual enemy.

After that famous meeting, the Soviet authorities had issued a decree announcing an amnesty for all Poles on Soviet soil. There was to be a new Polish army being formed in the South of Russia, under the leadership of General Anders, who had been imprisoned since September 1939. He had been released from Lubianka prison in August and notified of his appointment as Commander in chief of the re-formed Polish Army in the USSR. All Polish deportees and prisoners of war would, in theory at least, be free to travel there to sign up, and bring their families with them to the army bases.

'The NKVD officers will be coming to issue certificates of freedom and travel permits,' the commandant continued, 'So you can travel if you wish to leave.'

If you wish to leave? Who on earth would wish to stay in this hell? We looked at him as if he were out of his mind. Only crazy people would choose to stay in this land of starvation and darkness, where for nine months of the year the sun hardly rose and temperatures dropped to minus fifty degrees.

'God works in mysterious ways!' Mama was shaking

her head.

'He said we were free to leave the settlement and go wherever we liked. Can we go back home to Poland then? Right now? Today?' Antony was asking, his eyes full of hope. 'Perhaps Burek is still there.,,,'

Mama shrugged, but there was a glimmer of hope too in her gaunt face.

The following day not one of the Polish deportees went into the forest to chop trees. It was as if they were testing to see if we were really free. All the forest labourers stayed with their families. And there were no repercussions!

Now there was a growing excitement, but still unease. No one trusted Stalin. Even if he *had* made an agreement with General Sikorski, his past record showed he was no respecter of agreements or promises.

'But a newly forming Polish army in the Soviet Union? How can that be?'

'After all that the terrible things the Soviets had done to the Polish people – how could they even think that Polish men might now agree to help them?'

'Well, better to fight the Germans for the Soviets, than die prisoners in this pit of hell,' said Tata.

During the rest of the summer days, while picking wild raspberries and collecting forest mushrooms, and leaves and grass for the goat, we were all waiting all the time for the NKVD officers to arrive so we could be given our freedom papers and travel permits. 'Maybe we will not have to spend another winter here!' Mama said with feeling.

'Perhaps we will not all die here as Dziadziu did!'

So we waited and waited and waited, until the short, sweltering, mosquito infested summer was coming to an end, and the days were growing darker and colder, and still they had not arrived.

Antony and I would lie with our ears to the ground to see if we could hear the vibrations of the Soviet trucks. They were huge steam powered machines that the NKVD would arrive in. They shook the earth and made such a roar they could be heard and even felt for miles around.

But our hopes were dampened as our second summer turned into winter again. Our mother was now watching so anxiously every day for them to arrive. 'If they come when winter has started it will be too difficult to travel in the deep snow.' she worried.

But the snows came before the NKVD. When the temperatures dropped to minus 40 degrees, that was when the NKVD officers finally arrived on a sleigh.

The amnesty agreement was read out and eventually, slowly, with much queuing and waiting, freedom papers and precious travel permits were issued for those who wished to leave,. These were not train tickets – it was made clear that everyone had to pay for their own travel, and if they could not afford this, they would not be able to leave. Were we free to leave the Soviet Union, someone asked. It seemed we were.

'However,' the NKVD officer told them, 'There is no point in trying to go back to Poland, as it is now Nazi occupied. It is very hard at present to travel in Russia; you may have to wait a long time before arrangements can be made. You will have a good life if you stay here,' he said, 'Better than before. You will earn more money now, as free men,' he enticed them, 'You will have more bread, and things will be good for you'.

'Things will be good for you,'- we had heard that one before. I looked at him in utter contempt.

When the officer had finished talking, everyone walked away in silence. Once out of his hearing, little groups formed to discuss the situation.

'Are we really going to leave?' I asked Tata.

'But where would we go?'

You heard him say we can't go home to Poland.'

'I've heard America is a good place to live,' Antony put in hopefully.

Everyone on the settlement wanted to leave straight away. Not one family wanted to stay in Stalin's 'paradise'.

'But how do we get away?'

Even Ivaki town was too far to walk to in the deep snow.

'Help! Wait for me!'

All the Polish deportees in that forest settlement gathered together and held a meeting, and eventually decided to order sledges to take them, in groups, to the train station in Kiziel town.

Ivaki was the nearest little town, but the track to it was through the forest and too narrow for a sleigh.

So once again we were to pack all we possessed. This time though, it was with hope in our hearts, and the task was a simple one since most of the clothes most of us still owned we were wearing - layered one on top of another. We also packed some bread and dried nettles and mushrooms for the journey and our few vermin-infested blankets. Women and children and our small bundles of belongings were packed onto the sledges with sacks to cover us to stop us from freezing, while the men were to walk the whole distance through the forest.

There were only two sleighs, so not everyone could go at the same time. Each day a few families left. When our turn came, Antony was lifted up right at the end and put near the edge of the sleigh. Huddled under the sacks we finally set off. The ponies pulled hard, though once they got going, the sledge glided along the frozen snow, bumping occasionally when coming near the ruts at the side of the path. There was a deep ravine by the track. If you fell down there you'd be buried in snow and never be able to climb out. You'd freeze to death in minutes.

As we went round a bend in the track, the sledge jolted,

and Antony, who was precariously positioned right at the back, was thrown off the sleigh. He landed just centimetres away from the edge of the ravine. Everyone was looking to the front of the sledge and no one saw him fall off.

He lay there, stunned at first, not daring to move for fear of falling down the ravine, then, seeing the sleigh going on without him, started shouting, 'Help! Wait! Wait for me!' Screaming at the top of his voice. He was too scared to even wave in case he slipped into the ravine – they would never find him then! How awful to be lost now, on the way to freedom.

We heard his shouts, and stopped and ran to hold out hands to him, to pull him to safety away from the ravine. He was overwhelmed to tears with relief. For the rest of the journey he clung to the sledge for dear life, terrified of falling off again and being lost forever in this frozen land while everyone else escaped without him.

'We must get on that train!'

At the train station at Kiziel, there were such crowds of people already waiting to go south. Most of them were poor, emaciated, half-alive deportees like ourselves, desperate to escape south to join with the Polish army. The great mass of people, the noise, the confusion, the tremendous anxiety on everyone's face, brought back memories of the nightmarish journey that brought us there two winters previously. However, this time there were no cattle trucks waiting to take us away. Worryingly, there was no sign of any trains at all.

Everyone from our settlement was now there, families huddled under blankets, and so many people queuing and pushing and arguing heatedly at the ticket office, trying to secure a wagon to travel in. We soon learnt that it was not a case of buying individual or family tickets; the only way to travel south from there was to hire a whole wagon.

All the families from the settlement pooled almost every rouble we had and paid for a wagon. We had to pay extortionate rates; far, far more than we had been advised by the commandant. These, it seemed, were 'special' rates for freed deportees, to encourage us to stay. And if we couldn't be 'encouraged' to stay, then at least they would make sure we gave up everything we had before we left.

It took most of what we had, but there was no choice. We had very little left to buy food.

'You are lucky to be able to get a wagon at all!' we were told by those who simply didn't have the means. Some, desperate to leave, were talking about walking south - a journey of thousands of miles across frozen snow-covered land, uninhabited except for bears and wolves, and well-fed vultures. Many did set out on that epic journey by foot, and a few survived and have lived to tell their stories. Many, many more, however, died in the attempt.

It seemed now that it hadn't been by chance that the NKVD had waited till the winter temperatures had plummeted before giving out the freedom papers.

The temperature dropped as night fell. We tried to sleep, shivering, huddled together under blankets and sacks on the freezing waiting room floor. This waiting area had a roof but no walls or doors, and the icy wind blew through it relentlessly.

The next day there was a small piece of dried bread for breakfast that Mama shared out between us, with some Kipiatok which, thank God, was available at that station. We drank the hot water so gratefully, warming our hands on the pot it was in, so grateful that the boiler was working, not broken or out of fuel, as they sometimes were. In those freezing conditions, it was a matter of life or death.

'Mama is it time for lunch yet?' Albin was soon asking every few minutes.

'It's too early yet, child.'

Oh how slowly the minutes ticked away - to get that next little piece of dried bread to gnaw on. You bit into it two or three times and it was gone and you continued to starve. The next day we waited and waited with the crowds, which had doubled since our arrival, and ate another small slice of dried bread in the freezing cold and continued to shiver incessantly and huddle together, our breath freezing in our noses.

Night came again, and still there was no sign of any train. Was this whole thing just another cunning ruse of the Soviets to steal from the deportees and have us die here in the cold waiting for a train that never came? Two more days and nights we waited like this. The supplies of food brought for the journey were running low and we weren't even on the train. More people kept crowding into the station. A huge human river of walking skeletons desperate to escape from this hell. How on earth would we ever manage to all get onto one train? Antony, remembering his bitter experience of the pushing and shoving crowds at the bread queue, was determined we would push our way onto our wagon.

'We have the wagon ticket, child,' Tata reassured him. 'No one can take our carriage.' But he didn't sound convinced. This was not Poland. Here people were dying. Lives depended on getting on the train.

From time to time, to pass the long cold hours of waiting, and take our minds off our hunger, Antony and I would walk along the station platform. We saw many injured Soviet soldiers in uniform, some without an arm or leg, some lying on stretchers. We knew they would have priority on the trains. Worryingly, there were so many of them. What if they commandeered the wagon we had paid for?

At last, after several days of such intensely anxious waiting, a train finally arrived. We were all so tense and anxious as it approached the platform in a cloud of steam and smoke. Would we manage to find our wagon before others got to it? Clutching our bundles, all eyes were on the huge locomotive as with a screeching of unoiled brakes, it came to a hissing halt.

There was a panicky rush for the wagons. Mama and Tata and the others from the settlement too, all desperately searching for the number of our wagon in the pushing crowd.

It was soon located with great shouts of relief. Thanks be to God! A windowless cattle truck, similar to the one we had been brought out in, but we pushed our way to it desperately, helping each other to climb aboard, the men forming a guard round it while the women and children scrambled up.

Going backwards

It had the same filthy rough wooden planks for bunks as we'd had in the prison wagon we had arrived in, though this time the bunks weren't at either side of the wagon but along the length of it. An oil drum stove in the middle of the wagon was giving out enough heat to slightly warm the middle, but rest of the wagon was below freezing.

Eighty people squeezed into that one wagon. Once in, we were so crammed in that I felt the old panic at being trapped and unable to move.

'Close your eyes and say a Hail Mary,' Mama said, holding me close to her. 'We're on our way to freedom, child. It is good we are here. It will pass.'

'And we don't have to close the doors unless we want to,' Peter smiled, although equally squashed. Hey, brother! This is travelling in style!'

Eventually, Tata and Peter managed to get a space on the top bunk for Mama and little Albin, and another space on the lower one for Tosia and Antony and me. Tata and Peter had to stand with the other men.

As night fell, the train finally pulled away in the dark. By then everyone was exhausted, but it was so cramped, lying down to sleep was impossible. We had to take turns. Some stood while others slept sitting up or curled up tight. Later, with much difficulty, everyone would swap round places. It was so cold that if you were lying on the wooden planks, by morning your coat and trousers were frozen to the planks.

'But at least we're free!' Tata said in relief. 'And we're heading south where it will be warmer!'

When the sun rose the following morning and the train stopped at a station, we were free to open the door wide and let the icy fresh air in. We could jump out freely at the station to stretch our legs and get kipiatok.

From time to time, at the stops, with the few kopeks we had left, we bought some thin, watery soup that the locals sold, and brought it to the wagon in a bucket. It strengthened us a little.

'That's a lot of money to pay for such watery soup!' Antony complained looking down at the murky liquid with some bits of cabbage and potato peelings floating in it.

'Thank God for it, Antony. This soup is more precious than gold to us because it will help keep us alive.' Mama told him. 'And those poor people need money too. They will live in this miserable land for the rest of their lives. We have been given a chance to escape.'

After many days travelling, we arrived at a huge station.

There were twenty tracks side by side with no platforms in between, so you had to climb under the other parked wagons to reach the platform.

The wagons on the train were being shunted and sorted and attached onto other locomotives. Antony wanted to open the door and look out, but it was decided it was too dangerous while the crashing and shunting was going on, as in that overflowing wagon it would be easy to fall out onto the tracks.

Every now and then a locomotive would crash into our wagon and sent it hurtling down the track until it hit another train, and inside we would all be hurled around knocking heads and turning everyone upside down. After several such crashes, we were all bruised and battered.

'Well, that certainly is one way of moving wagons!' Peter said ruefully rubbing his aching bruised head.

'Perhaps they don't know there are people inside!' I spoke my anxious thoughts out loud. 'Surely they wouldn't do that if they knew we were inside?'

Later we were to find that I had been right, though with all my heart I wished I hadn't been. There had apparently been a mistake made, and because our doors had been closed, it had been assumed that our wagon was empty, so instead of continuing to head South for Tashkent, it was hitched up to a locomotive going back North to Siberia.

'Let your God give you water!'

'But how can they know where we're going?' I kept worrying aloud. 'No one has asked us! They keep shunting our wagon to different lines and hitching us to different locomotives. How can they possibly know which train to attach us to now?'

Our father and others were looking extremely anxious too. Everyone was murmuring and tense. Our father was ready to go and make some enquiries, but to do that, he would have to cross the twenty tracks, climbing under trains to reach the platform. It was a dangerous business, and there was no guarantee that he would find anyone on the platform who knew what was happening, and worst of all, there was no guarantee that the train would still be there by the time he got back. Russian trains had a habit of just taking off with no warning whistles, no indication beforehand. Many deportees travelling on these trains to freedom were split up from their families by being left behind on the platform while fetching water or soup when the train suddenly moved off, sometimes, never to be reunited.

'Don't go Tata!' Antony begged. 'We can ask later on at a smaller station.'

There was no time to discuss the matter, as the train suddenly and without warning jolted violently into motion. We went along fairly fast only stopping very occasionally for brief stops at small stations where there was no one to ask, and there was only time to fetch hot water and jump back on.

So it was only two long weeks later, when we should have been near our destination, and it should have been getting warmer, but instead was still freezing cold, that one of the men in the group recognised the name of the station we had stopped at. He looked aghast. 'It can't be possible!' he shook his head in disbelief and shock. But it was true! We were in Siberia. We finally realised we were being taken in completely the wrong direction, and were now even further north than the Urals from which we had come.

We all sat in horrified silence.

Our food supplies were gone, the cold was worse now than when we'd started our journey. We were so weak from having already spent nearly three weeks hardly moving, with next to no food, only to learn that we were now further from freedom than we had been when we'd started the journey.

The men from the truck ran to the driver shouting at the top of their voices in anger and alarm. When finally it was realised, that it was not horses in their wagon but people, people who should have been heading in the other direction, the wagon was unhitched.

After much waiting and shunting, (more gently this time) we were finally attached to a locomotive going in the right direction.

All in all, the journey took over three long, weary months. The last part of it was so painfully slow, it seemed to us that we would never make it. The train kept stopping at sidings. In these smaller stations there would be only one track and one siding. And there it would stand, sometimes for several days in the snow. When we asked what was happening and why the long delay, we were told it was because some important trains needed the track, either carrying soldiers or provisions for the Russian soldiers.

Once, as the train was moving away from one of these little stations, and the wagon doors were still open to let in the fresh air, a young Russian woman ran up to the open door. She was running alongside the slowly moving train, shouting and crying. She had a baby in her arms and was carrying a little bundle and a paraffin lamp. She ran breathless and desperate, begging us to take her baby, shouting that she had a lamp with paraffin in which would be useful to us. It was her whole treasure and she was begging us to take it in return for taking her baby away to freedom. 'Take my baby to freedom. Here he will die for sure!'

We held out our arms for the baby then my father, leaning out, holding onto the wagon with one hand, grabbed her arm and with Peter's help, pulled her and her little bundle and precious lamp in too. Tears of gratitude were flowing down her face.

Someone in the wagon grumbled about us taking on an extra passenger, as if there weren't already enough people crammed in. But Tata said that a woman desperate enough to give up her own baby couldn't just be left in despair. How could we not have helped her? 'And when it is as crowded as this,' he smiled kindly to her, 'One more is not going to make all that much difference!'

'God reward you, Sir! Oh may God reward you!' she repeated.

As the train rumbled and jolted along, Peter told us about a conversation he had had at the station while waiting at the Kipitok tap for boiled water (always keeping an eye on the driver's carriage to make sure the train wouldn't leave without him).

It was a girl his own age from Poland, from one of the other wagons, whose family had been deported to Siberia in June 1940 when the weather had been unbearably hot. It happened that there had been no stops and therefore nothing to eat and no water to drink for two days. Inside the carriage people were fainting from lack of air, dehydration and heat stroke. Even when the train finally stopped, the doors were not opened. They began to pray aloud in despair for God to save them. 'Silence!' the guards had shouted as they finally came round to open the wagon doors. They were ordering two volunteers from every carriage to fetch the water for the others in their carriages, but they missed out this particular carriage where the people had been praying. They opened the door of their wagon, but did not send volunteers to fetch water. One of the women called out to let them know that they had been missed out.

'Let us go and get water! We have a baby in here who is dying!' She called out. 'Please! We need water!'

'You have been praying to your God! Let your God provide you with water!' they jeered.

They were being punished for praying together, which

was forbidden by the Communists.

When the guards had gone to the station shelter, the woman who had begged the guards for water, climbed out of the carriage and asked everyone to join her on the platform to pray for water. Desperately, they all climbed out and knelt – all of them - on the ground and prayed for water.

It was so hot that even the beaten earth platform was burning their knees as they knelt, but suddenly, literally out of the blue, clouds were gathering in the sky. Dark ominous clouds, and within minutes, heavy rain was falling. With shouts of joy and utter amazement, they hurriedly fetched pots and cups and anything they could find that might hold water from the wagon and held them up to the sky as the heavens poured down water, providing them with not only enough to drink, but washing their faces and cooling them too. They raised their hands and faces up to the rain, thanking God in utter awe. Never ever would any of them forget that moment.

The guards were all in the station building, sheltering from the sudden, totally unexpected downpour.

We didn't spill a drop!

At last, it began to get warmer as we travelled south. The local people at the stations were different now, though the stations were still overflowing with Polish deportees. We were later to learn that thousands did not make it, dying from hunger, disease and exhaustion during this long and difficult migration south. Countless children were separated from a parent by trains moving off without warning, and left alone on trains or platforms, later being placed in Russian orphanages, never to see their parents or their homeland again.

At one of the stations, our mother gave me some of our last precious coins to buy soup. I put the coins in my shirt pocket as I always did – my mother had sewn me a little pocket on the inside of my shirt - to keep it safe. In the pushing crowd all heading for the hot water tap and soup sellers, I was jostled and shoved, but managed to reach the soup seller and get the soup. But when I put my hand into my pocket for the money, it was no longer there. Flushed, with my heart pounding, I searched that pocket three times, before I realised that it must have been stolen. I came back to the wagon in tears of shame and frustration, with an empty bucket and no soup. Everyone reassured me that it wasn't my fault, it could have happened to any of them, but I felt it so deeply, that I had let the money be stolen and the family go hungry. It grieved me to the depths of my soul.

'Witek, child, it wasn't your fault!' Mama hugged me as

I wept bitterly, but I was inconsolable.

When we were nearing Tashkent, we soon learnt that the station platforms there were crawling with thieves in the same way that our hut in the Ural forests had crawled with bedbugs. And like the bedbugs, they were most active at night, sneaking and prowling around the platforms trying to steal the few possessions any poor refugee might still be clinging to.

Even when travellers were sleeping on the platforms with their bundles underneath them, those Tashkent thieves still managed to steal them right from under their noses, so accomplished were they. It was rumoured that they held vials full of drugs under people's noses as they slept to drug them into a deeper sleep. Everything that could be possibly be moved was stolen. A person had to literally tie everything - every single one of their belongings - tightly to themselves and sleep on top of them and not move from that place, and have one person awake on guard.

We now know that in those days, the Tashkent thief was known and feared worldwide.

'They could even steal the boots off your feet without you knowing it!' Peter shook his head, seeing people crying in dismay each morning at their stolen belongings.

'In a way, child,' Mama nodded to me, 'Maybe it was a blessing that the soup money was stolen from you, because it made us all so much more careful. Who knows? Perhaps it saved us from having every single one of our things stolen, as has happened to so many others.'

She was right, no doubt, but even to this day, I cannot

remember that soup money loss without a painful feeling
of bitterness.

The train stopped for water and refuelling at
Werlowa station.

'No platform again!' I groaned at the thought of having
to crawl under fifteen wagons standing on more than
twenty tracks in order to get to the platform, and it was my
turn to fetch the hot water.

'I'll go and get it!' Antony offered, eager as always for
excitement. Mama wouldn't hear of him doing such a
thing at his age.

'I'll come with you, Wiciu!' Peter smiled. He was the
most agile of us all, so I was very glad of his help and off
we went together over the tracks and under waiting trains
carrying a kettle and a saucepan. We managed to fill up
with hot water and bought some soup.

'I think we've been cheated again,' Peter shrugged,
looking at the watery pale orange-brown liquid now in his
bucket. 'How on earth can they call this soup?'

It was not easy, crawling under the wagons on
uneven tracks, carrying hot water and soup to get back
to their wagon.

'Hurry up, Witek! We don't want the train to go without
us!' Peter urged me. We could see the driver climbing in
at the front.

I passed the bucket and water pot to Peter who had
already crawled out from under the first wagon, then he
crawled under the next wagon, and passed me the water

and soup, and so on with the other wagons. We got back to the train only just in time.

'And we didn't even spill a drop!' I proudly told our mother, as we passed the hot water and soup to her and clambered aboard. The locomotive creaked into motion and suddenly jolted forwards. Soup spilled over Mama's dress. 'Oh no! What a waste!' she cried in dismay.

'Oh Mama, don't worry!' Peter said with a grin, 'It looked quite horrible anyway. I don't think we've lost anything good!'

'And your dress is so stained already, a bit more won't make any difference!' Antony said, thinking to reassure her!

'If it croaks…'

By the time the train finally pulled into Tashkent, we were all, like most of the other travellers, in the last stages of exhaustion and starvation. Infested with lice, and filthy from weeks of lack of any kind of sanitation or washing facilities, we were almost too weak to stand.

The heat hit us as we climbed unsteadily down from the wagon. It had been the harshest of winters when we had left the Urals, and now it was sweltering hot.

At the military base, there was a river of people flowing in. The soldiers themselves were suffering from malnutrition. The supplies of food they were given by the

Soviets were so inadequate that at times they were not much better than the labour camp rations they had received in Siberia. The Soviet authorities were once again failing to keep their promises and failing to supply provisions. The newly organised Polish army was not only poorly equipped with no ammunition and, at that time, no uniforms, half of the soldiers didn't even have boots. They had been given as little training as they had been given food. The Polish soldiers were being given only a quarter of the usual army food ration, but they were willingly sharing it with the starving Polish children and their families.

The Polish soldiers were seen by Stalin as cannon fodder; he had ordered them to the front lines of battle without supplying adequate weapons and ammunition. It seemed he was understandably wary of allowing a strong Polish army to be built up on Russian soil.

General Anders refused to comply with the orders as his soldiers were so inadequately provided for. He realised that the only way to save at least some of his soldiers and their families was to get them out of the Soviet Union as quickly as possible. Because of the shortage of food supplies, Stalin was forced to admit that he could not provide rations for more than half the Polish army. He therefore reluctantly agreed for General Anders to transport half the Polish forces to the Middle East where they would be more adequately provided for by the British. They would be placed under British command to fight the Germans in Northern Africa and Southern Europe.

General Anders had insisted that the families of the

soldiers should also be allowed to leave the Soviet Union. He arranged for transport ships to take them from the Russian port of Krasnovodsk to the Persian port of Pahlevi. Anders knew that the number of ships and the time allowed for this evacuation were limited, and his concern was that the maximum number of people should be able to leave Russia. Each ship, therefore, was dangerously overloaded with human cargo. It was a risk he had to take in the attempt to save as many as possible. His orders were to include all children in the evacuation, even if they were sick or too weak to walk and had to be carried aboard.

This situation was explained to us when we arrived. We were given what little food was available and offered a corner of a hut to lodge in on a kolkhoz- a large collective farm - nearby.

Our father signed up for the army. We had missed the first evacuation, so we waited hopefully for the second (and last) one. Peter found work digging the irrigation canals for the cotton fields, and Mama and Tosia worked in the cotton fields, first weeding then picking cotton in the unrelenting heat. Every day people died of heatstroke and dehydration.

There was no clean water – only a muddy river a long, walk away, where people washed as well as drank, and rats were seen at night. This dirty water had to be carried in heavy wooden buckets, then it had to be left to stand for a while till the mud settled to the bottom. Then it was boiled, but even then, it was still contaminated, causing epidemics of typhus and dysentery which were taking the lives of both soldiers and civilians.

Peter came down with typhus. Our mother nursed him through the high fever, and he survived. Then she herself caught it and was so ill she had to be taken to the hospital a [illegible]. It was thought she would not survive the night, yet survive she did.

We younger children did not catch it, but our father, who had been nursing Mama through her sickness, both at home and at hospital, finally went down with it too. He too was so ill that he also had to be hospitalised.

With our sister Tosia at work all day in the cotton fields, and Peter away digging canals, even though he had not fully recovered from his own bout of typhus, in order to obtain a little food for the family, Antony and I were left to look after ourselves and Albin.

One day, when hunger was so unbearably strong, we decided to try and find some food for ourselves.

'You know, Witek,' Antony said, 'Someone told me that in France they eat frogs.

'Ugh!'

'No, not ugh! Apparently they are really tasty – a bit like chicken, only nicer.'

That evening, as the sun was setting, we went frog hunting, to the shallow muddy, rat-infested river, where everyone got their water (and their dysentery and typhus diseases) with a wooden bucket for catching our dinner. When you have been so terribly hungry for so long, anything is worth a try. We were pleased to find there was a lot of croaking going on in the early evening.

'How do we know which ones are frogs and which are toads?' I wondered aloud.

Antony thought about it, then shrugged. 'If it croaks, catch it!'

In the dark, they all looked the same anyway.

We quickly and easily caught a half dozen into our bucket, and very pleased with ourselves, and surprised and pleased that no one else seemed to have thought of the same wonderful idea. There would be plenty more for us to catch the following day. We took them back to the corner of our hut and put a pot of salted water on the stove to boil. We threw the frogs in and boiled them for a few minutes – then eagerly fished one out to taste.

We tasted it, and spat it straight out, gagging and retching in disgust. It was the foulest, most disgusting thing we had ever tasted in our lives.

'Perhaps we didn't cook them right?' Antony said.

I shook my head. 'No, for anything to taste that foul, it must be poisonous. Nothing edible could taste so disgusting. I don't think they were frogs, Antosh! That was toad soup we have just been eating!'

The saddest of times

Our mother was very weak when she came out of the hospital. Although she had survived the typhus, she was barely alive. Our father was still very ill in hospital but there was no way she could visit him, as this would have meant a several kilometre walk across fields, and she could hardly stand.

So it was Antony and I who had to visit Tata and take him some food.

'They mustn't go into the hospital, Mama!' Peter had said in concern. 'It's crawling with germs and unburied corpses!'

Mama nodded so wearily. 'But someone has got to go and visit your father and take him something to eat. You know they don't give enough food for a fly to survive on at the hospital. What else can we do? He needs nourishment.'

Mama handed us boys a card with our father's name written on it. 'But you must wait *outside* the hospital,' she told us so anxiously. 'Whatever you do, do not go inside! They will call your father. He will come out to you, if he is able to. But you are not to go in under any circumstances, do you hear me?

We nodded. Our mother gave us a couple of kopeks – some of Tosia's precious earning. She asked us to go to the market first to buy an apple for our father then on the way back to take it to him in the hospital.

I was glad that Antony took the coins – after being robbed of the soup money on the train journey, I had no wish to let the family down in such a way again. It wasn't a lot of money, but for us it was fortune, and we walked round the market looking very carefully at all the stalls on the market to find the very best and biggest apple for our father. But there were so many, we decided to split up for a few minutes so that we could quickly look at all the stalls to find the best bargain and meet together again before actually buying anything. Antony went off eagerly, checking out not only at the fruit stalls, but also keeping his eagle eyes to the ground, looking out hungrily for any food that might have been be dropped. To anyone watching him, he was just a very puny, ragged little foreign kid.

And someone *was* watching him. A big, tough, local Russian lad and his two friends. They followed him. They stopped when he stopped and watched him looking at the apples on the stall. As he walked away from one of the stalls, the hulking big lad, who was more than twice his size, approached him.

Antony looked up at him warily. He had been aware of them following him, and had been uneasy, but hadn't known what to do. If he'd run away, they would soon have caught him. He had a pocket that Mama had sewn onto his shirt, made from a bit of rag in which he had put Tosia's precious money.

'Look what we've got here, lads!' the big one jeered. 'Must be the last of the big spenders!' they all laughed.

He came threateningly close, leaned over and made a tight fist under Antony's nose. He whispered into his ear that if he shouted he would smash his nose to pulp. Then he put his two fingers inside Antony's pocket while the other two held him still. They took the kopeks. There was not a thing he could do about it.

When he came to meet me he had tears of anger welling up in his eyes.

We decided not to tell Mama what had happened as it would have upset her and she had enough to worry about already. We did not have anything to take to the hospital for our father.

Antony complained to me bitterly all the way home, and I knew how he felt. 'Until this war began, at home in Poland we used to leave our front door open and no one ever stole anything. Pigs and wolves tried to steal from us but not *people*! And when our cows wandered off, people looked after them and brought them back to us. No one robbed anyone!'

Then the thought of our father without any food made him choke up again with tears. We were so alone, so unprotected, strangers in an alien land.

The next morning, Antony and I saw Pani Jana, the woman who lived in the same hut with us. She had been out to the hospital early, visiting a relative of hers. When she saw us, she went pale and gave us such a sorrowful glance, a look of such compassion, that we knew at once that something wasn't right.

She came into the little kibitka hut and told our mother that our father was no longer alive.

Antony and I listened with thudding hearts, overwhelmed with guilt that we hadn't managed to take Tata the apple

Mama had asked us to buy him, and that he had been all alone when he died. No one had visited him that day.

We were both convinced it was our fault that he had died. It was awful to think that he had died hungry and lonely, in a harsh and dirty Soviet hospital.

It wasn't your fault!

Peter was away digging irrigation canals, so a message was sent to let him know of our father's passing on. He came back to the kolkhoz straight away and made ready to go to the hospital to ask where they had laid our father. The hospital had sent our mother a letter, informing us of Tata's death and asking if we wanted to bury him ourselves.

Our mother asked Peter to find out all the details of how Tata died and to find out how he could be buried. Peter would have to go on his own.

'The younger children mustn't go near the hospital or to the cemetery,' she told him. And she herself was still too weak to make the long journey.

Outside the hut, Antony and I whispered tearfully to Peter before he left, explaining to him what had happened at the market and how we failed to take out father an apple.

'Perhaps it was meant to be that you didn't go to the hospital,' he consoled us. 'Remember how Dziadziu used to say that there's a purpose and a reason for everything that happens? Tata wouldn't have wanted you there to catch the disease off him. You can be absolutely sure he wouldn't have wanted that. Maybe those bullying thieves saved your lives. Who knows?'

'But I knew that the apple would do him good!'

'If he had eaten an apple he might still be alive!'

Peter hugged us tightly. 'Who knows whether an apple would have helped? He may have been too ill even to eat it! It wasn't your fault he died! There was nothing you could have done about it.'

He was close to tears himself. We had been burdening him with our own worries while he was having to take on all the responsibility of burying our father alone.

'What will you do?' I asked him.

'I don't know,' he replied, shaking his head, tears welling up in his eyes again. To our mother, however, he was calm and reassuring.

'Mama, I will go to the hospital now,' he reassured her. 'I will see to it. Don't worry, I will sort it out.' He hugged her, said goodbye to us then set off for the hospital alone.

He told us later he'd been so scared of what he had to do. Even in the Urals, he'd had Antony and me with him to dig the grave, and the others from the settlement to help carry our grandfather to his grave. But now he would be totally alone.

As he hurried across the fields to the hospital – there was no road - he prayed for strength. He was still weak himself from the typhus, and although he was back at work he still suffered constantly from sweating and debility.

When he asked about our father, how he had died and where they had laid him, they said all they knew was his body had already been taken away to the cemetery. They asked if he wanted to bury our father himself, but Peter was now barely able to stand, let alone walk several more kilometres to the cemetery, then dig a deep grave.

He told them to bury Tata and he would come and visit the grave the following morning when he had regained his strength. He tried to get some sleep out in the fields that night.

Early the following morning, chilled, wet and hungry, he walked the several kilometres to the cemetery, to pay his last respects to our father. He tried to find the grave, but no one could help him. They buried so many people each day, often in communal graves. There had been no coffin. To have a coffin was very costly, as there was a shortage of wood in that region. They buried everyone in pits, and that is how they buried our father. They hadn't even marked the grave with his name.

Clinging on for dear life!

Peter stared at them as if unable to take in what they had said.

How could he go back and tell our mother what he had done? That he had abandoned our father to being buried by complete strangers in an unmarked pit?

Rationally he knew there had been no choice. He had been at the end of his strength, physically and emotionally. Yet irrationally, his heart ached with intense grief and remorse at the decision he had been forced to make.

Overcome with grief, he wept as he walked away, stumbling over the rough ground. He had not even prayed at his father's grave.

As he started the long walk back across the fields, the realisation that he was now the man of the family weighed heavily on his already burdened mind. Our mother was still weak from her illness; she couldn't work and needed support. What was he going to do? Our father had signed up for the army so that the family would be provided with at least survival rations, and above all, a chance to escape this brutal and oppressed land.

But now that Tata was gone, how could he look after Mama and the rest of us? The irrigation canal digging brought in a pittance that was barely enough to feed himself. Tosia was working in the cotton fields, but was also earning next to nothing for it. Dear God, what am I supposed to do? How am I to obtain food for us?'

The thought came to him that if he was to take Tata's

place he would have to join the army. The last thing he wanted to do was fight for Stalin in this war, but if he joined the Polish army, at least we would all have a chance to escape. He explained to me later, that if he helped to fight the Germans, then when this horrible war was over, we would be able to go back to our home in Poland.

He didn't have any money for the train fare to the army base, but he made his way to the station anyway. He jumped onto the first train that was going out to the base as it moved away, clinging to the bars at the end of one of the wagons. It was dangerous but he had no other way of getting there.

At the army base there were crowds of boys and men of all ages arriving to sign up, both Jewish and Polish. All were just as emaciated and ragged as he was himself; many were very sick. The queues were long and it was evening by the time Peter managed to get to the signing table. The first thing they wanted to find out was if he were truly Polish or Jewish. Many young Jewish men had been signing up for the Polish army, but once they had been transported to Persia, three thousand of them had deserted the ranks, claiming they wanted to go off and fight for the creation of Israel. They could not afford to feed, clothe, train and equip men who would then run away. Although many Jews *had* remained in Polish uniform, and some had died fighting against the Germans, there was now an understandable wariness of recruiting potential deserters.

They were told quietly to get into groups – the Polish in one group, Jewish in another. They gave the Jewish men some money for train fares to travel home, but Peter, to his relief was welcomed and allowed to sign up. He was also given a few roubles for his train fare back to his family.

There was no way he was going to waste that precious money on a train fare when it could buy food for his mother and younger brothers. So once again he jumped on as the train was moving away and clinging on for dear life to the rail between two wagons, that was how he made the journey. He was not the only one travelling that way. An older Polish man was doing the same.

They jumped off at the same station, a walk away from the Kolkhoz, and the older man offered Peter one of his lipioszki - flat breads - that he had in his sack, but when he went to take them out of his sack that he had on his back, they weren't there. Instead there was a slit in the sack - just big enough to take a little flat bread out. Someone must have been very cunning to have stolen them in this way.

So they went together instead to a canteen where they served a thick drink made of cooked dried plums. They had a little glass of that each. It was the first food Peter had had in two days, then they walked to where their families were.

By the time Peter reached the hut, it was two in the morning.

Cream!

Peter was given a soldier's uniform and, looking so smart and handsome, went to live at the army base. I joined the junior army cadets. I was given a cadets' uniform, which I loved, and stayed in the cadets' camp.

Our mother and sister with Antony and Albin continued to live at the kolkhoz - the collective farm – at Gurczekova. There were only six Polish families there. There were no beds for them in the little huts, not even any wooden planks to serve as beds. They slept on the floor. But at least, because there was no wood for beds, there were no bed bugs either. Peter and I came to visit on Sundays and we were all able to go to the huge outdoor Mass together.

We brought back with us to Mama some of the meagre rations we were given. Though we were always hungry ourselves, it was obvious that our mother and brothers and sister had even less than we had.

'We're free but still starving!' Antony remarked ruefully.

'It won't be like this for ever,' Mama reassured him, keeping our hopes up.

While we waited and prayed for a place on a train to take us to Krasnovodsk port, our mother started work with our sister in the cotton fields, first weeding, then later picking the cotton. It was sweltering hot and humid there in the summer – so hot that the Uzbeks wore thick woollen rug-like shawls over their heads, like thick tents, to keep from getting sunstroke.

Picking cotton is backbreaking work, and when you finish in the fields, the work is not finished for the day. In the evenings our mother and sister had to pick all the twigs and leaves out of the cotton they'd gathered during the day and pile it into sacks. Antony and Albin were able to help. Later in the evening they had to take the sacks of cotton to the Uzbek woman in charge and she would give them, for all that work, a little bit of milk - about a quarter of a jug. Sometimes when she had a bit of flour, Mama would pour the milk over it. There was never enough to satisfy their hunger, but it kept them alive.

One evening our mother was ill with terrible stomach cramps and couldn't take the cotton to the woman in charge, so my brothers Antek and Albin went alone.

The Uzbek woman gave them half a jug of milk for the cotton, but it was milk mixed with water. She no doubt thought that children would never know the difference.

When they took it back to our mother, walking carefully so as not to spill a drop of it, she knew at once they had been cheated. She looked at the liquid in the jug, frowned, had a little sip, then shook her head angrily. Even though she was in pain, she got up, wincing and pale, and went to the woman to tell her off.

To the Uzbek woman, maybe it was no big deal, cheating a couple of foreign kids, but to Mama it was a very serious matter – a matter of life and death. Her children desperately needed feeding, and she wasn't going to let this woman cheat them from the sustenance they had earned.

181

Mama scolded her in no uncertain terms, (by then we all spoke Russian well) telling her she should be ashamed of herself for cheating children.

The woman flushed and had the grace to look ashamed. She held out her palm to stop Mama's scolding, took the jug of watery milk and went to refill it. This time, instead of milk, she came with a bowl of cream. She handed the empty milk jug to Mama to hold, then poured into it some of the cream.

As we walked away, Mama was looking less pale and much happier, and when she poured that cream on the flour and water mixture that night, and they tasted it, they thought they had never before in their lives tasted anything so utterly and absolutely delicious.

'Mama, it was worth being cheated just to get this cream!' Antony said with satisfaction.

Mama smiled. 'Just like your Dziadziu used to say (God rest his soul) - there is no evil that happens that something good doesn't come from it.'

Antony nodded, licking out his bowl. He was quiet for a while, then asked her thoughtfully, 'But do you think any good can come from our Tata dying?'

Our mother looked at him, then nodded. 'Just because your father is no longer with us here on earth doesn't mean he's not still looking after us. Maybe from heaven he is able to look after us in a way that he never could before.'

'Do you think he's in heaven?

'Yes I do!'

'Can he see us then?'

'I think he is very close to us now. Maybe closer than ever before. And now that we have Tata as well as Dziadziu praying for us from eternity, we'll survive these hardships. You'll see.

'And if we don't, then at least we'll go and be with them in heaven!

'Well, that will happen one day anyway, child,' Mama smiled. 'And then what a celebration that will be!'

The gift of a storm

There was a huge pear tree on the collective farm, next to the administrator's office. The pears were quite large now but still green and hard, not yet ripe. Mama always looked on the ground as she passed by it hoping there might be some windfalls she could pick up and cook for us. But there never were. She worried constantly about how malnourished and thin we all were.

'Dear God, how am I to feed these children without your help?' she cried out one day, weary and distressed.

That evening, it was hotter even than normal, and very still.

All over the collective farm, people were putting out pots and bowls to catch the rain they knew would soon come. They could read the signs. Water was so precious in that arid land, they were grateful for every storm.

Mama too placed every pot outside to catch every

drop possible.

When the storm finally came, the rain poured down in torrents, thunder crashed and lightning was flashing across the whole sky repeatedly.

Well, if there was no food, at least God was providing clean water, Mama thought, and like everyone else, was immensely grateful for it.

The next morning, as she was going to deliver the sacks of cotton that they had sorted and cleaned the previous night, (it had been raining too hard to deliver them during the storm), they passed the commandant's office and saw that all the green pears from the huge pear tree had been knocked to the ground by the rain.

Our mother took Antony and Albin with her to the commandant and asked for permission to pick the windfall pears off the ground. He granted this quite readily, so even before delivering the cotton, they went quickly and collected two large sacks full of the hard, green, unripe pears.

From then on it was pears for breakfast, pear soup for lunch, pears in the evenings, pears here, pears there, pears everywhere! A bonanza of pears. Mama boiled them, she made soup with them, and she sliced them up for eating raw. She made sure Peter and I had some when we came to visit, and how grateful we were for them. And always before we ate, our mother thanked God with all her heart for the storm that had brought them down.

Sharing a little pot of soup

A whole cotton season passed, the wheat had ripened and been harvested in the fields around the Kolkhoz, and we were still waiting to be taken on one of the transports to Persia.

After the wheat harvest, our mother went into the rutted stubble fields to glean. There were always some stalks of wheat remaining in the stubble. Mama and Tosia and Antony and Albin would go and pick up any wheat stalks they could find lying on the ground. It made their backs ache from constantly bending. They scoured every part of the long field for a few leftover grains. It took a long time; patience was not an option for them but a necessity.

Back in the hut they would rub the stalks between the palms of their hands to separate the wheat grain from the chaff, then blow on them to get rid of the all the bits of straw and the outer husks.

One hot day, they had collected quite a nice little pile of wheat grains, and were really happy about that. Mama put some of it to soak to make a soup that evening.

The Uzbek woman who owned the hut where they had been allocated their tiny, dark corner, saw their wheat and went off and reported to the administrator of the farm that they were stealing grain.

He came to see Mama about the accusations of theft that had been made about her, and asked where they had got the wheat. Mama told him. She explained angrily of how long they had spent doubled over and on their knees in the fields, she showed him their rough grimy sunburnt hands. Tosia, Antony and Albin were angry and indignant too. The administrator looked at the pile of wheat, and waved his hand and went away.

'It's because she is poor, too,' Mama excused the woman. 'And we are strangers in their land.'

Poor Mama.

Perhaps it was from the lack of food, perhaps from the dirty water, or maybe it was just that her body had had enough, or her soul couldn't take any more, but soon after that, Mama became so ill she had to go to hospital.

The hospital was a more than a couple of kilometres from the collective farm. Tosia was working all day, so Antony and Albin had to make the long walk there and back each day to visit our mother, and take her some food. Peter and I also went whenever we had time off from the army and cadets.

We saved some of our rations for her on Sundays, and sometimes Tosia received enough kopeks for her work to buy an apple for her, but the most important food each day was the soup Antony and Albin made with the wheat grains they gleaned each day.

They would soak the grains overnight to soften them a little, then boil the water with a bit of salt and simmer. They would take Mama a bowl of this soup to hospital each day. It was the first thing they did each morning; they never missed a single day.

They would carry it to the hospital in a small clay pot with a handle made from a bit of string. Antony would carry it, very carefully, covered with a cloth. The first time they went, they took her an apple as well, from our sister, but Mama shook her head and refused it. 'The soup is enough for me, boys. You have the apple!'

'No Mama! We have enough of them too!, 'This is for you.'

But she wouldn't take it.

Nearly every day, she would be waiting for them on the veranda of the hospital. If she wasn't, they would knock on the window and she would come to the door to eat the soup. Before giving them back the pot, she always first took some in to share with the woman in the bed next to her.

'But Mama, there is hardly enough there even for you!' Antony said worriedly. 'The soup is for you. You have to eat it all to get better!'

But she couldn't just eat it herself, not when the woman begged her each day for some. She was a Russian woman, and was even poorer than we were.

'Child, it will be all right.' Mama reassured them. 'God has our health and our lives in his hands. Of course we must do our best to look after these bodies he has given us, and try to stay strong, and you are looking after me so well!' She hugged them. 'But you know, He also told us to share what we have with those who have less. This woman has no one to bring her soup.'

After visiting Mama at the hospital, Antony and Albin would then continue gleaning in the fields. Their legs and backs ached each evening, but they knew their lives and our mother's life depended on it.

Chased by an angry
man with an axe

Once when Antony was coming back alone from the hospital across fields where loganberries and plums grew, there were some windfall plums rotting on the ground. He picked them up eagerly.

An Uzbek boy the same age as he saw him from a distance and screamed angrily at the top of his voice, 'Kradczuk! Thief!'

Antony nearly jumped out of his skin in fright and dropped the plums. He held out his hands apologetically to the boy, wanting to explain that he hadn't stolen them, but had only picked the windfalls off the ground, but there was no chance of that! The boy began to shout, and the boy's father, who must have been a worker or manager of the field, suddenly appeared from behind some trees, and was coming towards him with an axe.

Antony decided this was not the time for explanations. He started running away as fast as he could, absolutely terrified that he was going to get murdered.

He was running for his life and this huge raging man was running after him, furiously wielding the axe.

Luckily, it was a well-irrigated, well-watered field, making the ground soft and soggy. Antek being small and extremely thin and light (and also extremely scared!) ran over the surface of the mud, but that big burly angry man sank into it at each step practically to his ankles, which slowed him down.

When Antony told me about it later, I said, 'But, Antosh, maybe he had no indication of how they grew. Maybe he just wanted the plums back!'

'Oh no! I'm sure he must have seen me dropping them!' Antony shook his head, 'He could see my hands were empty! Witek, you didn't see the crazy look on his face!'

Spat-out cherry stones

With so little to eat, and having to make the long walk to the hospital each day on an empty stomach, all Antony could think about was food. He was so hungry he went to walk around the market in the town, hoping to find something dropped on the ground that was edible.

There were stalls selling melons and watermelons, apples and apricots and cherries and sunflower seeds. How he yearned to be able to taste some of the fruit, but he didn't even have a kopek. Eventually, wilting from the heat and faint with hunger, he sat down by a little wall, where some local men were sitting and eating. He watched them eating apricots and morello cherries, spitting out the stones into their hands and putting them in a neat pile next to them, to throw away later. They were tidy people and no one littered the ground.

It gave him an idea - the sort of idea that you had to be truly desperate to have. He went and asked the men if he could have the fruit stones they had spat out. Of course they let him take them – willingly! To them these fruit stones were just little heap of rubbish to throw away; giving them to this ragged boy would save them the bother of disposing of them later.

Antony carried his precious treasure back to the Kolkhoz. He found two large stones and hammered the apricot and cherry stones one by one, prising out the kernels from inside. These he ate hungrily. Each day he went back for more cherry and apricot stones. He took some of the kernels for Mama at the hospital, and shared them with the rest of us.

One Sunday Antony and I also managed to obtain another ingredient to add to the daily soup, which nourished our mother a little. The Uzbeks grew fields full of sunflowers. The seeds would be crushed and pressed to extract the oil, then the leftover husks piled into carts in baskets to be taken as fodder for the cows and pigs.

We were standing watching them one morning, loading the carts with these sunflower husks, ruefully thinking how much better the cows here ate than we did. As the workers climbed onto the cart to drive away, we jumped up as they were setting off, to grab a handful each of these sunflower husks.

We tried to eat them, but the woody husks were too hard to swallow. They stuck in your throat and choked you. But just sucking them and chewing on them gave them a little taste of the sunflower oil, and that was something. After that, Antony often 'happened' to walk past the sunflower husk carts, and always pocketed a handful or two. One day he put some of those husks into the soup he made for Mama – and oh what a difference that made! The soup tasted so delicious he just couldn't get over it, and was very pleased with himself for being able to provide something extra for our mother. It would strengthen her, he told me happily when I next came to visit. I nodded in agreement; yes, it would be good for her bones! And then we giggled as we realised how much like our mother we were beginning to sound!

One weekend, when once again, there was next to nothing to eat, and Peter and I were visiting our sister and brothers, Peter decided to use his wits to obtain a little nourishment. He needed to eat. There was a war to fight, and he couldn't fight if he died of starvation.

He had grown taller now, and in his khaki uniform and his blond hair bleached in the sun, and his grey eyes always ready to smile, he looked so handsome and grown up now, though still painfully thin.

'I have an idea!' he told us as he set off for the market. I'm going to eat some cherries!

'But you don't have any money!' I protested.

Peter smiled to me. 'Then I will have to use my brains!'

He came back after a while, flushed but still smiling and proudly told us he had eaten five cherries. A veritable feast!

'I'm just sorry I couldn't bring you some.' He said regretfully, 'But you might try the same yourselves another day. Tosia, you might get away with it. Not you though Antony. You're still too young.'

'What did you do?' We were full of curiosity. To have eaten five cherries seemed an impressive achievement.

'I went to a stall selling cherries and I took one to taste as if intending to taste before buying.' It was not an unusual thing to do on the market, many of the locals did it.

'I ate the cherry then pulled a face as if it were really sour, saying, 'No, they aren't as sweet as they look!' and then I walked away frowning.'

Then he went to another stall and did the same there, and then to another stall and another.

We looked at him in admiration, though he was shaking his head regretfully.

Five measly cherries. I looked at my brother and thought back wistfully to our heavily laden cherry trees in Poland, and my heart ached again for all we had lost.

Storing up treasure

There was no time for the rest of us to try out Peter's cherry tasting idea, because at last, at last, the last transport had been arranged which would take us to the port and across the Caspian sea to freedom. Peter would be leaving with the army; I would be going with the boy cadets, and our mother and the others with the civilian transport.

Mama was out of hospital now, though she was still weak. She was so relieved and grateful to hear of the transport.

She had a beautiful brightly coloured cotton headscarf scarf, a Polish 'Babuszka', that she had never thought of bartering for food. It had been a necessity - for warmth in the winter and to protect her from the sun in the summer. The administrator of the collective farm had admired it greatly. He had offered to buy it from her, but Mama had refused, needing it as she worked in the heat of the day in the cotton fields.

However, just as she was leaving the collective farm for the last time, she took it off her head, folded it neatly and went to the administrator and handed it to him. 'Here!' she smiled, 'It's for you!'

He looked at her, too stunned to speak. He looked as if he couldn't believe his good fortune. He looked as happy as a man who has just been given a thousand dollars.

Antony was watching and was thinking, 'Oh no! She could have bartered that on the market for some apples or milk!' He was frowning, not understanding why she had done such a foolish thing. Wasn't this the man who had complained when they had arrived, muttering about having to accommodate foreign deportees. And here was our mother giving away to him her lovely colourful headscarf! Just *giving* it to him – for nothing!

'Antony,' Mama explained to him, 'We are on our way to freedom. Life will be better for us now. I am so grateful that you children will not have to grow up and live on in this communist hell. I wanted to thank God for this blessing of freedom.'

Antony nodded, 'But why did you have to give away your beautiful scarf?'

'I didn't have to. I wanted to.'

'But couldn't we just have thanked God in our prayers'? Antony still wasn't convinced. 'Why did you have to give your beautiful babuszka away!'

She paused for a moment. 'Antosh, when we do something kind to another person, God takes it as if it had been done to him personally. So it really was a thank-you gift to God.'

Antony sighed, but he had to grin in the end. 'You think God liked your cotton scarf, then?'

'Yes I do! 'Mama smiled. 'I'm sure he liked it very much!' she nodded. 'I think he liked it every bit as much as the administrator did!'

It was so good to see our mother laughing again.

'But I still wish you still had it. You looked so pretty in it.'

It was true. Even in her old, threadbare, stained old

dress that hung so loosely on her bones, in the sunshine, with her colourful scarf covering her hair, she had still looked beautiful.

'It's like you gave away something so precious!'

'You are right, child,' she nodded, understanding how he felt. 'It *was* precious. And it was beautiful, and I will miss it. But, you know, *that* was the whole point. To give away something worthless is no big deal. But when we give away something that is precious to us on this earth, God repays us by storing up for us treasures in heaven.'

'What kind of treasures?'

'I don't know. I don't suppose we'll know till we get there! But then, just think what a lovely surprise we'll have!'

'Well, our treasures on this earth sure do have a way of disappearing!' Antony was thinking of his kopeks at the market, and the stolen sack of our food on the journey, and my stolen soup money, not to mention our home in Poland, our barn and cowsheds, cows and horse and chickens and even our beloved dog. Everything!

Mama nodded. 'At least what we store up in heaven, we'll keep for ever and ever, throughout all of eternity! There are no thieves in heaven!'

'No thieves or cheats or sly, dishonest and greedy people allowed!' Antony nodded. But the earth was certainly full of them, and especially so in this cruel and fear-filled land. He looked down at the small, threadbare bundle Mama was holding on her lap. Inside it just a few worn rags that were all that was left of their clothes now. It was all they owned in the whole world. He looked at his mother with

195

new respect. And the memory of our grandfather sitting reading his Bible to us in the hut in the Urals in the evenings came back to him. 'Blessed are the poor.' He'd read it to us so often, so very often, by the light of the stove, as we had sat, weary, depressed, homesick and hungry. 'Blessed are you who weep now, for one day you will laugh.'

As the cart that was taking us to the station was setting off, the administrator came running after it, carrying a small sack of wheat. He handed it up to our mother with a look of immense gratitude and respect. It was Mama's turn to be surprised and delighted. 'May God repay you!' she said to him, gratefully.

He looked at her shaking his head in happiness and confusion, as if he just couldn't make her out.

The good man who threatened to shoot the water-sellers

There were thousands of deportees at the station, all, like us, waiting for the train to Krasnovodsk port. Everyone knew this was the last transport that Stalin was allowing to leave the country. Those who didn't get on board would be left behind forever.

In theory, according to the agreement made with General Sikorski, Polish deportees were still free, but we all understood now that there was no such thing as freedom under communist regime. Just as there was no such thing as a promise that would be honoured. We understood that this didn't apply just to us, but to the ordinary, decent Russian citizens who lived their lives in quiet desperation, mostly in abject poverty and in constant fear and oppression.

General Anders had suspected for some time that our so-called freedom would be short lived and had done everything he could to take as many Poles as possible to Persia.

Peter and I had been on the army ship that had sailed a few days before the last transport ship that our mother was on. We had amazingly managed to find each other amidst the crowds and had stayed together. Peter had been given some dried army biscuits and we clung to these for dear life. We gnawed at them, dry-mouthed, as there was no water to drink. Everyone was so thirsty, but again, no one complained. We all understood what a great blessing it was to be on that overloaded, waterless cargo ship.

Many were very sea sick. Because of the vomit and dysentery and severe shortage of toilets for such crowds, there was a foul, nauseating stench, making the sea-sickness even worse. It was a hellish journey but it was taking us out of hell.

When the train that our mother was to take arrived, people were climbing on even before it had stopped. Crowds of desperate people surging forward, pushing, shouting, panicking.

My brother Antony told me later how he and Mama, Tosia, and Albin had been waiting anxiously for a long time right at the edge of the platform. They had been determined not to be pushed away. When the train pulled in, they tried to climb up into the first carriage, which was the nearest one to them, but others around them were even more determined and such a rough crowd pushed in front of them, they were not able to get on. Mama shouted to the children to hold tightly onto one another and to push for dear life as hard as they could together. They had travel papers, but these wouldn't be worth a fig if they couldn't even get on the train!

Antony's heart was pounding, nightmarish memories of being trampled on in bread queues flashing to mind. He pushed with all his might, but there were so many others doing the same, it seemed there was no way they would be able to get on this precious last train. The wagons were filling up so fast – what if it suddenly moved off without them?

Then, thanks be to God, Polish soldiers arrived. They surrounded the train and forced people back with rifles to stop the terrible panic, to stop people from getting hurt, and to stop the train from being so overloaded that it would be dangerous.

With the soldiers' help, Mama and the children made it to a carriage, though they had been pushed right down to the middle of the long train. They had their papers checked and were finally able to climb up.

They stood squashed in, right against the door of the

wagon; there wasn't room to get further in, but they had made it onto the last transport.

Looking out at the thousands still on the platform, without papers, unable to board, was heartbreaking. And there were so many left behind. A sea of anguished faces. There would be no rescue for them now. Some tried to cling to the train as it moved off. Some jumped onto the links between the wagons. Some, in despair, threw themselves under the train. Everyone was weeping. Those on the train wept too. They were on their way to freedom, but how could they rejoice when so many of their own people had been left behind in that inhuman land?

When the train stopped at the first station, no one dared get out for fear of the train moving off suddenly without them. Local sellers ran up to the windows holding out jars and kettles of hot water to sell.

'Go away!' the Polish officer in charge of the train shouted at the top of his voice. He ran from wagon to wagon, along the platform, ordering the Polish exiles not to touch the water the Uzbeks offered as it had only been warmed up and not boiled. During the previous transports so many people had died from dysentery caused by this contaminated unboiled water, and he was not going to let this transport die in the same way.

This good man threatened these dishonest, dirty-water sellers with a pistol if they tried to come near the train. At every station, he ran from wagon to wagon to make sure everyone understood the danger.

Everyone on that train arrived at the port parched and thirsty, but no one caught typhus or dysentery. It was the only transport that had avoided these. This one man's unstinting efforts saved the lives of so many. He really cared. He was later to receive an award for bringing across the border the healthiest transport without any major diseases.

May God reward him!

Train crash

Day after day they journeyed through arid desert land and sand dunes, occasionally seeing beautiful lakes and trees and even houses, which they were told by those who had travelled through such landscapes before, weren't really there at all. They were simply mirages.

'But they *must* be real!' Antony protested heatedly. 'I can see them so clearly!'

Someone tried to explain to him that they were indeed real, just that they weren't actually there! They were caused by the sun reflecting things that might be hundreds of miles away.

After a week, when the train was only one day from its destination, it crashed with a Russian train coming the other way at full speed. It was a huge crash that threw everyone violently against the doors and wooden seats. Many were badly bruised, but being so tightly squeezed in together actually saved most of the passengers from greater injuries. However, most of the people in the first carriage were killed or seriously injured. That was the carriage our mother and Tosia, Antony and Albin would have been in had it not been for those who had so rudely pushed in front of them.

At Krasnovosk port, there were tents on the beach to sleep in while we waiting for the ship. Orders were given not to go in the water, as it was badly polluted, but this was too much for Antony, who had never seen so much water in his life before. Hot, sweaty and grubby, and not being able to see the harm in just splashing in the water a bit, he persuaded Albin to go into the sea with him. They stripped off and waded in to take a quick cooling dip, then were horrified to find themselves coming out dirtier than when they'd gone in! They were covered in tar; black, thick, greasy oil.

There had been an oil spill and the whole beach and water's edge was polluted. Our poor mother tried to scrub them clean with sand and water, and someone offered them some red wine to drink to prevent them from getting ill from the oil. Mama agreed it might help, but after this 'medicine' had been administered, to their very empty stomachs, Antony's head was spinning, and he thought it was the oil that had caused this strange dizziness!

There was not enough room in the tents for all the incoming refugees. Our mother, Tosia, Antony and Albin slept on the beach. After sleeping on the hard floor of the hut in the collective farm, this was no hardship for them. It was warm, the sand was soft and there were no bedbugs.

When the ship came in, they were taken out to it by tender boats, since the huge cargo ships couldn't come right into the port. Each little tender carried about three to four hundred people. Those little boats kept fetching more and more exiles, and the cargo ship kept sinking deeper and deeper into the sea, getting more and more crowded till it was packed as tightly we had been in the trains. No one complained. Everyone understood that this was a desperate attempt to save as many as possible. Even small children sat quietly in the immense discomfort and baking heat. None of these Polish children cried any more. They lay, crammed together, curled up in silence.

As they sailed away, people knelt in thanksgiving for leaving that land of such immense misery. They sang Polish hymns and wept, not just because it was a moment of great relief, but also because it was a moment of immense sadness for those left behind, and for loved ones who had not survived and been buried in that alien land so far from home.

Antony told us later that Albin had been terribly sea sick, and vomited and retched, but didn't cry. Like all the other children, except for the very smallest ones and the babies, they had all seen too much and lived through too much to cry over being sick.

'It won't be long now,' Mama comforted him, 'And then we'll be in Persia.'

'What will it be like?'

'Better than Russia, that's all I know, child,' she said. ''We'll soon be there. We'll be free.'

But in the middle of the sea, their overburdened boat [illegible] strain, and they had to wait for forty-eight long hours in the middle of the Caspian sea, in the heat, while it was repaired. They then sailed on for two more days to Pachlevi Port. There was no fresh water to drink. In the sweltering heat, people were getting severely dehydrated. Children were fainting. Some did not survive.

For those who did make it to the shores of Persia, sick and so weak that many had to be carried ashore, the sight in front of them made them stand and stare in awe.

It was such a beautiful place with snow-capped mountains in the distance, and a clean, white sandy beach. The sea so sparkling and clear and blue, and on the sand, rows upon rows white cotton tents right by the water's edge.

Those who had the strength, knelt down and kissed the ground, and weeping, and thanking God for having brought them there.

Persia

Songs and camp fires

The beach tents were to shelter new arrivals for a period of quarantine. This was necessary as so many had brought infectious diseases from the Soviet Union. But this time of waiting on the beach was no hardship for us. We were told to bathe each day in the clean warm waters. After surviving for so long in filthy, vermin-infested clothes without a bath or even a proper wash, the warm sea water was an absolute delight.

Food was cooked for everyone in huge, communal outdoor kitchens, though after such a long period of starvation much of it was difficult for us to digest, especially the greasy mutton stew that was served. This was a staple food in Persia, and considered a great delicacy, but our half starved digestive systems could not cope with it at first. It was quite some time before we were able to eat small but normal amounts of food other than bread or potatoes.

There were four temporary camps set up, one for the soldiers, one for the cadets, and the other two for families. Peter was in the fourth, I was in the third and Mama and the others in the second, living in tents with hundreds and hundreds of other refugees. It wasn't home, but it was freedom, and there was kindness and warm hospitality from the gracious Shah of Persia, and charity aid from the American and British Red Cross.

It was not by any means the end of the road. There were still many more miles to travel over arid, mosquito-infested lands, but it was the beginning of some kind of normality. The cadets were reunited with their families, while the soldiers went to join the war.

Temporary outdoor schools were set up to occupy the children and young people and allow us to try and catch up on years of missed education, though in fact, life had educated us in so many ways; it had just been a very different kind of education.

Scout and guide groups were set up too, with games and songs and camp fires, and gymnastics sessions were organised each morning, to establish some order and gentle discipline into our lives. It was all carried out with such kindness and compassion as we were all of us in need of emotional healing. Most children had lost at least one parent, most hearts had been broken and souls damaged by the years of severe hardship and depravation.

Peter, and the other young men in Polish forces, went on to win the respect of all the allied armies for their honesty and integrity and their courage in battle. In the Battle of Britain the Polish squadrons won special renown. Two hundred and fifty German aircraft were shot down by Polish Pilots. For every lost Polish plane, the Poles shot down nine German aircraft. (In the RAF, the ratio was one to three.)

The Polish navy took part in well over a thousand naval operations, sinking fourteen enemy warships, thirty-nine enemy transport vessels, and damaging a further twenty-nine, as well as shooting down thirty enemy aircraft. They had also been the bravest fighters at the battle of Monte Cassino in Italy, (which is where Peter was sent and where he was wounded), securing the victory. Having been prisoners and exiles for so long, they passionately believed in freedom, and fought accordingly, yet at the end of the war, they were the only nation that had no homeland to return to.

Although Hitler had been defeated, the 'great and mighty' Stalin still had exactly what he wanted. He still had Poland. Churchill and Roosevelt had given in to his demands, sacrificing Poland in order to placate an evil, mass-murdering tyrant.

Countries all over the world, hearing of the plight of the Poles, were opening their hearts and borders to Polish exiles. The world was beginning to understand that this bravest of nations had suffered more than any other during these terrible war years, and had also the suffered the greatest betrayal and injustice when the war ended.

The strangest of fruit

Persia, though beautiful, was only meant to be a stopover place. It was announced that there was to be a transport soon going to Africa.

'That's where the storks fly from Poland in the winter!' Antony cried. 'There won't be any snow and freezing winters in Africa! It will be sunny there all the time! And who knows, one day, like the storks, we might be able to go back to Poland from there!'

So, not having the faintest idea of what Africa would be like, but having had enough of travelling somewhere in our lifetime, we signed up to go with the transport that would take us over the Indian Ocean to yet another strange and foreign land.

The most memorable part of our journey there for many of us young people, was being given our first banana on the train to Rhodesia. Most people got a bright yellow one, but my group were given ones with brown spots on. I looked at this strange mottled 'fruit' suspiciously. For a start it didn't look like any fruit I'd ever had before, and then, comparing it with the yellow skinned bananas that most other people had been given, I came to the conclusion that we had been given bad ones.

I watched what everyone else was doing and did the same. I peeled it, took a bite, and gagged on it! It was the strangest, most disgusting texture. Convinced it was because it was a bad one, and would give me food poisoning, though not wanting to seem ungrateful, and feeling overwhelmed with guilt at wasting food, when no one was watching, I surreptitiously threw it out of the window.

At one of the stations, it came as a shock to see hundreds of half naked black-skinned people on the platform, running towards the train. None of us from Eastern

Poland had ever seen a native African before, let alone a half naked one. We stared open-mouthed in amazement. There was also a crowd of white, uniformed policemen with truncheons, who chased the blacks away, hitting them so they writhed in pain.

We stared out of the windows horrified, our hearts sinking in dismay. What was this country we had come to? Had we left one brutal land just to come to another?

Our final destination was Lusaka, which was then a very small town with just one main road, one cinema, and a few shops. Outside the town, out in the bush, a huge camp had been set up for Polish refugees. It was divided into sections, and in spite of those first misgivings on the train, we found it a peaceful, hospitable place.

We lived in a simple, small, African mud hut with a straw roof with just an opening for a window - no glass was needed in that climate - and another opening for a door.

There was an outdoor school set up, and there were even outings organised occasionally for the pupils and students, sometimes a day on safari, sometimes to a lake not far away where you could take a dip.

A choir was organised and all the activities that you would find in a normal high school, except that we didn't have books, and everything took place, not in classrooms but outside under the blue African sky.

What a change from the dark skies of Siberia! The main sports were volleyball and football, and sometimes there were dances in the youth club barn in the evenings.

The teachers, some of them clever, some not quite so gifted, had very few resources, but they taught us as best they could from memory. On Saturday nights, there was always a camp fire and singing, which I loved, and on Sunday mornings a huge outdoor Mass. There was a pattern to the days and weeks; routine and order, and a sense of security.

It was not a place of luxury or comfort, but it was warm, there was enough to eat, and we were free. We could walk into the bush if we wanted to take a stroll, or into the town. We were free to speak without fear, free to pray, and to sing Polish songs and to dance. Unlike the Soviet Union, in Africa, as in Poland before the war, people smiled.

It was there we spent the days of our youth. I was fourteen when I arrived there and twenty when I left to sail to England.

My brother Antony later said of those years: 'They weren't rich years; there were no luxuries or comforts, but they were our most beautiful years because we were young. It was good to be alive!

What we lacked we didn't notice. We had enough to eat (though never enough to feel full). We could freely walk beyond the confines of the camp. The world was, once again, a beautiful place.'

During our time there, young Antony, to his delight, found his Polish storks nesting high up in a Baobab tree, but me, I found something much, much better.

Who was she?

After we'd been in Africa for nearly a year, a new transport of Polish refugees arrived at our camp from Persia. There was much excitement, as always over new arrivals, with everyone coming out and gathering round to welcome them, all of us hoping to see someone we knew from back home.

I was fifteen years old now. Since I was one of the oldest of the children and a bit taller than the other boys, I stood at the back watching as the new refugees were being helped off the transport lorries.

A slender dark-haired girl about my own age caught my eye. She stood out among the short-haired, blond Polish girls with her tanned olive skin and long wavy dark hair. She glanced my way, and gave me a brief shy smile before being led away with the other new arrivals to their new quarters.

I stood looking after her.

Suddenly, the hot African sun felt even warmer than before, and the surrounding bush more beautiful than I'd ever seen it looking before.

Suddenly, life was glorious, and this poor refugee camp in Africa the best place in the whole world to be.

A few days later I met her properly for the first time. She was sitting with a friend out in the bush not far from the camp, under a huge shady Baobab tree. They were reading, and I walked by with a friend. We stopped to say hello.

We introduced ourselves and chatted for a while. Before continuing on our way, we asked them if they would meet us at the youth club barn than evening. Most of the young people went there in the evenings to chat, play a game of chess or table tennis and sometimes there was music and dancing.

They agreed!

All I knew then was that her name was Alinka, and that I couldn't get her out of my heart and mind.

Part Two
Alinka's Story

Tonight we will eat well!

Alinka took a horrified look at what her elder brother Marianek and his friend Edek had proudly dumped on the dirt floor, and burst into tears.

The boys looked at her in surprise.

'Oh how *could* you?'

'Tonight we will eat well!' Marianek grinned, rubbing his hands together in anticipation.

'No way! You can't *eat* him!'

'Sssh, now!' their mother, warned, glancing anxiously out of the door.

'It's no different than eating a lamb or a pig,' Marianek shrugged, wiping his rain soaked face with his sleeve. 'Tata always killed the pig every year, didn't he? And chickens - all the time! It's no different than killing a chicken!'

'Yes it is! It *is* different! It's nothing like killing a chicken at all!'

Their mother was looking out nervously. 'If anyone catches us, there will be such trouble.'

Alinka, glancing across at her mother's thin anxious face, was silenced. They all knew that people 'disappeared' for lesser crimes in that inhuman land.

But there was no way they were going to eat him. It was unthinkable. She couldn't just stand there and let them do such a horrible, horrible thing. Running to the large cooking pot that stood over the stove (it was the only one they had) she grabbed it and ran out of the hut, slipping and falling in the mud and as she ran.

215

Soaked to the skin by the relentless Siberian rain, she kept running until breathless and faint, she reached the Kolkhoz barn by the old milking sheds. Peering into the gloom to check there was no one there, she crept inside and hid the pot deep under a straw bale. Then she sat on the bale, shivering and dripping wet. With a heartache even greater than the hunger gnawing in her stomach, she wept for that poor old brown dog. She had seen him around. He'd had gentle eyes. He'd belonged to someone.

She hated this disgusting war that made people do such foul things. Hated the Soviets who had taken away her father, stolen their home and land and dumped them in this treeless, waterless wasteland a million miles from home, with no way of escaping. She hated her stupid brother and his stupid friend. Hated this brutal, stinking place where everywhere you walked there were piles of human waste that you trod in with bare feet, and no stream to wash in, no well for fresh water.

How much longer could they survive?

It wasn't just the starvation, the dirt, the disease and the extreme cold that killed people here; every day was so dark and bleak and dreary and painful, so terribly bitter, people just lost the will to live.

Her heart ached for her father. He would have understood. And for Boyik, their faithful old dog, left behind with strangers, in some village that he hated.

She was so weary of the endless misery.

Marianek turned up, peering into the darkness of the barn. 'Mama wants you!' he said. 'Now!'

She ignored him. Dog-murderer.

'You'll be in for it if you don't come straight away. '

Slowly, reluctantly, she stood up. She followed him back. She stood outside the door in the rain, soaked to the skin in her one, outgrown, cotton dress. Well, at least they wouldn't be able to eat him now! He needed to be buried and a cross put on his grave, not cooked in a pot and eaten. What if everyone started doing that? Her heart sank. What if they were doing that in Poland now, since people were starving there too? What if someone had done the same to Boyik? This brought on a fresh flood of tears; she stood alone and defiant, missing her father so badly.

'Alinka!' Mama came to the door. 'Go and bring back the pot this minute, you hear me?'

She stared down in silence at her muddy, bare feet.

'Do you hear me, child? Now! Go and fetch it right now! For goodness sake, we have to eat! Do you *want* us all to die? Where have you hidden it?'

She stood biting her lip.

'Listen, my girl, if you don't go and get it this minute, I'll give you such a beating that …. that you'll wish you had!'

Alinka went to fetch the pot.

Mama cooked the poor dog. In waste whey water and salt. Marianek and Edek buried the skin to hide the evidence of their crime.

As it started cooking, it began to smell so good, so very delicious, that Mama was worried that someone in one of the other mud huts would smell it and suspect what they'd done.

By the time it was cooked, Alinka was so hungry, that, to her shame, she was the first one ready with her bowl.

Marianek and Edek were laughing at her, and she didn't know whether to laugh with them or cry.

Mama invited Pani Szarajkowa and Honoria, as well as Edek, to share the meal.

Everyone had a piece of meat in the soup. Pani Szarajkowa asked God's blessing on the food and they gave thanks for it together, then Alinka began to wolf it down in silence. Marianek and Edek, however, kept giggling and barking to each other as they ate. Everyone ignored them and kept eating. Honoria was saying how delicious it was – it looked like chicken and tasted like veal. But those two kept barking, and in the end Honoria said in exasperation, 'What are you two fooling around for?' turning to her mother to complain about them, but her brother interrupted and said, 'Do you know, Honoria, just what you are eating - where it came from?'

She looked at him, puzzled, then shrugged, 'Well Pani Pietrzak must have exchanged something on the baraholki market for a piece of meat. But they shook their heads and, laughing, put her right. She stared at them aghast, then turned pale, ran to the door and vomited it all up.

What a terrible waste of food, was all Alinka could think, and then felt thoroughly ashamed for not feeling sick herself.

It had been the best meal they'd had since leaving Poland.

It was then she understood why there were no dogs

barking, no cats, no birds singing, not even any frogs croaking or crickets chirping, why, apart from the wolves and the howling wind, the Steppes of Siberia were as silent as the grave.

Cats and dogs with the strangest haircuts

Alinka remembers:

When I was a child in Eastern Poland, I used to think, as children do, that I would live forever, that the sun would always rise in the mornings and I would always be provided for.

Until the war began, we lived a peaceful life in Ros, (pronounced Rosh), a quiet, small town on the river Ros. It wasn't much bigger than villages are today, with just one quiet main road with a few small roads off it, a little primary school, a few small shops. The church had pride of place in the centre of the town with a leafy park opposite. There were benches in the park for people to sit and chat, and linden trees with their heavenly-scented blossom in June, silver birches, oaks and sweet chestnut trees for shade and for playing hide and seek.

After Mass on Sundays everyone went for a stroll in the park, on special occasions in the summer we children would be treated to the great luxury of an ice cream.

It was safe for children to run around freely as there were no cars in that part of the world in those days; people walked when they needed to go somewhere, or occasionally used a horse-drawn cart or carriage. There was a train station in the big town where my grandparents lived, and my grandfather worked in the station office, but

I had never been on a train. People tended to grow where they were planted, and travelling any distance was rare.

Had the war not come and changed everything, no doubt I would have grown up there; I probably would have married a local boy (there were the villages of boys my own age) and would perhaps still have been living there to this day. But life, I now know, is rarely as predictable and comfortable as we would like it to be. Never, ever, would I have imaged then that I would be taken across half the world in the harshest of circumstances before I was to meet my future husband.

But in those sunny, peaceful days of childhood before the war, we lived on the quiet main road of our little town. We occupied the middle house of a small terrace of three. On one side of us was the police station, where my father was the well-loved chief of police, and on the other side, a widowed schoolteacher lived with her son Zbyszek. We didn't own our house; it belonged to the police and came with my father's job.

Opposite our little police house was the town jail, and down the road and round the corner was the little primary school where my younger brother Tad and I went, (our elder brother Marianek was at the secondary school in Wolkowysk, our nearest big town where our grandparents lived. During term time he lodged with them). Next to the church was the priest's house and garden from where we once stole his raspberries. But only the once - because when our mother found out, she sent us off to Confession to him to confess what we'd done! That was enough to put anyone off stealing again for life! It's not even as if we didn't have raspberries in our garden too, but his looked bigger!

There was a long garden at the back of our house where cherry trees provided shade and fruit in the summer. There was also a huge pear tree in which my father and elder brother had built the base of a tree house. In the summer, when I sat high up there in the dappled sunlight, with yellow pears hanging all around, and the birds twittering and bees humming, I could see the whole of our beautiful world: the gardens and trees, the meadows with horses and cows grazing and chickens free-ranging and clucking and pecking contentedly, and then the fields and forests and fishery lakes beyond.

We didn't own much and there wasn't a lot of space inside the house; like most of the houses in Eastern Poland in those days it was built of wooden planking and all on the one floor. There was one bedroom, which we all shared. Mama and Tata had one bed, Tad and I another, and lucky Marianek, being the eldest, had a bed all to himself.

My father came from a family of thriving market gardeners, and had a great love of flowers. There were always masses of flowers in the front garden, greeting visitors and passers by with their colours and scents. Under each window of the house, he planted jasmine, night-scented stock, honeysuckle, rambling roses and many other scented flowers, so whenever the windows were opened, in wafted the heavenly scent.

In the back garden, we had tall lilac bushes shaped into an arch that created shade to sit under in the summer.

There was a table under the arch and a bench to sit on. In May when the lilac was in flower, it was another one of my favourite places to sit and read and just breathe it all in; birds and bees and butterflies (as well as children!) thrived there.

At the bottom of the garden, like most people in those days, we kept a pig, and some chickens and ducks, for meat and eggs. Self-sufficiency was the normal way of life, even in a little town, and what a tremendous blessing that was to be when the war began.

Nearer the back of the house was our large, well-kept kitchen garden with everything we needed: cabbages and carrots, lettuces, radishes, tomatoes, cucumbers, spring onions, parsley and dill, all in neat straight rows and well watered and weeded. For a snack we would be given bread and butter with chopped spring onions on top, or bread dipped very quickly in water then sugar sprinkled on the top. Or – best of all on a hot, summer's day - long wedges of cucumber fresh from the garden dipped in sugar. When you're hungry and thirsty, oh how good that was!

Once a girl came to stay for a visit in our little town from America and we saw her eating bread with butter and jam. We thought it was a strange and sickly thing to do, spreading both on one slice of bread, since butter for us was a savoury thing. We either had jam or butter; never both together.

Food in those days for most people in that region of Poland was home-grown and home-made. For breakfast, a slice of bread and butter or some sweet semolina with milk which we all liked a lot. For school lunch we would be given whatever there was - usually some bread and butter or bread and jam and a small ridge cucumber or an apple. But although this is what we were *given*, it is not however what I actually ate most days! My best friend Helenka, whose father owned the cooked-meats shop, was always given thick slices of ham or salami or other sausage on her bread, every single day, (poor girl!) and she was sick of it, so I generously offered to do a swap; my apple and bread and butter, or bread and jam, for her thick ham or Salami sandwich and we were both very happy indeed!

Very occasionally, on a special occasion, our mother would send us to Helenka's shop to buy half a kilo of 'rozmaitosci' (mixed sliced meats and sausage). I used to love that. We all did, and we would have liked it more often, but there wasn't the money. There were some advantages to being the family of the chief of police, but being rich wasn't one of them! We weren't poor, as there was enough to eat, - though I nearly always would have liked more - and we had clothes, but there wasn't the money for luxuries.

However, because of my father's job, we were the only family in the town with a wireless. Now that was really something in a little town where the only music most people ever heard was at Mass on Sundays when a little folk band enthusiastically accompanied the hymns with fiddle and accordion, mandolin and guitar. On warm summer days, our generous-hearted, music-loving mother would put the wireless by the open window so the people passing by could enjoy the music too! My father taught me to dance.

We also had the privilege of having the only telephone in the town, which again was quite something.

Until just before the war, we didn't have electricity; we had paraffin lamps which had to be cleaned each morning, as after an evening of burning, the glass would be all greasy and blackened. When electric lights were finally brought in and we were just getting used to this wonderful new convenience, it was all taken away from us when we were deported to a land where for most of the year, darkness lasted eighteen hours a day, and where even candles were impossible to come by.

For washing, there was a communal water pump down the road, and we'd carry the water home in a bucket to put in our water container. This container had a little tap at the bottom with a basin underneath it for washing our hands and faces. The used water was then poured out on the garden. Not a drop was ever wasted. In the winter, the water that dripped or was spilled around the pump would freeze solid and was treacherous. The women would complain that you could kill yourself going to fetch the water, and we children would make it even worse by making slides over it which made the older ladies grumble and shout at us if they caught us at it.

We went barefoot throughout the summer, though we did have a pair of winter boots each. Clothes-wise, we had just one spare change of clothes, underwear included; one lot to wash once a week, and one to wear. I also had a black pinafore that the girls wore to school, (the boys just wore ordinary clothes).

Everyone walked to school. There was no option; there were no cars or buses at all in that region of Poland. Tad and I had it easy as the school was just down the road from us, but some of the children who lived out in the forest regions, had to walk several kilometres each morning then back again in the afternoons. My friend Claudia used to have to walk over an hour to school. I used to feel so sorry for her in the winter, as she'd arrive tired and wet, and blue with cold. The Norwegians say there's no such thing as bad weather, only the wrong clothes, but Claudia, like many in those days, had neither the right clothes nor the right boots.

School finished early in the afternoon, but then we had lots of homework. My mother was always too busy cooking, washing, sewing or cleaning and tending the vegetable garden to help with this and my father too busy with his many police duties to help in the daytime. However, he allowed the younger police officers, who were not so busy, to help me. He told them not to do it for me; just to show me how to do it. In practice, though, they usually ended up doing it for me, since it was a lot quicker that way, so I was always one of the first to get outdoors to play!

There were several children my age who used to play with us. Zbyszek the teacher's son from next door would often come and call for us. Sometimes, to my joy, he would bring me a comic he'd finished with. His mother was quite well off and could afford such things, which was lucky for me as they were always generous and passed things on to us.

Jurek Gileski, also used to come over; he lived down the road. I'd go off with my two brothers and the other boys to the park where we'd climb trees and swing up and down from their branches. I was a real tomboy then. Once a circus had visited our little town and everyone had turned out to watch it. Afterwards we children had taught ourselves to do circus acrobatics. We'd sit in a tree, on a high branch and then fall backwards with our knees bent so we'd end up hanging upside down in the tree. Tata would shout at me in alarm if he caught me at it, but we all did it, even little Tad.

When Helenka, my best friend, was over, we used to play doctors and patients and also hairdressers. We really liked to practice cutting hair. As we had no human volunteers for either game, we mainly used the local dogs and cats – however many we could catch. Consequently, there were many dogs in our little town with the strangest of haircuts – cats too if they'd been foolish enough to be caught by us!

In the summer, we'd often go down to the river and sometimes catch a fish, or to the woods, taking a picnic. There was nothing much else to do, but we didn't need anything else; we were happy.

Everyone would walk to these outings since there was no other way of getting about for most people. It was a fair way, but quite a few families from our town would go together. We children ran and played in the forest while the grown ups would sit and chat, enjoying the sunshine and the company. It was the way we socialised. We walked together, sang together, prayed together in the church, and played together.

As for toys and games, the few we had, we made ourselves. With my father's help, I made a set of scales out of a couple of empty shoe polish tins and we played shops with these, weighing things out endlessly. We also used to play five-stones. I think it's a game children play all over the world - you sit on the ground and put one stone on the back of your hand, throw it up, turn your hand over quickly and try and catch it in the palm of your hand, then try it with two stones, then three stones till you got to five. Whenever I managed to do all five I was very proud of myself.

In the winter, the very best times for me were when went skating on the large fishery lakes not far from the other end of the town. I loved that. There were no skating lessons; we just taught ourselves. Nearly everyone in the town used to go – mostly with blades that screwed onto winter boots. Putting these on took ages, but it was really worth the effort.

At the other end of the main road, just beyond my friend Buba's house, was a hill where we'd go sledging when it snowed. That too was good fun for the whole little town. Tragically, that hill was later to be the execution place of all the men of the town by the Germans.

Once the war started, and the Soviets invaded

Eastern Poland, such neighbourly gatherings were no longer allowed. People meeting in groups were seen as a threat. You'd think that Communism would encourage communal gatherings, but in fact, it forced people into fearful isolation.

The war changed everything. My father used to say that there is no such thing as a just war. In a just war, innocent women and children are not killed or hurt.

I do not know of anyone – man, woman or child, who was not badly hurt in some way during that terrible war. Most children lost their fathers; many their mothers too. Hundreds of thousands of men, women and children were killed in the most brutal ways, and of those who survived, there wasn't no one who was not in some way broken.

Blazing like a furnace!

I remember very clearly the day the war started because we'd been staying over at my friend Buba's house, Tad and I, just down the road from our house. We'd been sleeping up in their barn loft. It was a glorious, hay-scented summer morning. The cockerel was crowing joyfully at the top of his voice and sunshine streaming in through the barn window.

I was already half awake when the sound of footsteps running towards the barn disturbed the peace of the morning. I knew something was up even before Stefan, their farm-hand, started shouting.

'Get up children!' He sounded all out of breath. 'Wake up! They need to be getting home!'

Buba groaned sleepily, and rolled over.

'Come *on*! You need to get up!'

'Go away, Stefan!' she shouted back, 'Or I'll tell Tata that you woke us up!'

'Get up, I tell you!' he called up, 'It was your father who sent me to tell you! The war has started!'

Somehow, after that moment, nothing was ever the same again.

Buba's father ruefully repeated to us what Stefan had called out. He had already been down the road to our police station to check the news. Roads and bridges in the cities had been bombed, schools and homes and churches destroyed and thousands of ordinary people killed as well as many soldiers.

'But they're nowhere near *us* yet so why do we have to go home right now, even before breakfast?' Tad was complaining as we ran home.

I knew exactly how he felt. Breakfast at Buba's was not something to be missed. Their father kept beehives in the meadow, and the sweet drippy honey with waxy bits of honeycomb, on crusty bread with bowls of creamy milk fresh from their cow was for me, at the time, the nearest thing to heaven on this earth. And now here was Hitler spoiling it all with his ill-timed war.

'Couldn't he at least have waited till after breakfast!' we laughed, as we ran into the police station.

Our wireless was out on the windowsill with people clustering round it, listening intently. But there was no music coming from it now as there usually was; it was just the news - serious voices droning on and on like wasps.

What we saw when we dashed in to our father's normally very neat and ordered office made us stand back in open-mouthed amazement. Great piles of papers and files cluttered the floor and every available surface. Our father and the police officers were ripping them up and burning them. Heaps of papers everywhere from the shelves and open cabinets they were slinging into the open stove which was blazing like a furnace.

'Tata! What are you *doing*?'

He looked up, his face flushed with the heat of the fire and smiled when he saw us.

'What's happening? Why are you burning all the papers?'

He came to give us a hug, reassuring us with 'It's all right sweetheart! It's just what we have to do because of the war. We're having a big clearout.'

He gave us both a little push towards the door that led to the house. 'Now off you go and help your mother to pack. You're going to stay at Babcia's for a while.'

Hoping for breakfast, we ran through into our kitchen next door, and once again, stopped in surprise. Our mother was packing food into boxes and baskets. The table was stacked with jars and pots, there were bundles wrapped in sheets and bedspreads by the door. There was no sign of any breakfast semolina on the stove, not even any bread and milk on the table.

231

'Mama, why are we going to Babcia's?'

'Your father will be going away for a while with the other policemen.'

'He's not coming with us?'

'He will join us when he can.' Mama turned away to the shelves behind her.

'Where's he going?' Tad asked.

'Tad, go and pack your clothes,' she repeated.

When he'd gone, I asked the same question. 'Mama, is Tata going to fight in the war?' Surely he couldn't be? Not my gentle, peace-loving father who served everyone with such kindness?

My mother didn't reply.

'Mama, what's the matter? The Germans are right away on the other side of Poland aren't they?'

'They're still a long way away, child.'

'So why is he going away?'

'It's just something he has to do! Too may questions! Alinka! Just go and pack your things now. It's all right. Everything will be all right.'

But if everything was going to be all right, why was my normally cheerful mother looking so tense and close to tears?

'What about Boyik?' I persisted, 'Is he coming with us?' But I knew the answer even before I'd asked, and one look at my mother's face told me I was right.

'He isn't, is he?'

'Alinka. It's for his own good! If the Germans came they would...' she broke off and shook her head. 'Your father has to do what's best for him.'

'But Boyik *hated* going away last time there were rumours of war! You *know* he did! He ran away and found his way back to us! We can't send him away again! It's not fair!' I turned and stomped determinedly back into the police office through the open door. Surely my father wouldn't be so heartless! How could he even think of doing such a thing? But my father didn't hear me coming back in. None of them did. The window was closed now, the wireless switched off. They were all sitting now at the table at the far end of the office, their backs to the roaring stove, heads together, talking low, a large map spread out in front of them.

I stood at the door hesitating, then quietly crept away, back into the kitchen and through the open back door into the garden.

Shading my eyes from the bright morning sun, I anxiously scanned the long garden. Boyik wasn't there.

He wasn't in his usual place on the grass run, he wasn't sniffing anywhere in the garden, or sleeping in a sunny patch.

I ran to the kennel, and suddenly, slowly, sleepily, there he was, coming out from his kennel, stretching and yawning, short stubby tail wagging to greet me, as if nothing had happened. As if stoves weren't roaring with flames, as if things weren't being packed into bedspreads and baskets, as if he weren't about to be exiled from his family and home.

Overwhelmed with relief, I crouched by him, stroking

his ears. 'We're going away too, you know,' I tried to explain. 'We'll come and get you back as soon as we get home again. I promise.'

I knew dogs could sense fear and sadness in people, so perhaps somehow, he would be able to understand what I was telling him. 'Maybe this war will all be over in a few days, but even if it's a week or two, don't you go running away and coming back here this time, Boyik, because we won't be here. Do you hear me? You have to stay where Tata takes you, Boyik!'

Hearing the word 'stay', he lay down in front of me obediently, looking up expectantly, very pleased with himself, his black stubby tail thumping the ground.

'Oh Boyik! I didn't mean *stay* right now!' I had to smile, 'I mean when you're at the village!'

He was a well trained police dog. He would never accept food from anyone who tried to feed him from their right hand, and he would have given his life to protect any one of us. He'd been with us since he was a puppy, and yet now we were about to send him away, and there was no way I could really explain to him why - and anyway, how could I? I couldn't even understand it myself.

'Alinka! Come and pack your things!' my mother was calling from the doorway. 'Hurry!'

Sad and scared talk at night

We were on the road to Wolkowysk, where Babcia Maria and Dziadziu Jan, our maternal grandparents lived, in [illegible] the same names were often found in families in those days since children were quite frequently named after parents or grandparents.

The normally quiet road was crowded with people. We had never seen so many people along that road before. People burdened with baskets and bags, and bundles wrapped in bedspreads. Some pulling carts, others pushing heavily laden prams. There were a few horses and carts too. Everyone looked so anxious and seemed to be in a hurry.

'Mama – why is everyone else going the other way? We're the only ones going towards the town!'

'They're escaping from the Germans,' Mama explained. 'They want to get across the border and out of Poland to safety. Most of them are Jewish.'

Whole families were carrying suitcases, or wheeling bicycles piled high with belongings, bags on their backs, babies in their arms and little children on their shoulders - a streaming river of people flowing towards the eastern Polish border. Mama asked our cart driver to stop for a moment while she offered a drink of water and some bread and pears to an exhausted looking family with several little children.

'May God repay you!'

'And may He keep you safe!' Mama replied.

That evening at Babcia's we had chicken soup and dumplings, and Babcia's plum cake so sweet and good that for a while I was happy. Perhaps war wouldn't be so bad, as long as it ended soon so we could go back home and have Boyik back with us again.

But later that night, there was a lot of quiet talk when we children were in bed and Tad was fast asleep. I could hear Mama and Babcia and Dziadziu's voices in the kitchen.

'Marianek!'

'What?'

'Do you think Tata and the others are going to fight in the war?'

'No.'

'Are you sure? Isn't that why he's going away?'

'I'm sure.'

I looked out of the open window. The air was warm and scented, the stars were shining and for a moment, hope filled my heart. If my father wasn't going to fight, then he'd be safe.

'But if Tata's not going to war, where *is* he going?'

My brother looked across at me in the dark, without replying.

'Marianek?'

There was no reply.

'Marianek! *Where is* Tata going? When will we be going back home?'

'We won't be, not if the Germans arrive.'

'But Tata's chief of police! He's the commandant! He won't let them…'

'Alinka!' Marianek sighed with exasperation, 'Tata and the others are running away for their lives. Tata won't *be* a police officer any more when the Germans get here. They have their own police and you can be sure they will get rid of all Polish ones.'

I sat up in bed, shocked. 'You mean they will take over the *police station*? But it's our *home*!'

Marianek was silent.

'What about Jurek next door? What will happen to him?'

There was no reply.

'Marianek?'

'Go to sleep Alinka!'

'What about Boyik? When will we get him back?'

Marianek turned over in bed. 'We'll have to wait and see. Maybe everything will turn out all right. It will just be different that's all. Boyik will be all right.'

But his words sounded unconvincing in the darkness, and in the kitchen the low voices sounded sad and scared.

A plague of locusts

Soldiers and civilians were dying by the thousand, and all over Poland cities were in ruins, but the warm September sun continued to shine.

Tad and I were out barefoot by the stream at the bottom of Aunty Anna's and Uncle Juzek's garden. Their big house was just down the road from Babcia's rented rooms, and we often used to go there to play. We were building a dam with twigs and pebbles, listening to the birds twittering and frogs croaking, when suddenly the peace of the day was shattered as wailing air raid sirens started. Tad shielded his eyes from the sun to catch sight of the planes.

'Tad! We're supposed to hide, not stand admiring them!' I grabbed his hand and dragged him towards the shelter of the old apple tree.

'But look!' he cried pointing up from the shelter of the tree. 'It's not the swastika on the wings.'

I looked up as they passed over us, hands over my ears because of the deafening roar, and saw the red star. So it was true, what everyone had been talking about it.

'It's the Russians, isn't it?'

We both looked up to where the planes had left their trails of smoke in the cloudless summer sky, and for once, neither of us spoke.

Soon after that, those red stars were everywhere as the communists marched into our little town like a plague of greedy locusts. In their long coats, fur lined caps and black leather boots, they stripped all the wheat and fruit and vegetables from the farms and stores. They took over the bakery and the shops. Within days there was nothing left. They had emptied every shelf.

Every night I prayed for our father to be safe and for him to come back to us. How could he escape across the border now, if the Russians had invaded now too? Perhaps he'd be able to go through the Ukraine to escape, but that would also be dangerous. The Ukrainians had been seen welcoming the Soviets with flowers and flags. They had long wanted the borderlands of Poland for themselves. Now they were eagerly joining with the Russian forces to drive the Polish people living in the remote borderland areas from their homes. They had been harassing, stealing, burning barns and homes, and torturing and killing any Polish 'capitalist' who dared to stand up to them.

In the afternoons, I took to walking up and down Aunty Anne's long garden, as my father used to do in our garden at home while he prayed the Rosary and I prayed with all my heart for his safe return.

A few days later, there was a gentle tapping at the front door, and when Babcia went to open it, what a joyful shout of surprise! And then the sound of our dear Tata's warm voice and his laughter. Mama was running to the door, and there were hugs and happy tears and cries of 'Thank God! God be praised!'

That night, there was a celebration supper at Aunty Anna's house. There was vegetable soup and a chicken with carrots and potatoes, with an apple crumble cake for pudding. There were no sad voices that evening. Our mother was smiling and Tad and I sat snuggled close to our dear Tata, feeling safe as chicks under a hen's wings. It was easy to feel that everything would be all right when our father was with us.

'Tata, why did you come back?' Marianek asked him quietly. 'Why didn't you carry on with the others to the border? Will you be safe here?'

The Soviet Secret Police were arresting so many people: police officers, soldiers, teachers, professors, university students and priests; anyone at all who was educated or had any kind of authority was seen as a threat. They were deported to Siberia.

'I turned back when the Russians crossed over our borders. We were there when they entered Poland,' he rubbed his forehead wearily. 'They were assuring the border guards that they were coming to liberate the Polish people, so no attempt was made to stop them.' He paused, his face clouding over, then continued, ' Then they began to arrest and shoot the guards and brutally hurt the women whose husbands were away fighting. By then it was too late to do anything.' He shrugged and hugged us closer to him. 'What will be, will be,' he said, 'but at least I'll be here with you. At least we'll be together.'

Marianek was looking at him uncertainly,

'Marianek, one day, when you have a wife and children, you will understand. There are some things that are more important even than freedom.'

'But they won't find you anyway, Tata, will they?' I interrupted, annoyed with my brother for spoiling the evening with his questions. 'It's not as if we're in our police house, anymore, is it? How will they ever know you're a police officer now? The p̲ ̲m̲ ̲'̲ ̲l̲ ̲m̲ ̲̲̲ ̲l̲ ̲̲̲ ̲̲̲ ̲̲̲ ̲̲̲ ̲̲̲ ̲̲̲ ̲̲̲ ̲̲̲ ̲̲̲ I turned to my brother, 'Tata isn't wearing his uniform any more, is he? And all the papers are burnt. They won't ever know who he is if we stay here. How could they?'

Unexpected egg bath

For weeks the sky stayed blue and the sun kept shining, and our father was with us.

In Aunty Anna's house there were always children playing and people chatting, so in the early evenings, my father walked in the long garden to have his daily time of quiet prayer. I would sit on the bench behind the house and watch him and I thanked God with all my heart that he was back. Sometimes I walked by his side, listening to his peaceful prayers, sometimes joining in a little.

Before he had met my mother, when she'd been just sixteen, he'd been studying to be a priest.

'Was Mama very beautiful when you first met her?' I asked when he had finished his prayers, and we were sitting together on a log by the stream.

'Yes she was,' he nodded. 'As beautiful and dark-haired as you are now.'

I wanted to hear the story all over again, even though I'd heard it many times before.

'You were walking along the street one hot sunny day, weren't you? And she was sitting by an open window sewing at a sewing machine?' My mother had worked as a seamstress.

Tata eyes lit up. 'And I went over to the window and smiled to her and said, 'Good morning!' And that was that. We arranged to meet that evening, and we fell in love. I asked her to marry me soon after. She was still only sixteen.' After a long pause, he added, 'You are very much like your mother, you know.'

'Well, when I get married, I would like a dark-haired husband. I want all my children to be just like you!'

He gave me a hug, 'Never mind the colour of his hair! Just make sure he loves God and has a good, kind heart!' he laughed.

Back in the house, everyone had gathered round the wireless that we had brought with us from the police station. Yet again there was more bad news. Thousands more Polish soldiers and civilians had been killed. The allied help from France and Britain had not arrived as promised. More broken agreements. All over Poland, families were in mourning. Sadness and fear hung in the air.

In the cities people were suffering with hunger. But at least at Aunty Anna's house, there was still food to eat. In the garden there were still vegetables and fruit, and Uncle Juzek worked in the meat factory in the town and sometimes brought home slices of sausage or ham or some other meats. Then also, Aunty's chickens clucked and pecked all over the big garden and gave us eggs, though at one point, for a while, they didn't seem to be laying as well as usual. None of the hens were missing, or broody, but, mysteriously, there were fewer eggs each morning than normal. With so many people to feed, it made a difference. Aunty was puzzled. 'Perhaps the air raids and sirens have upset them?' she wondered.

But even with fewer eggs, there were still carrots and onions and cabbages in the garden, and late apples and pears to pick and store in the attic.

I loved helping with the fruit picking; tasting, as far as I was concerned, was part of the job.

The pears were still hard and crunchy when we picked them but they would gradually soften, stored up in the attic, and eventually we'd be eating them very soft and over ripe. I loved them however they came.

'Just save a few to actually store away for the winter!' Mama said, as she caught me yet again with my mouth full!

Just as the fruit picking was coming to an end, and we were all out helping in the garden, the sirens shrieked and my father shouted to us children to hide. All in a panic, as the deafening roar approached, I dashed to a low growing, wide-leafed shrub and dived under it just as the planes came roaring by. I landed headfirst not on soft soil as expected but, ugh, on a heap of something that cracked and splattered all over me! I had to lie there in a pool of slime until the noise in the sky had passed over. Crawling out after the planes had gone, I didn't know whether to laugh or cry, covered as I was in broken egg shell and raw egg. 'Now I know why there haven't been so many eggs!' I called to Aunty Anna, ruefully. 'One of the chickens must have been hiding them here!'

Mama explained to me with a smile as she helped to wash me down, that raw egg was very good for the skin. 'You will be very beautiful now when you grow up.'

The rumours of Soviet brutality increased. More Russian soldiers were moving in with their huge steam-powered tanks and lorries, bigger than anything anyone had ever seen before.

There were terrible, shocking things happening that the grown ups only whispered about. We were later to learn that in every town and village women were abused in such terrible ways by gangs of soldiers that they died. Stalin had not only turned a blind eye to this but encouraged it, saying his troops needed some recreation. We heard of a village in which the women and girls, on hearing that the Soviet soldiers were on their way, had tied themselves together and jumped into the lake to drown. They had preferred to die that way than to be brutally abused to death as so many other innocent women had been. Wives and mothers, sisters and daughters, all left unprotected as the men were away fighting.

Now on the radio, there was no more Polish news. No more Polish music. Chopin and all Polish composers were banned; Polish dance music and folk songs were banned; Christian songs were banned, even on Sundays. The

Russians had taken over the radio broadcasts. Now it was all Communist propaganda and songs about Joseph Stalin and the mighty Soviet Union.

They took over the big police station in Wolkowysk, and a neighbour told our father they had taken over our little police station in Ros too, our house with it. Like fat cuckoos, they were also taking every spare room in Polish peoples' houses. Everyone who had a spare room had to allow the Soviets to lodge with them, eat their food, drink their drink, and you had to watch every word you said and everything you did.

That was when Aunty Anna and Uncle Juzek urged everyone to come and live together in their house. Aunty Anna had no intention of letting the Communists take over any of their rooms, not if they could fill them with family instead.

Babcia and Dziadziu's rooms in the town were rented, but Aunty Anna and Uncle Juzek's big house belonged to them. They had three children - our cousins - Wiesio, Niunka, and Mirka. But it was a big house, with room to spare.

So we all moved in: Babcia Maria, Dziadziu Jan, Tata, Mama, Marianek, Tad and me, Aunty Stefa, (Mama's sister),her husband Uncle Kazik, and their son Rysiu. Uncle Kazik was our father's brother; Mama and her sister had married two brothers.

Fifteen of us all in one house.

'There's safety in numbers!' Aunty Anna declared.

If only that had been true.

Just before Christmas, 1939
Arrested.

Logs were burning in the stove and everyone was busy with preparations for Christmas Eve.

A big fir tree had been felled from the forest and was now filling the living room with its scent. There were little white candles clipped onto the ends of its branches, and a silver star right at the top. It was always put there as a reminder of the other star, a long time ago, that led the wise men to Bethlehem.

The house was warm and filled with the sweet and spicy scents of Christmas biscuits. I was beating butter and sugar and brandy with a wooden spoon (and tasting, as always).

'Alinka! Will you please leave some to actually put on the cake!' Mama scolded, as she caught me licking the spoon yet again. It reminded me of when we were still living in our little police house in Ros, when my brother Marianek got into trouble one Christmas Eve for being greedy. Mama had baked a special large yeasted raisin cake for Christmas Eve, and had put it in the pantry to store. Now, we children were always wanting something to eat, especially if there was something really tasty around, and raisin cake was a rare treat.

My brother Marianek decided to taste just a raisin or two before the celebrations, being careful to pick them out of the side of the cake, where it wouldn't show. But, once he'd tasted them, since they were so delicious, he went back and picked out a few more from the other side of the cake. And then back again for a few more. By the time Christmas Eve came and Mama proudly carried the cake out of the pantry and took off the tea-towel that had ⬚⬚⬚⬚ ⬚⬚⬚⬚⬚⬚ ⬚⬚ ⬚⬚ ⬚⬚⬚⬚ ⬚⬚ ⬚⬚ ⬚⬚⬚⬚⬚⬚ ⬚⬚ ⬚⬚⬚⬚⬚ ⬚⬚⬚ ⬚⬚⬚⬚⬚⬚⬚ ⬚ raisin cake but just a large yeast cake full of holes where my greedy brother had picked out every single raisin!

How life had changed since then. Instead of just the five of us in our own home, and Boyik, there were now fifteen of us living together and any food that was prepared had to always be shared by fifteen, so the portions were always too small. All our clothes were getting very loose, and we always left the table wishing there was more. Mama often gave her share of anything especially tasty to us children, saying she'd eaten enough, but she was getting thin too.

My musings were suddenly interrupted by the sound of a heavy lorry coming along the street, which stopped outside the house. No one but the Russians had vehicles in our town. We could hear doors slamming and footsteps approaching. As the front gate creaked, Babcia looked up all flushed from checking her honey cake in the oven. She and my mother exchanged an anxious glance and wiping hands on aprons, went together to open the door.

I took an extra lick of the cake mixture, then dropping the wooden spoon in the mixing bowl, ran across to peep through the lace curtains at the front window. Two soldiers in long boots and long coats and hats with earflaps were standing at the door. It was beginning to snow.

'Roch and Kazik Pietrzak?' they enquired in Polish.

'They live here, is that not so?'

Mama nodded.

'We have orders for them to be taken to a court hearing.'

There was a pause. Well, at least that didn't sound like Siberia, I thought in relief as I crept to where I could see better what was happening at the door.

'They are at the barber's,' I heard Babcia reply politely, 'having their hair cut. They will be back shortly.'

'We will wait!' they announced, making a move towards the door expectantly. Babcia hesitated. She and Mama exchanged another glance, then reluctantly they stood back to let them in. One of them positioned himself at the back window, one by the door. I went to stand by the front window again, hoping Tata would see the army lorry and understand what was happening. Perhaps he would be able to turn away before they saw him, and escape and hide. Maybe go to the village where Boyik was and hide there with Boyik, since it was no longer possible to escape from Poland across the borders.

But there were soldiers in the truck too, and all my hopes were dashed because suddenly, there he was, my father, with Uncle Kazik, walking down the road. The snow was falling more heavily now but I knew it was them. I stood very still, as if I'd seen nothing, though my cheeks were blazing. I could see that Tata had noticed the lorry and had changed direction suddenly and was heading for the back of the house. Maybe they'd hide in the shed until the soldiers had gone. Perhaps through the thick snow, they wouldn't be seen.

But one of the soldiers on guard in the lorry saw them heading for the garden and called out to alert the others. They hurried out and I could hear voices, and then my ⁣⁣ their hands tied behind their backs.

The soldiers explained to Mama that they would have to be taken to jail until the court hearing.

'But what are they charged with?'

'We do not know when they will return,' was all they said in reply.

As my father was being led away, one of the younger soldiers, seeing my mother's tearful face said to her more gently, 'It will be all right. You will be able to go there, to the prison. You will be able to see them, and you can take them a parcel.' He told them where they would be and that was that. They were gone.

I had not even kissed my father goodbye.

'Stay close to me.'

Mama and Aunty Stefa took parcels of food for them in prison, but as these had to be left with the soldiers in charge, we were never sure whether they actually received them. There were rumours that the Soviet soldiers kept the parcels and gifts for themselves.

But at least it's better than Siberia, I kept reassuring

myself. At least he is not far away. And he'd be back home after the court hearing. They would soon see that he'd done nothing wrong.

'But why do they have to go to a court hearing like criminals? What crime are they charged with?' Marianek was asking angrily some days later. Our father and uncle Kazik were still in jail and there still had not been any court hearing. 'How can they just arrest them like that when they've not done anything wrong?'

'All army and police officers are considered undesirables,' Dziadziu explained.

As Christmas Eve drew near, I was full of hope. Maybe the trial would be held soon, and Tata would be released. Maybe they would let all the prisoners out in time for Christmas.

Marianek looked at me cynically. 'Alinka,' he sighed. 'Communists *hate* God,' he said, 'They do not celebrate Christmas. God is just another threat to them, just as Tata is – only more so!'

Normally on Christmas Eve, we children would have been glued to the window, looking out for the first star of Christmas, so that Wigilia, the special Christmas Eve supper could begin. But that afternoon, the sky was heavy with clouds. Eventually it grew dark and we broke and shared the traditional blessed Christmas wafer, and wished each other peace and blessings as is always done at the start of the Wigilia. But because Uncle Kazik and Tata were still in prison, everyone ended up in tears.

It was a relief to say grace and sit down and eat. It was a meal I was to bring to mind many times in the years of hunger to come. Hot, tangy beetroot soup to start with, with mouthful mouthwatering ravioli pierogi. Then all the other traditional dishes: baked fish, and fried fish, potato and vegetable salad, pickled herrings, pickled cabbage, cream cheese pierogi, then mixed fruit compote and Babcia's heavenly apple crumble cake to follow, and finally the brandy-butter-iced nut torte, with barley and chicory root coffee.

Now, I was always wishing there weren't so many of us to share the food at mealtimes. But that Christmas Eve, even though the portions were much too small as always, I would gladly have gone without food altogether, if only we could have had our father back with us.

The candles were lit on the tree and we switched off the lights. Dziadziu and Babcia led the carol singing round the table that night, not our father. Mama had to leave the table for a while in tears.

Later, as Christmas bells were ringing out from the church, we walked through the snow to Midnight Mass. The church was lit up with flickering candlelight, with the scent of hay from the life-sized crib and pine from the huge Christmas tree. Even though the accordion and fiddle and guitar accompanied the Christmas carols, the singing was subdued, and in the normally packed church there were empty seats. So many of the men were missing.

After Mass our mother stayed to pray by the crib. For a

long time she knelt with her head bowed and eyes closed. It was only many years later that she told me that as she had knelt there in prayer, she'd heard quite clearly in her heart, words from Our Lady, 'Don't ever walk away from me, my child. There will be much suffering, but stay close to me.'

From that time, whenever she had a moment of rest in the evenings, her rosary beads were in her hands, and in this way she was at least joined together in spirit with our father.

January 1940
Two match-flames in the dark

It was just after Christmas. I was over at my best friend Helenka's house. Helenka's mother had been into the town and had come hurrying back earlier than expected, looking all upset and out of breath from running.

'Mama! What's the matter? ' Helenka asked in concern, seeing her flushed face.

'You know, Alinka,' she said to me urgently, giving me a look of such compassion, 'They are taking prisoners from that jail where your father is and taking them away to the train station!'

I ran all the way home. I have never run faster in my life. Then with Mama and Marianek and Tad, we ran as fast as if our lives depended on it, to the train station.

What we saw when we arrived there made us stop and gasp in amazement.

The normally quiet station was a heaving mass of people. There was confusion, crowds, noise. Soldiers with rifles were guarding the platform and train wagons. Orders were being shouted, people running up and down, calling out names and crying.

The train was nothing like the little Wolkowysk passenger train. It was a huge black locomotive with the red Soviet star on it, and there were no passenger wagons. I stood staring at it. Surely there must be a mistake, I thought. Helenka's mother must have got it wrong. These were just old cattle trucks, snaking out beyond the platform way into the distance. Each had a tiny barred oblong ventilation hole near top. You could smell the stench of the animals from them from the platform.

But there was no sound of sheep bleating or cows stamping coming from inside. As I gazed up at the ventilation holes, it finally dawned on me that there weren't any pigs or cows or horses in them; even though the doors were locked, I could tell that there were people inside.

'Wow! Look at that engine!' Tad was whistling in admiration, oblivious to what was going on. I squeezed his hand, looking round at all the wailing, panic rising up in me. Mama too was looking up at the barred ventilation holes, her face pale.

All along the platform women were shouting out names, children crying, and so many anguished people running up and down yelling, 'Tata! It's Marysia!' 'Tata it's Edek!' 'Tadzio! Zbyszek Koszynski! Where are you? What's happening? Where are they taking you? It's Aniela!' Shouting out names and surnames, trying desperately to catch a glimpse of a loved one locked inside.

Marianek pushed his way through the crowd, as close to the wagons as he could get, screaming over all the voices, 'Tata! Tata! It's Marianek! Pietrzak! Roch Pietrzak! We're looking for Roch Pietrzak! Tata! Where are you? It's Marianek! Tata! It's Marianek! Pietrzak. Pietrzak! Roch Pietrzak!' He was crying out desperately at the top of his voice. He kept screaming it out till he was hoarse.

Suddenly in one of the carriages just beyond the platform, they started to shout back to him. 'Marianek! Pietrzak! Here's Roch Pietrzak! In here! Here! Roch Pietrzak is in here!'

We pushed our way through the crowd to the wagon. Never had I seen my polite mother push like that before, tears streaming down her face. 'Roch! Roch! It's Maria!'

'Tata! It's Alinka! We're all here!' I shouted up to the little barred ventilation hole, over all the noise surrounding us. We could hear people moving inside the truck, urging others out of the way, we craned our necks to see, but it was pitch black in the hole and it was so high up, we could see nothing.

Then the shouting stopped and all went quiet in the wagon. We were staring up expectantly at the barred dark hole, when suddenly on either side of it, two matches were struck at the same time, one on either side of the hole, and there, in the light of the two match flames, for a few seconds was my father's face. The window was so narrow you could only just see him. He looked so pale and thin. It was just for a couple of seconds, then the match flames burnt out and there was just darkness.

'Roch!' Mama cried, tears flowing down her face. 'Are you all right? Are you well? Where are they taking you?' But a whistle was shrieking, drowning her voice. The piercing whistle blew again and smoke billowed out over us, as the huge engine groaned and creaked and pulled away.

We stood watching as the trucks were towed away, with my father locked inside one of them.

The crowds on the platform surged after the wagons. We ran with them. Even Marianek had tears streaming down his face. 'Tata! Tata!' He screamed as we ran after the wagon, 'We'll ask them where they are taking you! We'll come and find you!'

But the engine picked up speed and we were left behind.

'God go with you!' Mama cried at the top of her voice, but it was lost in the noise of the engine and shouting and wailing of the crowds. And then it was gone.

The crowd of people on the platform now stood in stunned silence, the train now just a wisp of smoke in the distance.

I wiped my face with the back of my hand. 'But they can't take him away without us!' I cried. 'He came back to us so we would be together!'

I was ten years old.

That was the last time I saw my father.

How can a person just disappear?

'It wasn't just men from our local jail on that train; they've taken all the police and army officers from the whole town,' said Uncle Juzek. He had heard it from other workers at the meat factory. 'Every single one. They were all on that train!'

There had been no court hearings. All the assurances we had received that everything would be all right had been a ruse to stop people causing trouble.

Mama and Aunty Stefa (who was both Mama's sister and Uncle Kazik's wife), boldly and desperately went to the NKVD office to ask where their husbands had been taken, taking Uncle Juzek with them for support since he was their brother. The NKVD officer told them he did not know the destination of the train, but he would notify them as soon as he knew. They waited a week then went back to ask again, and received the same response. Back again the week after that, with the same anxious questions and again and again in the weeks to come. They always received the same reply.

The rest of that winter, the bitterly cold winds blew in from Siberia, but of Tata and Uncle Kazik there was nothing. We waited each morning for the postman hoping for a letter, but it never came. Day after day, week after week, no news.

Then one day, Uncle Juzek went off to work at the meat factory as usual. He kissed our cousins and Aunty Anna, and ruffled my hair as he always did, promising to try and bring home a bit of salt pork to have with our bread for tea.

He never returned.

He didn't come home for tea as he normally did. He didn't come back that night, or the next day, or the day after that. No one knew why he had been taken, or where he had gone. There was just nothing. No news, no explanation no goodbye. We didn't know if he had been murdered or deported. He just disappeared. None of us ever saw him again.

Aunty Anna went with our mother and Dziadziu Jan to make enquiries about him, but were told nothing.

'How can a person just disappear?' I was wondering aloud to Marianek one night when we were in bed.

'In the same way that Tata and Uncle Kazik have disappeared,' he replied bitterly, 'Only with Uncle Juzek, they didn't even try and pretend it was going to be legal.'

'But why would they arrest him? What has he done?'

'Maybe it was because he went with Mama and Aunty Stefa to ask for information about Tata and Uncle Kazik,' Marianek shrugged, 'That would no doubt be enough to have him labelled a trouble maker. I don't know. Maybe he just made some slight remark against communism and someone overheard and reported it. Who knows?' he shrugged. 'There are spies and traitors everywhere now - even among the Polish people.'

With Uncle Juzek gone, Aunty Anna was often standing by the window crying.

Tata was gone, Uncle Kazik was gone, now Uncle Juzek

too. The house was full of heartache and tears.

Just before Easter, we heard whispered warnings that there were more deportations to come.

'Well, at least they can't take anyone else from our family.' I reassured Tad on the way home from evening Mass. 'All the men have gone now, and Dziadziu is too old.'

The night before Easter Sunday, I slept well. I dreamt I was flying. It was a bright morning in my dream, full of sunlight. I was over a meadow full of wild flowers and in the distance was the ocean with clean white sand. And Tata was there, looking so happy, walking towards me, smiling and holding out his arms to greet me.

When I woke, I closed my eyes trying to go back to my dream.

'Alinka! What the matter?' Tad asked me sleepily. 'Why are you crying?'

'I had such a beautiful dream!' I whispered and turned over, not wanting to talk, because to say it had been a dream did not feel right; it had seemed so real.

'What was it about?'

I kept my eyes closed, longing for my father, wanting to go back to him.

'Alinka! What was your dream about?'

Marianek was awake now too. 'If it was so beautiful, why are you crying?'

But I couldn't reply. I just lay there for a long time with my eyes closed. I wasn't able to get back to my dream, but I never forgot it.

13th April 1940
When the whole town was silent and asleep.

It was cold. Snow was still on the fields with winter refusing to give way to spring. Deep in the middle of the night, when the whole town was asleep, a truck pulled up outside the house. There were heavy footsteps and a sharp knocking at the door. It could only be the Russians. But why were they here in the middle of the night? I lay awake listening. I could hear the door being opened and the sound of voices; we children were soon creeping out to the kitchen to see what was happening.

Our mother was there, and Aunty Anna and Babcia Maria and Dziadziu Jan, anxiety on all their faces. They were talking about us.

'…Not all of you,' the soldiers were saying quite politely but firmly. 'Just Maria Pietrzak and her children. We have orders for their transportation.'

'But why? Where are you taking them?' Aunty Anna was asking.

'It will be all right,' he replied to Mama, ignoring Aunty Anna. 'There you will have work, the children will be able to learn. Things will be good for you.'

I was ten years old, and this sounded all right to me. Things would be good for us! I would be going to a new school. I'd make new friends. And although my grandfather, Dziadziu Jan, worked on the railway, I'd never been on a train before. The thought of a journey was exciting, as was the thought of moving to a new place. But above all, above all, was the most wonderful hope: 'Are they taking us to join Tata, do you think?' I whispered excitedly to Babcia who had come to put her arm around me protectively.

'You must pack now,' they were ordering Mama, 'Take what you want, but do not pack knives.'

They were not unpleasant men. One of them wasn't much older than my brother. Mama said later they were just doing their job, but they sat down at the kitchen table without being invited, and watched everything while our poor Mother, flushed and nervous, started packing. Babcia and Aunty Anna were helping.

Mama was packing Tata's warm sheepskin jacket into a bedspread with her things, and so even though everyone seemed so shocked and scared, I was glad we were going. If our mother was packing father's things that meant we'd be seeing him again! How glad he'd be to have that warm jacket to wear again! How could he have survived a winter in Siberia without his warm jacket?

No one stopped me from going into the bedroom when Aunty Anna called me to help her pack a few things for me. We kept the door open as commanded, but the soldiers couldn't see us when we stood behind the open door. Aunty Anna put a finger to her lips and crouching down slipped a knife inside my long woollen ribbed socks.

'It will come in useful for bread' she whispered, 'When

you go back into the kitchen, don't look down at it! Don't look down at all. Because this knife will be useful to you - to cut bread or something, because otherwise you have nothing. But you have to pretend it's not there.'

Marianek had packed a penknife in his rucksack but they'd searched it and thrown it out. They repeated angrily, 'Take everything you want, but no knives!' I could hear them shouting this as I came back into the kitchen, my heart pounding. I was sure they'd see how guilty I looked or notice the bulge in my sock.

The packing did not take long as there was so little to pack. I had one spare dress, one cardigan, my black school pinafore, one spare vest, one spare pair of knickers and socks, and I put on my one pair of winter boots, my coat, and my scarf and woollen gloves that Babcia had knitted.

'Dress warmly,' the soldiers called out. 'It will be a long journey. It will be very cold.' Babcia brought a bottle of vodka and handed it to Mama. 'In case of typhoid,' she said.

And so, while it was still dark, even before the cocks were crowing, while most people in the town were still sleeping, they hurried us out to the lorry - Mama, Marianek, little Tad and me - the policeman's family.

There were a few people on the street now, though it was still dark, and they stopped and looked at us in silence and made the Sign of the Cross.

By the time we arrived at the railway station, the sky was turning grey.

It was Sunday morning, I remember; the church bells were ringing for the early morning Mass.

They won't catch us!

At the station, the same kind of dirty trucks that Tata had been taken away in awaited us. They stretched from one end of the station to the other and then way out beyond into the distance. All the way along, Russian soldiers with rifles and fixed bayonets were guarding the train.

Still full of hope about seeing my father again, I was excited at the prospect of a journey into the unknown, but that excitement lasted only until we were herded into one of the wagons. When I saw what it was like inside, I wanted to go back home. It was dark, damp and airless. The rough wooden slats that had been fixed along the sides of the truck for sitting on, like a lower and higher bunk, were filthy, the floors wet and soiled, there was no toilet that I could see, though it smelt worse than one. There were no windows. So many people were being pushed in that there wasn't even enough space for everyone to sit. We sat crammed into a small dark, frozen corner of a bottom bunk, with our bundles on our knees, as more and more women and children were pushed up into the wagon. There was no more room, and yet still they kept pushing them in. The doors of the wagon were still open, but what would it be like when they shut them?

Well, we wouldn't be in there for long, I told myself firmly, to stop the panic rising up in me. It was just for the journey. Perhaps we'd arrive at our new destination before it got dark, and surely it would be worth any amount of discomfort to be with Tata again.

'They said we'll be able to go to school,' I tried to distract Tad who was looking as though he was about to be sick. 'So we'll make new friends. Look, I brought my friendship album.' I opened it to show him my favourite page. 'See what Tata drew for me; it's a picture of him in uniform and Boyik by his side.' And Tad was successfully distracted. 'And look what Buba drew for me – a beehive and a bee and a pot of honey! Remember breakfast at Buba's? And listen, I'll read out to you the verse that Helenka wrote.' I wasn't doing it just for him. In that little wooden-covered album engraved with flowers, I carried the love of my father, the memory of Boyik and the affection of my best friends. It was my link with our home in Ros, the only thing I possessed that I really treasured.

Shouts outside on the platform made me look up. Although our wagon was overflowing, outside there was still a river of people arriving, and there were others now running up and down, as we had done when Tata was being taken away, shouting out names. We sat quietly, listening. Eventually, to our joy, our names were being shouted out too.

'Maria Pietrzak! Maria Pietrzak! Marianek Pietrzak! Alinka! Tad! Tad! Tadziu!'

'Tutaj! Here! Here we are!' we screamed as loudly as we could, we could just about see out when we stood up, but were unable to move to the open door because we were so tightly crammed in. But there was no keeping my brother Marianek back. He wriggled and pushed his way through like a rat, shouting at the top of his voice.

It was Aunty Anna with our Babcia, hurrying across, flushed and breathless. They lifted up to him a bundle wrapped in a tablecloth, but the soldier on guard took it from them and carefully inspected the contents before he allowed it to be passed up.

'Maria!' they called into the wagon. 'We brought you some fresh bread and boiled eggs and blankets. Write and let us know where they take you!'

Without any warning, soldiers were slamming the wagon doors shut and locking the iron bolts on the outside of the doors.

'God go with you!'

Marianek jumped away only just in time to avoid having his fingers crushed. In the next carriage someone was screaming in pain. Maybe they had not been so lucky.

As the train began to creak and groan into motion, a woman sitting next to us with two children our age, made the Sign of the Cross and began to pray the Our Father. Mama joined in, as did others in that foul, dark, airless wagon. Soon, one small child began to cry, 'Mama I need to go to the toilet!' His mother didn't know what to do. There was no toilet. When he soiled himself I began to understand why the wagon stank like a toilet. After that, some of the women and older boys hacked out a hole in the rotten floorboards.

I stared at the toilet hole in horror. 'There's no way I am going in that!' I shook my head in disgust. With the wind blowing up and everyone looking, I made up my mind to wait till we got to our destination. Little did I know how many long weary weeks we would be locked up in that wagon.

Nearly everyone had slept for a while, lulled by the motion of the train and tired out since we had all been taken from our beds in the middle of the night.

Now people were waking and taking out food and beginning to eat. Mama sliced some of the bread that Aunty had brought for us, with the knife from my sock, and peeled the boiled eggs.

Strengthened by the food, the women revived a little and began to talk; to introduce themselves and tell how they had been arrested. There were no men in the wagon, just women and children – all wives and children of police and army officers. The lady next to us who had prayed the Our Father, introduced herself as Pani Szarejkowa and her children Honoria and Edek.

Later, when people started to need the toilet, another woman who had two older daughters went to stand by the hole, holding a blanket up so there would be some privacy. That's what everyone did after that. Even I had to go in the end, to my acute embarrassment. It wasn't easy crouching and balancing while the train juddered and swayed and the air came rushing in through the hole. You had to be careful to aim well, which not everyone had managed, as the floor was sodden and dirty and slippery around the hole. It was the most disgusting toilet visit of my whole life.

For the rest of that long day and the following night we travelled without stopping. Although it was dark in the carriage, there were slits between some of the wooden planked walls that let in enough light to be able to tell if it was day or night.

Two days later the locomotive brakes screeched as the train slowed and juddered to a stop. Chains were taken away, bolts lifted and doors opened. Daylight streamed in, hurting our eyes that had been in the dark for days.

'Are we there?' Tad asked hopefully.

We were at a little railway station. The name sign of the place was covered with a sack. It was just a dirt platform with one small wooden building. But there was a tap for hot boiled water.

'We are not in Poland anymore,' someone said.

The guards were shouting for two people from every carriage to come out for water and food. Each was given a bucket – one of boiled water which they called Kipiatok, and the other a half bucket of watery buckwheat soup to take back to the carriage. No one else was allowed out.

It was not enough for so many people, so everyone carefully took just half a cup of water and a few spoonfuls of the soup. We were all very thirsty as, although most people had brought some food for the journey, most had not brought anything to drink. When you are forced to pack in the middle of the night, it's hard to remember everything.

Far from being the end of the journey, as my brother had been hoping, it was just the beginning. For three more long weeks we travelled. Each morning Pani Szarejkowa led us in prayers, and the beautiful morning hymn *Kiedy ranne staja zorze*, about the earth and sea and all of creation singing praises to God. And each evening, we joined her in the Rosary meditations. The younger children fell asleep to the soothing sound of the prayers. Every evening when Pani Szarejkowa took out her rosary beads and began the 'I believe in God', my thoughts went back to my father, picturing him as he used to walk in the garden. I always wanted to stay awake to the end of the Rosary, to feel close to him, but was always asleep before it finished.

Most days we stopped for Kipiatok and grey, watery soup, but not everyday. Soon all the food we had brought had gone. No one had imagined the journey would be so long. It felt like we'd already travelled a million miles.

After a week, the train stopped on a siding in marshy land. The guards allowed everyone out to relieve themselves outside. Climbing out of the trucks which were high off the ground, where there was no station platform, wasn't easy for legs unaccustomed to moving for so long, and certainly not dignified. The tracks and grass around the tracks was already covered in human waste, no doubt from previous trainloads of deportees. Everywhere was crawling with flies. There didn't seem to be any toilets anywhere.

'If you try to run away you will sink in the quick sand, or be shot,' we were warned.

My brother Marianek had been whispering in the wagon to two other boys his age. He came to quietly explain to Mama that they were planning on running away and he wanted to go with them.

'No Marianek!' Mama begged him not to go. 'It's too

dangerous. You'll be shot if they catch you!'

'They won't catch us!' he said.

In the middle of nowhere

Although Marianek went back to the boys who were planning to escape, he later returned to us. The other boys did not return. When the soldiers were ordering everyone back onto the wagons, it was discovered that they were missing.

'They will be found!' The soldiers warned angrily. 'They cannot escape!

The food we had brought with us had ran out, so we were hungry all the time. The small drink of boiled Kipiatok water that was given once a day or sometimes every other day, was never enough to stop our thirst. Lice from the filthy wooden boards were soon crawling all over us, in our hair and our clothes; their bites made us itch to distraction and scratch till we bled. No one had washed or changed their clothes for three weeks, so the body odour smells from so many unwashed people was worse than anything I had ever experienced before. The toilet hole smelt so disgusting it made you retch, and the air inside the locked wagon was always foul. If horrible smells could kill you, I thought, I would most definitely already be dead.

Just when it seemed the journey would never end, and

that we would all eventually die from hunger or thirst, as many already had, after three weeks of travelling, the train pulled into a tiny station in the middle of nowhere, and stopped.

The sliding doors of the wagons were unlocked one by one and opened wide. People were blinking and shading their eyes from the unaccustomed light. We were all stiff, aching and dirty; our faces pale and drawn, our clothes hanging loose, filthy and crumpled. Everyone was ordered out of the wagons. Anxiously clutching bundles and bags, we were half crawling, half falling out, hardly able to pick ourselves up off the ground.

When we left Poland it was still winter; now it was May, and very hot. How good it was to feel the sun again.

We were at a small station with one small rough shelter, a kipiatok tap, and that was it; nothing else. I gazed around in bewilderment. All around us was nothing. I had never seen such a flat empty landscape, so vast and wide stretching out into the distance as far as you could see in all directions. There were no houses, no woods, no trees, no mountains or hills in the distance, no bushes, no lakes or rivers, just flat empty earth and an endless sky.

Not a drop of water anywhere

'Where are we?' someone asked the guards.

'Here you will work and learn!' was all the reply we received.

There were carts and ponies waiting. Names were called off lists and people ordered onto the carts, which heavily laden, set off, their ponies straining.

'Maria Pietrzak, Marianek Pietrzak, Alina Pietrzak, Tadeusz Pietrzak.' I was relieved to see we were put on the same cart as Pani Szarajkowa and her children.

We were taken over narrow dirt tracks, over the monotonous land, under a vast hot sky. Eventually we stopped at a few poor mud huts. Dug-outs. They were basically a hole in the ground with low mud and straw walls and a straw roof. But each had a door and a small glass window. There was a rough barn in the distance. This, it was explained to us was a saffhoz - a very small collective farm settlement.

A few of the local people from the settlement had come to stare at us new arrivals in silence, people such as we had never seen before in our lives. They were native Kazakhs of Mongolian race, with narrow slanty eyes, gaps in their discoloured teeth, and dark sun dried skin. We children stared back at them warily, never having seen such strange looking people before. We were soon to learn that, although they hardly ever spoke without cursing and swearing, they had kind, hospitable hearts and a mistrust of the Soviets as great as that of any Polish deportee.

There was a hut where the Communist party chief commissar lived. There was also a shack that opened twice a day that provided bread for work ration cards. There was a small primary school building, and a nursery hut for all babies and little children too young for school. Caring for your own children was not an option under Communist regime; all mothers were forced to work long hours in the fields.

The Soviet Secret Police office was in a small town nearby about five kilometres away.

We stood, clutching our few belongings, and were welcomed by the commissar with, 'Kto nie rabotayet tot ne yest!' He then repeated it loudly in Polish. 'Everyone has to work here,' he told us. 'He who does not work, does not eat!'

Most of us were fainting with hunger and thirst. Many who had started the journey had not survived; their corpses had been left behind along the tracks of the railway, and those of us who had survived, were barely alive. How could our Mama and the other women work when they could barely stand?

But that wasn't the question that bothered me most right then. I was looking round desperately. There was no sign of a toilet anywhere, not even a hut with a hole in the ground. And no sign of any water anywhere either. I could see no public water pump like the one we'd had in Ros. There seemed to be no well, not even a natural spring or stream.

'Where do we get our water?' Someone asked, voicing the anxieties of us all. We had been parched with thirst for the whole three weeks of the journey and could think of nothing else. We were also infested with lice and crabs, soiled and filthy and desperately in need of a wash. The commissar informed us that there was no water there at all.

We stared at him. What was he saying?

How was it possible to live without water? It could not be true!

But we found it was true.

There was not a drop of water anywhere near the settlement, apart from what was brought into the saffhoz in barrels, which was precious little, and which was very severely rationed.

However, the commissar explained, there were cows in the fields beyond the milking barn and the cheese-making barn where they produced Brindza. This was a soft salty, skimmed milk cheese that looked like the feta cheese we have in the shops today. When all the goodness had been extracted from it, the salty, sour waste liquid left over was thrown out into huge urns. As it was of no use to them and would otherwise be thrown away, it was available to anyone to use as a water substitute. No wonder the locals smelt so sour; that's all they had to wash in.

Every day I had to go with a bucket and fetch some back to the hut in a bucket. We made soup with it and we washed in it. Soon our scent was just as sour as the locals'!

No Capitalist luxuries here!

Some of the mud huts had small rough animal shelters attached. It was forbidden to keep more than one or two animals per household, and for each animal kept, the government demanded a large percentage of the milk or meat produced, so even the animal owners were barely producing enough for themselves and their families to eat.

At the back of the hut there were small lean-to porches for storage.

For the first night, we were all assigned to the barn. This barn was used to store animal foods in winter and straw from wheat and barley crops, but that May, 1940, it was Polish deportees that were being stored there. There was no kitchen, no toilet, and of course, no water. It seems not only did the Communists not believe in God, they didn't believe in any kind of sanitation either! And they even boasted of it. 'No capitalist luxuries here!'

This posed a tremendous problem for a self-conscious eleven-year-old girl. Since there were no trees or bushes to hide behind, what did people do when they needed to go? After treading on piles of human excrement that lay everywhere, and seeing locals crouching anywhere to do their business in public, without any shame or modesty, we soon found out.

Once the Commissar had left us for the night, the gentle Pani Szarejkowa said quietly, 'It is May now. Let us pray together the Litany to Our Lady.'

In Poland, May is the month dedicated to honouring

the mother of Jesus and asking her to pray for us. Pani Szarejkowa knelt on the barn floor and her children knelt too. Everyone joined them - even the smallest children listened as this devout lady read out the litany from a battered old prayer book. She prayed quietly so as not to be heard by the Russians:

'....Mary, Help of Christians, pray for us,

Queen of Peace, pray for us,

Help of Sinners, pray for us,

Comfort of the Afflicted, pray for us,

Queen of heaven and earth, pray for us...'

For a little while, hunger and thirst were forgotten. As the beautiful familiar words were recited, it took me back to those warm May evenings in Poland when our father would take us by the hand to church each evening for the May devotions. No matter how much we wanted to stay outside and play, it was always- feet washing time and sandals on, and then the short walk together to the church. I could still picture my father singing the hymns with his rich, strong wholehearted voice – *'Chwalcie laki umajone, 'Praise the meadows in blossom and the mountains and forests and sparkling streams'.*

My heart ached for him. Where was he now? There was no sign of any Polish officers anywhere here. Where had they taken them? This land was so terribly vast. Would we ever see him again?

After sleeping rough and unwashed on the floor that night, stiff and aching all over and weak with hunger and thirst, each family was allotted a space or a room in one of the small dug-out huts. Each tiny mud hut was dark and low and half buried in the ground and divided in two by a thin partition that didn't reach to the ceiling. You could hear everything through it, but at least it gave a little privacy.

We were given one half of one of these huts with Pani Szarejkowa and her children being allotted the other half.

There was a flimsy steel-barrel stove in each half, though no sign of any wood to burn, and a small table with rough, dirty wooden planks for seats and bunks. The fleas and lice were even worse in these huts than in the train. Every evening, we would sit and crush them with finger nails from each others' hair and clothes. Or we'd just catch them one by one and throw them onto the stove. But no matter how many we crushed, they just kept multiplying.

Even worse, at night, disgusting blood-coloured bedbugs crawled out by the hundreds from every plank of wood, intent on one thing only - sucking our blood. Their bites were truly deep and nasty and in those dirty surroundings often became infected. When we crushed them, the stench from their crushed bodies was so sickening and vile, that even though we were on a starvation diet, they still made me sick.

A risky thing

At dawn each day, Mama and my brother Marianek had to go out with everyone else who was sixteen or over, to the vast, seemingly endless wheat and sunflower fields to weed the already sown crops. They worked a ten day week from dawn to dusk, with only water and a slice of bread to nourish them. There was no rest on a Sunday. In order to make sure that God would not be honoured in any way, the communists forced people to work even longer on that day.

My mother and brother came back to the hut when it was dark, hardly able to walk after bending and stooping all day in the hot relentless sun and the constant scorching wind. Whistling sand storms came that blew thick swirling dust into their faces so they couldn't breathe. But they were not allowed to shelter. Even when the workers were choking and coughing, the work still had to go on. The wind dried out their bodies and irritated their eyes and ears and skin. The lack of water caused constant dehydration.

What a shame there were no fruit trees there, I would think ruefully, or mushrooms, since it was ideal weather for drying sliced apples or burowiki (porcini or ceps), and for making prunes from plums. But there were no trees of any kind, and not one bush anywhere for even a toadstool to hide under. The only things drying in the sun and wind out there were emaciated human beings, human excrement and cow dung. Flies and maggots thrived and crawled over everything.

Since all the women were forced to work on the fields, we children were left alone to go to school and take care of ourselves and each other as best we could.

Tad and I worked hard at the schoolwork and were soon fluent in Russian language and communist propaganda. It was hard, though, to concentrate for long on anything other than the thought of food. Thirty grams of grey bread was what Mama and Marianek got for the backbreaking work they did each day. We children got a little bit too for going to school. But as with the rations given to us on the train, it was hardly enough to fill your caved-in stomach.

Occasionally the workers were given a bonus of sugar. When our bodies were crying out for fruit and vegetables, protein and oils, we were given instead, as a treat, the one thing that not only had no nutritional value whatsoever - it depleted the body of vitamins and rotted teeth already loose from malnutrition. This was to cause suffering too, as there were no dentists or doctors for deportees. This was the so-called bliss of collective farming; Stalin's Communist paradise.

Once, on Stalin's birthday, we children were given a few boiled sweets each at school. It was a great national feast day. I saved mine to take home, guarding them carefully, wanting to make them last as long as possible. That evening I had one slowly with my supper; one small bite of bread, one sip of water and one suck at the sweet. Poison to my health and teeth it may have been, but oh how good it tasted! I still remember it to this day.

If we hadn't bartered everything pretty we owned and every item of our spare clothing, we would have starved to death, as so many others had.

There was a little town about five or six kilometres away; you could see it in the distance since the land was so totally flat. It was a long walk for people already weakened by back-breaking work and inadequate food, but Mama would make the long trek there occasionally to sell some item of clothing we still had from Poland. We had very little, as far as clothes went but the locals had even less. There were no shops, and clothes could not be bought anywhere, apart from extortionately expensive fufaika jackets and felt boots. The locals were willing and eager to barter for any items of clothing, giving some flour in exchange, or half a cabbage or a bit of cheese or an egg.

As soon as the wheat started to ripen, Marianek and Mama came back to the hut after a hard day on the fields with some of the wheat grains in their pockets.

Our mother put her finger to her mouth as she emptied the contents of her pockets.

I stared at her. Was this my honest mother who had sent us off to confession to Fr Jan when we'd stolen his raspberries?

'Oh, my dear child, this isn't Fr Jan's back garden,' she shook her head wearily at me. 'We've had everything stolen from us by the Communists. Everything. Our home and all our crops and animals, they've stolen it all. Yet they say their Communism is all about sharing everything according to the need.'

'But it isn't, is it?' Marianek said, as he carefully took every grain out of his pocket and placed it in the pot. 'The local people here are almost as poor and hungry as we are. They have to work till they drop like us, and the few clothes they have are patched and dirty and worn, They live with the lice and bedbugs, and with no washing facilities, no toilets. Their teeth rot and fall out!'

'They took your Tata away from us too.' Mama added quietly. 'So if we now take some of this so called 'communal' wheat from the 'communal' wheat fields that we're breaking our backs on from dawn till dusk in order to barely survive, I do not call that stealing.

Next day Mama came home with her trousers tied with string at the bottom, and wheat grain inside the trouser legs.

'But you could get sent away if they catch you!' I worried. At school, we were learning a lot about what went on. I knew that to be found stealing was a terribly risky and dangerous thing.

'If we don't eat, we will die. It's a chance we have to take.'

Mama sent me to find two flat stones, and with these she crushed the wheat a little and poured some waste whey water over it, and let it soak a bit. And that's what we ate. I tried to be grateful. It was food after all, it was keeping us alive.

At harvest time, Mama was given the job of driving the combine harvester. In Eastern Poland the hay and corn were still cut with scythes, and until the Russians invaded, there had been no vehicles in our little town. Yet within a day, our mother had learnt to drive and work this giant powerful machine. It was dusty, noisy work, but she did it well. It was better than weeding the fields, and she was expecting those who worked hard to be given a share of the harvested wheat for their labours. That is what we had been told in Poland about the great rewards of collective farming. We were soon to learn, however, that most of the crops were commandeered by the government, with precious little left for the saffhoz workers, no matter how hard they worked.

Communist coal!

Suddenly and unexpectedly, the scorching hot summer came to an end. There was no beautiful autumn season as in Poland, no signs of nature giving glory to God, of leaves on trees changing from green to gold and red and yellow, crunching beneath your feet, and seeds twirling and dancing in the wind, and everywhere the scent of ripe pears and apples, and mushrooms in the woods. Here there were no trees, no autumn leaves, and very worryingly, there were no logs piled up in the shed, or anywhere. How could there be with not a tree in sight?

Overnight, summer simply and silently, turned to the bitterest winter we had ever known. Cold easterly winds blew in the first snows, and the temperature dropped to minus forty degrees.

We had no food stored up apart from a small sack of flour that Mama had bartered for, and some wheat grain. Our heap of straw and sunflower stalks, that we had gleaned from the harvested fields was fast being depleted. There was nothing else to burn on the stove. How would we survive in such arctic conditions?

Coming from a land where minus four was the coldest we'd ever had, we could never have imagined just how bitterly and painfully cold it would get, and we were not prepared for it. In that vast flat land, there was no shelter at all from the winds and raging blizzards. It was like nothing we had ever experienced before.

With most of our clothes bartered for food over the summer, our winter clothing was totally inadequate for these temperatures. In one night the snow covered the whole of our hut, burying us alive. We were trapped inside in total darkness. With no kindling for the stove and no candles for light, it was like being in a dark airless tomb.

We were there for several hours until a neighbouring deportee finally dug a tunnel to our door and Marianek managed to squeeze out and finished digging us out.

From then on, as the winter snows continued, everything we had that could be burned was burned: baskets, boxes, even straw bedding all went on the stove. Without some heat we would have frozen to death, even inside the hut, just as the salty whey water froze solid in the pot on the table.

When there was nothing left to burn, in desperation, my brother went out one night to search for something to burn. He was gone far too long. Our mother was so worried about him, but to our huge relief, he did eventually come back, frozen and barely able to breathe, but with a bulge under his jacket. 'This is what they use to burn in their stoves!' he announced triumphantly showing us his find.

'Dung!' Cow dung. I'd seen them mixing it with straw in the summer but had thought they were making bricks for building with.

'Nope!' Marianek grinned, shivering and blue in the face, but pleased with himself. 'It's communist coal! '

We lit a fire with this 'cow coal' and put on a pot of whey water. There was enough to boil some water and make a thin flour and salt soup.

Once, Mama had made the long cold journey out to the little town to barter for food. She was wearing her winter coat. When she came back she took out from under her coat a chicken that had frozen in the snow. She had hidden it under her coat for fear someone would see it and take it from her. It must have wandered away from home as chickens do, and frozen to death.

Our mother was truly sorry that someone would be missing it, but whoever this chicken belonged to, she said, they probably had eggs through the summer, and chicken in the winter, while her children had nothing.

She made chicken soup, which we ate that night, sharing

it with Pani Szarejkowa and her children. It was a meal I would never forget. It was one of the two times we had meat in the Soviet Union.

Fall asleep and you die!

It was three days before Christmas Eve 1940, our first Christmas as exiles in the Soviet Union, and our second Christmas without our father.

I looked at Mama as she sat picking the lice out of my brother's hair, and my heart ached for her. I wondered again if Tata would recognise any of us now. Our dark-haired pretty mother, who had always taken such a pride in her appearance, and had always dressed attractively, her dresses always clean and ironed, her hair shining. She was now so thin, with her dress crumpled and stained, hanging limp and loose as an old rag. Her face and scalp were covered in bites and scabs, her hands were rough, scarred and grimy with ingrained dirt from the fields, which would not wash out without soap. There was no soap - this was another Capitalist luxury the communists didn't believe in.

In the winter there was no way we could wash and dry clothes - no one even attempted to. We all lived and slept in the same clothes day after day week after week. The stench from others I found unbearable at first, but when you start smelling the same yourself, you get used to it.

It wasn't just our mother who had changed. We all had.

'If we don't have some more food soon,' I began to voice my thoughts, then broke off, seeing the look of pain in my mother's face.

'We'll die won't we?' Marianek finished the sentence.

That's when our mother decided it was time to sell Tata's sheepskin police jacket. She would barter it for food to keep us alive through the rest of the winter. She would get a lot for it, she was sure. One of the other Polish deportees who worked alongside her in the fields had told her that the town in the opposite direction to Kidziali had a better baracholka (local market).

It was a lot further away though, too far to walk there and back in a day, but it was worth making the journey as you got better exchanges there. Mama went to see the commissar of our saffhoz and boldly asked for permission to borrow the farm cart and ox to go to that town before Christmas. She showed him our father's jacket and promised him, in return, a share of the food she planned to obtain for it. The farm ox and cart would get her there and back in a day.

Permission was granted, and Honoria, Pani Szarejkowa's daughter, who was the same age as our Marianek, offered to go with her, and barter some small items of clothing for their family too.

And so, two days before Christmas Eve, wrapped in coats and a blanket each, our mother and Honaria set off early in the morning while it was still dark, promising to be back that evening.

I stood by the door of the hut waving into the darkness until they were out of sight. It was snowing. When I next looked out, the tracks of the ox and cart were completely covered over.

All day Tad and Marianek and I waited eagerly for our mother to return with food. That night we would eat well! All day we talked about what she might bring. I kept going to the door to look out expectantly. The snow kept falling.

The short dark Siberian day soon turned into a long, cold Siberian night, and still they didn't come back. All night I sat by the window waiting for them. I could hear Pani Szarejkowa praying her Rosary quietly in the other half of the hut. All night long she prayed, and I prayed along with her in a whisper so as not to wake my brothers.

The following morning, when they still had not returned, Marianek went anxiously to ask the commissar if he had had any news of them. But there was nothing.

Pani Szarejkowa walked the five kilometres the deep snow to the little town of Kidziali, to ask at the NKVD office there. There was no news of them there either, but she did learn that a buran, a Siberian blizzard, had been raging over in that direction since the previous evening.

I stared at her. Buran. Out on the Steppes, even the very word brought a chill to the heart. In a buran, the snow fell like a swirling, raging fog, blinding you and making you lose all sense of direction; even horses and whole carts had been buried under the snow in minutes and never discovered until the thaws in the spring. We had been warned about these blizzards often enough by the locals. You would freeze to death very quickly, they said. You began to feel sleepy and warm. In blizzard conditions, it was vital to keep moving. If you gave in to the temptation to rest, you would freeze. 'Fall asleep and you die,' they repeated to us. 'Whatever you do keep moving and stay awake.'

The following day, Christmas Eve, my brother Marianek walked the long journey through the deep snow into Kidziali to ask again if there was any news of them, but again there was nothing.

As he returned to the hut, weak and weary, Pani Szarejkowa made the decision to go with her son Edek again to the NKVD office, to beg for a search party to be sent out. She knew they would not do it. No one would knowingly venture out in a buran, and to search for someone who had already been missing for three days and two nights would be considered madness. It had never been heard of that anyone had ever survived even a few hours in such conditions. But she said she had to at least try; she couldn't just sit in the hut waiting and feeling helpless.

They did not return that night.

Marianek went out again as darkness fell, and I sat alone by the window. He came back with dried dung, and for just long enough to boil up the frozen waste water, we had a smoky fire in the stove. I threw in the last of the flour into the pot, and some salt, and that was our Christmas Eve supper.

The only sound was the howling of wolves getting closer, the shrieking of the wind, and Tad's coughing. It was the most silent Christmas Eve ever. There were no church bells ringing, no tramping of boots and cheerful voices of people on their way to midnight Mass singing carols; there was no church. Tata was not with us to sing his beloved carols, nor Mama, not even the good-hearted Pani Szarejkowa.

With Tata's jacket gone, it was as if all hope of seeing him again had gone too. And with Mama gone now too, what would become of us? How would we survive?

To keep back the tears, I took deep breaths and tried to picture my father walking in the garden in Poland. I remembered how he would encourage us each evening to say our prayers before bed. 'When you pray you are like a little light shining in the darkness,' he used to say to us. So I continued the most miserable vigil of my life by the frozen window, whispering my desperate prayers into the darkness. If tears could save a person, then my mother would be saved. I understood it was impossible for anyone to survive in such conditions, but if by any chance Mama was still alive, she would be in terrible need of a little light shining in the darkness.

Amazing rescue

Four days after Christmas, when we had given up hope of ever seeing out mother again alive, the administrator came and told us that she and Honoria were in hospital. He didn't know how they were but at least, amazingly, it seemed, they were still alive!

There was no way we could visit, not even Pani Szarejewicz could venture out that far in those conditions, it was not possible (and the Saffhoz ox and cart had been lost). If it had been in Kidziali, we could have walked through the snow, but not to that distant town.

Our mother was released from hospital after the New Year and Honoria a few days after that.

Mama, was so thin, and so weak she was hardly able to walk, but she was overwhelmed with tears of gratitude at still being alive and back with us again. Bit by bit, she recounted to us what had happened.

They had made it safely to the town and bartered Tata's sheepskin jacket for lots of good things to eat - flour and butter and eggs and... – 'But it's no use even thinking of these things now,' she shook her head. 'They are not so important now.'

'You've come back! That's the important thing,' I said, and I meant it with all my heart. For the second time in my life I truly didn't care about food, even though my stomach was hurting with hunger, just so long as we had our mother back.

'Mama, don't ever go away again!' I said, 'I don't care

if we have no bread. I prefer to starve to death, but at least be together!'

'But Mama, tell us the rest of what happened!' Tad urged her.

'Oh, dear child,' Mama hugged him and held him close, 'We were on our way home and we were so happy, talking about what we would cook for our Wigilia, and hurrying the ox on as the sky was getting dark, but before we know it, the wind starts picking up and the snow is falling and swirling like a thick fog, and we're caught in the middle of a full-blown raging buran.

We couldn't see a thing, and you just lose all sense of direction, and before long everything around us is buried in snow. The ox, bless him, went plodding on through it, with his head down low, until he must have gone off the track into a ditch because he was suddenly in such deep snow that he couldn't move. We tried to pull him out, but soon he was covered in snow and it was getting dark.

We're just standing there and I knew we were beginning to freeze. So I said to Honoria, 'Listen to me, Honoria, we have to keep moving, we have to start walking!'

She was afraid of leaving the cart. 'In what direction?' she said. 'We can't see anything! There's no way we can walk in this!' And she was right - everywhere we looked all we could see was endless snow, no sign of a track, nothing in the distance, no landmarks. But I was feeling sleepy and I knew I had to move, so in the end, I said, 'All right, Honoria, I'll go and try and find help. You stay here then, with our things, but you must keep moving or you'll freeze to death.'

"But where would I be able to find help out in such a blizzard? How was I even going to walk in that terrible wind and snow? I could hear wolves baying, but I set off - had no choice - saying to myself, 'God is with me.'"

'And I was praying for you that whole night!'

Mama nodded, her eyes filling with tears, then continued, 'So I started walking, though at every step my feet were sinking so deep into the snow, it was hard to take the next step. Very soon I was just surrounded by pitch black darkness with the wind hurling snow at me with such a force, that I could hardly breathe. When wolves started to howl from closer, I was so scared I wet myself. And it froze to my legs, so I had ice stuck to the length of my legs, and that made it even harder to walk. I kept stumbling and falling into deep drifts. It was such hard work crawling out of them, each time I fell, I didn't want to get up again. The temptation was so strong to just lie there and go to sleep! It is not a bad way to die, you know. But I kept thinking of you all left here alone, and I kept praying for strength. I kept forcing myself to get up. There was nothing else to do.

'As for Honoria, she told me later in the hospital, that she stayed near the cart, getting more and more scared as it got darker, and the wolves were getting closer and closer. She tried to keep moving so she wouldn't freeze, but she too began to feel sleepy and she knew she was dying. Then when she saw that the ox was already dead, and the howling of the wolves was getting even closer, no doubt at the smell of a dead animal. She knew she wouldn't stand a chance against a pack of hungry wolves, she knew she had to walk away.

Terrified, she climbed out of the cart while she still had the strength and began to walk too, into the darkness; she had no idea in what direction she was going.

'Children you just can't begin to imagine what it's like to be out in the middle of a blizzard like that!' Mama's voice was shaky, 'The darkness is so thick, you just can't see a thing, your lungs hurt, you can't breathe. You feel so totally disorientated, and suffocated by snow.' She paused, looking down at her now crippled fingers.

'Honoria was picked up first. Amazingly, in those conditions, when no one would ever venture out, exactly at that moment, a man came riding by on horseback and found her in the snow. He picked her up and took her to the hospital in the big town.'

I was giving up all hope and was falling asleep even as I walked, I stumbled and fell for the last time, no longer having the strength to get up again. I was too sleepy even to pray anymore or even think of you all. Sleep was overwhelming me and I knew I was dying.' Mama paused, taking a deep breath to try and stop her tears.

'After that I don't remember anything until I was being shaken and by a man who lifted me onto his horse. I will never forget his strength and the kindness in his eyes.' She was crying now, and couldn't stop. We sat close to her in silence, holding her tight, until she was able to continue.

'I just cannot understand how we were both rescued

291

out in that blizzard.' She shook her head incredulously. 'Why those lone travellers were out in such conditions. I've never heard of anyone being rescued in such a way, ever, because no one would ever knowingly venture out in such a blizzard. And that both of us were rescued,' she shook her head in awe.

'But Pani Szarejkowa and I were praying for you all the time!'

Mama nodded, crying again, 'Someone in heaven was definitely looking after us.'

'Maybe it was angels who helped you?'

She nodded, 'I surely have never seen such kindness in anyone's eyes before.'

The hospital they'd both been taken to was in Pietrepavlosk, a long way away from where they had been found.

'With Honoria they had to cut off two fingers as they were totally dead and useless from frostbite. They wanted to do the same with mine, but I wouldn't let them.' Mama put her hand out to show us. On one hand three of her fingers were bent and damaged (and they stayed like that for the rest of her life, but at least they were still on her hand; though after that they were always white.)

Even to this day I wonder at the courage of those two women, and at their amazing rescue.

Somewhere out there, under the snow, was the dead ox and the cart and our food that Mama and Honoria had exchanged at such great cost.

Spring 1941
'Don't eat anymore soup!'

We longed for spring to come, remembering the end of
winters in Poland. At home, buds would be bursting into
new leaf in every imaginable shade of green, birds would
be nesting, and storks flying back from hot countries to
their old nests. There would be twittering and cheeping
and squawking from the trees and sky.

Here, though, spring came not with bird song but floods.

As the deep snows thawed, they turned into oceans
of icy water, flooding everything and everywhere. As the
dug-out mud huts were lower than ground level, the earth
floor of our hut was soon as sodden, muddy and slippery
inside as it was outside. The straw roof leaked, wetting
the wooden bunks and our blankets. All our clothes were
constantly wet, and there was so little to burn on the stove
that it was impossible to dry out. There was never enough
daylight to dry anything outside, since the nights still
lasted for most of the day. Lice multiplied in those slightly
warmer wet conditions, as did the bedbugs. We would sit
miserably scratching our bleeding sores, huddled under a
wet, flea-infested blanket.

It was actually a relief to go to school each day. When
I came back to the hut, I busied myself getting everything
ready for when Mama and Marianek would come home
soaking wet and worn out. Even in those days, I liked
everything tidy and everything on time, just as I do now.
I always tried to have some hot whey-water and flour soup

ready for Mama when she came back. That, together with the small daily ration of bread was what we lived on.

One evening, I poured some of the sour whey water into the pot as usual and put it on the stove to boil. Marianek had been out the night before gleaning cow coal from the communal barn and milking shed, so there was a fire in the stove. I mixed some flour with water to make a flour and water crumble; there was never any oil or butter or any fat, just flour and water. When the water in the pot boiled, I threw in the flour crumble and some salt. I tried not to look at the ugly grey centipedes that crawled around over my head on the straw roof, especially over the place near the stove where it was warmest. They were always there; like the bedbugs and fleas, you had no choice but to share the hut with them all. These centipedes had the most disgusting soft, grey bodies that really sickened me.

When Mama and Marianek got home, I stirred the soup and served it. I always served Mama and Marianek first, and they had the biggest portions because they had to work so hard outside all day, then Tad, and myself last. Marianek was so ravenous that he was wolfing it down even before grace was said.

'Mmm,' he said in surprise, 'It's seems nice and thick today!'

This puzzled me, as I had added nothing different to it than I had the day before.

As Mama was saying grace, I peered into my bowl in the darkness of the hut and realised what had happened. Those disgusting fat grey centipedes had fallen from the ceiling as the pot had boiled, perhaps from the heat of the stove, and landed into the pot. I watched my brother eating it and had a moment of meanness. Memories of the dog murder came to mind and the way he and Edek had teased Honoria, and I was tempted to let him eat it all and then explain why the soup was so thick! But in the end, seeing his thin caved-in cheeks, I didn't have the heart to do it.

'Don't eat anymore! I cried, 'I think I know why it is thicker today!' and pointed to the centipedes on the roof. A few were still falling off into the space where the pot had been. Marianek pulled a disgusted face, then shrugged looking uncertain. Mama looked at her bowl and then said firmly, 'Well we can't waste it!' One by one she picked the centipedes out with her spoon, and threw them into the fire, then continued to eat her soup. Tad and I did the same. While we were doing this, I kept glancing at Marianek with interest, wondering whether he would finish the soup as it was, keeping it 'nice and thick! But even the dog murderer picked out the remainder of the bugs and threw them on the fire before finishing the rest of his soup.

We all licked out the bowls as we always did, not to waste the smallest drop.

Gypsy girl

As spring thaws turned into summer, once again the work in the wheat and sunflower fields increased and everyone had to work from dawn till dark sowing and planting and weeding the vast expanses of open fields. Even children had to work in the summer for their ration of bread, in the fields or in the dairy.

I did extra work for a while cleaning the milking sheds; sweeping up the cow dung, and washing the dirty buckets. There was thick, dried-up filth everywhere, and such work would have been physically demanding for a well fed adult, but for a starving child it was very hard. Also, it was such a long walk in the heat from our hut to get to the milking sheds, that by the time I arrived there in the morning I was already feeling faint and wobbly on my feet. Sometimes I would sit down feeling I just couldn't carry on. So when the opportunity came up for a job looking after a baby for a Russian woman, I took it gratefully, thinking that at least it would be easier than cleaning up after cows.

However, the baby was a very young one and even though I was twelve now, and no longer felt like a child myself, this miserable infant cried and cried and cried and wouldn't stop no matter what I did for him, until I felt like shaking him just to make him stop. I knew I had to find other work.

It was Pani Szarejkowa's idea. She could see that I was in a state of nervous exhaustion at the end of each day, and she pitied me. She had also realised that the local people were extremely superstitious. The Communists actively encouraged superstition and occult practices of all kinds, the idea being that if people believed in superstition, they would stop believing in God.

'Those who don't believe in God,' my father used to say, end up believing, not in nothing but in anything and everything.'

So good Pani Szarejkowa said to me in her compassion, 'You're such a little gipsy, Alinka, with your olive skin and long wavy dark hair. You know, perhaps you could earn a bit from it.'

Now, children out there in the Steppes had nothing to do after work. The days were so short and dreary. Darkness fell in the middle of the afternoon. There was no radio or television, no comics or books to read and even if there had been, no light to read by. No trees to climb or games to play, no animals to play with, no toys. There was nothing much to do apart from watching everyone's comings and goings. The most interesting things around were other people. So we knew everything that went on in the saffhoz; all the local gossip.

I knew that real fortune telling was bad, our father had taught us the dangers of such things, but when you are forced to live on sour water and flour soup, you'd do almost anything to obtain a little food, and I was desperate. So, in spite of misgivings, I determined to give it a try. I put on my spotted red cotton headscarf, tying it gypsy style behind and under my hair at the back, and set off, not without some trepidation.

There was a local woman there whose husband had left her and gone off with another woman. All of us children knew of it, and this particular lady wanted her fortune told. She wasn't very old, but old enough to have known better! By now, having attended school daily, I spoke Russian well. With a pounding heart I walked to her hut and knocked on her door, and to my surprise and relief she welcomed me in.

I spent some time seriously examining the palm of her hand which was not quite as grubby with ingrained dirt as Mama's hands were, then I told her very accurately, how her husband had gone off with another and that if she went to such and such a place she would see him again. We kids knew all his comings and goings and had worked it all out. All that I told her I knew to be fact, and when it all 'turned out to be true', she was so impressed she recommended me to others and I was suddenly in business! In return for my 'palm readings,' I was always given something small, not roubles but a bit of something to eat.

I was so proud to be taken for a real gyspy and to be bringing home something to add to our family's nourishment.

Look what came in the post!

Whenever the post lorry came, I ran over eagerly, hoping for a letter or even better - a parcel - from Poland. We had received a parcel twice during our first winter, once with a bit of salt pork fat in, which had been a godsend, but after that nothing more. The people in Poland were hungry themselves no doubt, if they were still alive. (We heard later that in our little town of Ros, there had been a German soldier killed, and in retaliation, the Nazis had lined up all the men of the village, on the hill where we used to go sledging, and shot them all.)

This time though, although there was no letter or parcel, something even more unexpected arrived!

As I hurried towards the lorry, I could see a man climbing stiffly out from the passenger seat. He was skeletally thin, like all of us, and stooped, and filthy as a tramp, but he looked familiar. I stopped in surprise, my heart missing a beat. It couldn't be, surely? Tata?

But as I ran nearer, with my heart pounding, cheeks flushed with excitement, I saw to my disappointment that it was not my father, but Uncle Kazik, his brother. As I approached, he recognised me and smiled in delight and put his arms out to give me a big hug. I thought he would swing me round as he used to do in Poland (I was taller now but certainly no heavier!) but he put me down, coughing and bending over in pain. He was so very thin and weak, and I could see lice crawling all over him.

'What happened to Tata?' was all I could say to him,

299

so sharp was the disappointment and so deep the ache in my heart that it wasn't my father.

The way he looked at me made me take a deep breath, wanting to cover my ears. I didn't want to hear what he was going to say.

'I can't say,' he replied. 'We got separated. He was a police officer and had to go with the police officers. I was with the soldiers.'

When Mama and Marianek came back from the fields there were cries of astonishment, but I could see the same disappointment in their eyes that I had felt.

'He came with the post!" I told them with a grin.

Uncle explained that he had managed to escape and made his way here, but he didn't give details. When Mama asked about Tata, he told her what he had told me. When she asked how they'd been treated at the prisoner of war camp, he looked at her, then shook his head. 'It's time to look forward now,' he said quietly.

'But if you got here, perhaps Tata will find his way to us too!' said Tad hopefully, and I wanted to ask more about this too, but Uncle nodded briefly and changed the subject. He told us the news that Hitler had broken his alliance with the Soviets and was now invading Russia. Since Stalin was now in desperate need of more soldiers to fight against his powerful former ally, he had agreed to an amnesty for all Polish deportees.

'It means all Polish prisoners from all over the Soviet Union are free to leave and travel south.'

We stared at him incredulously.

'But how can they think our men will ever agree to fight for them?' Mama asked in amazement.

'After all they've taken from us! How could we ever be on their side?' I added heatedly.

'Just thank God it is so for now, Alinka,' Uncle said. 'Because all Polish deportees are included in this amnesty, not just men.'

'You mean *we* are free?' Mama looked stunned.

Uncle nodded.

'Since when? What does this mean? But why has no one told us this?'

'Can we go back home to Poland then, to Ros?' Tad asked excited.

'To Poland, no,' he shook his head, 'Not at present. We might be free, in theory, but Poland isn't. But there is a Polish army being formed in Tashkent and Guzar in the South of Russia. That's where Polish deportees will be safest.'

'Can we go back with you then?'

Uncle shook his head. 'It's not so easy getting tickets for the train. You need travel papers too, and permits and health-check papers. The authorities aren't making things easy for us. The Russians here don't want to lose their labour force. But I'll arrange it all through the Polish army when I go back, and I'll send for you.'

'If all prisoners are being freed, then Tata will be free too!' Tad was saying excitedly.

With rest and many hours spent delousing him, Uncle Kazik was soon strong enough to work. Each morning he went off, and he was crafty enough to come home each day not just with a bit of grain, but whole sacks full that he distributed among all the Polish deportees, and sacks of potatoes. 'May God repay you!' everyone wept on receiving this food. It was the first act of generosity they had received since leaving Poland.

We never found out where or how he had managed to obtain them. It made us anxious though, because it couldn't have been legal. If he had been caught he would have been shot. He saved the lives of some of the deportees and strengthened us all while he was there.

Eventually, when he was leaving to go south to Tashkent, to join the newly forming Polish army under General Anders, every one of the Polish deportees came to say goodbye to him.

Marianek was very quiet and withdrawn much of the time that Uncle Kazik was with us. I had never seen him so solitary and lost in thought. When Uncle Kazik was due to leave, my brother announced that he had made up his mind to go with him to the army base. He wanted to join the navy and fight for Poland from the sea. Uncle had agreed, and Mama had no choice but to let him go.

Our family was getting smaller and smaller.

Slippers in the mud

Mama, Tad and I were out in the fields in the rain, gleaning sunflower stalks to dry for kindling, when one of the boys from the saffhoz came running across the mud towards us.

'Pani Pietrazak! Alinka! Come! Come quick! Someone from the army has come to your hut!'

We looked up in surprise not knowing what to think.

'To us?' Mama said. 'Are you sure?'

Why was she suddenly looking so anxious? Were we in trouble? What if it were news of Tata? Now my heart was anxious too.

Picking up our precious bundles of damp stalks, we hurried to the hut where a young soldier was sitting waiting. At least it wasn't a Russian uniform. He was very young and blond and looked Polish.

He stood up respectfully and smiled and held out his hand to Mama. He introduced himself politely and explained that our Uncle had sent him to fetch us, and gave us a note from him. He had obtained all the necessary travel papers and train tickets. The journey was all arranged.

'We're *leaving*?' Mama asked as if she couldn't believe it.

He smiled. 'Everything is arranged, but we must hurry. The train will be leaving soon.'

None of the other deportees had been able to leave yet. We were the first family on our settlement. Tad started leaping around the hut for joy and in his excitement kicked the stove which broke. Mama didn't even shush him. We wouldn't be needing that smoky old tin can stove anymore!

The young soldiers asked us to pack our things quickly, while he went to ask the administrator to borrow the new saffhoz pony and cart to take us to the station. It had started to rain again.

Mama took one look at my muddy bare feet (my outgrown shoes had fallen apart some time before) and began to cut up one of our blankets and with her poor rough hands, to quickly sew me a pair of slippers.

'We won't be needing this blanket where we are going,' she said, 'It will be warm there.' Uncle had explained this to us in his note. 'And you can't set off for the train with no shoes, dear child.'

There was very little to pack. Every last bit of furniture had been burnt on the stove for warmth. Every last bit of spare clothing bartered for food. I was searching for my precious little autograph album. I was puzzled. It wasn't where I had always kept it - under the wooden slats where I slept. I knew I hadn't moved it, not for a long time, and Mama and Tad didn't know where it was. There weren't many places for a little book to be lost in the hut since it was so small and unfurnished, but it had to be here somewhere! Mama had finished making my slippers and I was still searching for it anxiously.

'Come on, Alinka! He's here with the cart!'

'But I can't leave without it!'

'Come on! We'll miss the train! It's just a book!' Tad shouted from the cart.

'It's not just a book!'

'Alinka! If you don't come now, we'll have to go without you!'

I quickly searched again behind the stove and once again under the bunks. It couldn't have just disappeared. Had someone stolen it? Or exchanged it for food? The local Kazak people didn't have books and were willing to give butter or even a chicken for something really pretty. My heart sank as the thought grew into a certainty. Had it been Marianek? Or Uncle Kazik when he had been here?

It was supposed to be a happy day, leaving that miserable dark place. I was glad we were going, but the little friendship album was all I'd had left of our life in Poland. My one small reminder of my father and friends. And now even that had been taken from me.

It was still raining as we left. Mud everywhere. As I ran to the cart that was already moving off, my brand new slippers stuck in the mud and there was no time to stop and dig them out. It was just the last straw! This horrible land had taken everything from us: Tata's warm sheepskin jacket, every single pretty thing we'd had to wear, and even now at the very last minute it had taken my precious little friendship book and the new slippers that my mother had sewn for me. Hot tears spilled down my face. It was as if all the suffering, stress and sadness of the past two years was coming to the surface now that we were leaving. I wept not just for myself, but for my mother, who had made those slippers for me, who had struggled so long and hard and alone to keep us alive.

'Alinka!' Tad looked at me puzzled and impatient, 'We're going away to freedom, why are you crying?'

I had never imagined that freedom could be so sad.

Come with me!

Tad was so different now from the little boy he'd been when we'd set out from Poland. Not once this time did he mention the train journey. I didn't want to think about it either. Would we be in another dark, flea-infested wagon again for weeks without food, water or sanitation of any kind?

Our young Polish soldier had been right; the train was already waiting at the station. The platform was noisy and crowded. People were desperately trying to climb aboard, although it already looked full to bursting. The carriages, which to my huge relief, were passenger ones and had windows, were overflowing; even the doorways were jam-packed with people. How on earth could we ever squeeze on, never mind find a place to sit?

Our young Polish soldier was looking as flushed and anxious as we were. As we stood uncertainly, with people pushing and shouting all around us, I looked down at my muddy bare feet, and was suddenly aware how short my dress was, though looser than it had been two years before, how dirty and smelly and wet it was, and crumpled. It was the same one I had been wearing when we had arrived there two years before. I glanced at my mother clutching her small grubby bundle wrapped in the cut-up blanket, which was all we now possessed in the whole world, her face so worried, her cheeks grey and scabby and scarred, she who had been so beautiful in Poland. On top of it all, it looked like we'd never be able to get on the train. Once again the tears flowed. And I stood there thinking, how can I still cry? How could there be any tears left inside me, I had cried so much already -even a deep well has to run dry eventually doesn't it? I felt so weary and sad I just wanted to curl up in a ball away from the pushing crowds, where no one could see me and go to sleep.

Our young soldier hurried off to make enquiries about our seats at the office, but we could see there were long queues waiting outside the office, and Mama kept looking round so very anxiously for him. Our dear mother, who had once been so confident and cheerful, so sure of herself and everything.

'Smile, Alinka!' she leaned over and whispered to me nervously, 'Stop that crying! People are looking at us. Don't let anyone notice you, or they might arrest us again and make us stay.'

I gulped down my tears and was wiping my eyes with the back of my hand when to my absolute horror, I saw two Russian officers in uniform with guns in their belts, approaching us.

'Oh God help us!' I prayed silently. 'Don't let them send

us back. Blessed Mother of God pray for us!'

Mama was frantically searching the crowds for our Polish soldier. The officers stopped in front of us. I was trembling. I knew it was all my fault, yet far from stopping me crying, more tears came spilling out. I stood with my head bowed, ashamed of my tears and dirtiness and abject poverty, and waited in terror for us to be sent back to the settlement.

One of the Russian officers was peering at me and said to Mama gently, 'So, where are you going?'

'We're supposed to be going to Guzar,' our Polish soldier who had just returned to us breathlessly replied for us, shrugging and looking very flushed.

The officer looked at my mother's anxious face, and my terrified tearful one, and said kindly, 'We have room in our carriage. Come with me!'

Astonished, Mama followed him, holding Tad tightly by the hand. The officer carried our precious little bundle wrapped in a blanket, and I followed with our young Polish soldier.

They were all Russian officers, in a carriage all to themselves. The one who had invited us to join them explained that this carriage would be hooked on to a different locomotive when they had to change trains, 'So you will not have to get out to change wagons right until we get to Tashkent, which is quite far south. After that you will not be far from your destination.'

Two officers who had been sitting by the window moved over to make room for Tad and me by the window. Tad was beginning to look excited as he looked out with wonder as the smoke and steam puffed out and the whistle blew and the train creaked and chugged away from the station.

I could feel the kind officer looking at my bare muddy feet with pity, and felt my face grow hot with embarrassment They all had shiny boots and clean, ironed uniforms. He's so smart and he's thinking how filthy I am, I sat there thinking. We must smell so bad to them! We must smell as sour and disgusting as the locals did when we first arrived here and what if they notice the lice? Perhaps he'll be sorry he brought us into his carriage. Perhaps they'll throw us out in disgust. I didn't dare move.

There was a table in the middle of the carriage, and the Russian officer pulled out a game to play, and when he spoke to me it was with gentleness, not disgust as I'd been expecting.

'You are hungry?' he said.

I replied with a nod. Yes I was hungry. So was Mama, so was Tad. We had been hungry for over two years.

They shared their food generously with us, which we just sat and stared at, at first, overwhelmed at the sight of it, before eating it very quickly. They even gave us sweets.

I felt they'd been sent by God. I was overwhelmed with gratitude, thinking that someone, somewhere must have been praying for us.

'What's the matter?'

In Tashkent it was the end of the journey for the officers. They explained that we would have to make the rest of the journey without them since we were going on to Guzar.

But instead of being happy that we were nearing the end of the journey, I was once again in tears, holding the side of my cheek with the palm of my hand. A tooth that had occasionally given me some pain and a few sleepless nights in the hut, was now aching and throbbing and making my whole head hurt.

The kind Russian officer said to me, 'What's the matter, little girl? Why are you crying?'

I hesitated. I knew only too well what happened to people who had toothache. There was only one remedy for deportees; the tooth had to be pulled out. I had seen it happen to Pani Szarejkowa when we had first moved into the hut. It had to be tied with strong thread, the thread tied to a door, then the door slammed shut. Blood everywhere and moans of pain. I felt faint and sick just thinking about it. Was there never going to be an end to the constant suffering?

Mama explained to him about my troublesome tooth.

'Come with me, dzieweczka (little girl).'

I looked at him fearfully.

'To a dentist,' he explained kindly, glancing at his watch. 'You know, we just have time to go into the town and have it made better. Your Mama and brother can come with us. It won't hurt.'

It was a proper dentist with a dentist's chair and my tooth wasn't even pulled out, but a little filling put in. No blood, no doors slamming and the pain had gone and we even arrived back at the station in time to catch our train to Guzar.

Without them we would never have managed to board the crowded train, but with their authority, they made sure we were settled in seats, before bidding us goodbye and a good journey.

'May God repay you!' Mama said to them, so overwhelmed by their kindness, that she forgot about the communist taboo of mentioning God. I looked at them expecting frowns and condemnation, but this kind-hearted Russian officer only smiled. I couldn't speak as I was crying again. There are no words to express the gratitude I felt towards these good Russian officers.

We were now on our way alone for the last part of the journey.

At a station stop some time later, our young Polish soldier jumped out, as many did at the stops, to relieve himself and get us some kipiatok. However, the train, suddenly moved off again almost immediately, without giving any warning, not even a whistle blow, leaving him and many others stranded. It was in this way, we later learned, that many Polish children had lost their only parent and landed up in Soviet orphanages.

But at the time it was our own fate that worried us. We were suddenly on our own on the train. There were no kind Russian officers looking after us now. The stranded young Polish soldier had our tickets, our travel permits, our freedom papers.

Night was falling, and we were alone, travelling illegally and unprotected.

'What will happen to us?'

'Mama! What will happen to us?' I whispered anxiously. 'What if the ticket collector comes and throws us off the train? What if they arrest us because they think we've run away, and they don't believe that it was Uncle Kazik who sent for us?'

We sat tense and flushed, but the train was so crowded it would have been almost impossible for a guard to pass through. Eventually, with the rhythmic rolling of the train, I closed my eyes, and knew nothing more until it was dawn. As the sun was rising, the train was pulling into Guzar station, and there was Uncle Kazik waiting to meet us. Later our stranded young Polish soldier arrived back safely too.

The heat hit us as we climbed down from the train. It had been chilly and wet when we had left the Siberian Steppes; now it was, even at that early hour, sweltering hot and humid.

Uncle Kazik took us to the army camp, which was such an amazing joy to see. There were so many rows of dazzling white cotton army tents, and Polish soldiers in uniform, and then also so many poor living skeletons streaming in looking and smelling like tramps, most of them half dead, so ill and weak they could barely walk. I wept with relief. I just couldn't believe we were here. It was so warm, and there was food to eat. The soldiers gave us a little piece of chocolate and a tin of corned beef. Their own rations were inadequate, yet they shared them with us and with all the women and children who kept arriving, sick and hungry.

Tad was asking excitedly if we could start looking for Tata straight away. Since it was a newly forming army made up of prisoners of war and deportees, surely our father would be among them? But Uncle told us we couldn't stay in the camp because it was just for the soldiers. He had found Mama a tiny room in a hut owned by a rather unpleasant Russian woman on a collective farm nearby. It wouldn't be for long, he explained apologetically. It was just for a little while, and Tad and I would be able to stay at the children's camp.

General Anders had good reason to mistrust Stalin's agreement on the amnesty; he had already broken the agreement to supply the Polish soldiers with food. He was therefore desperate to get as many of us as possible, as quickly as possible, away from the Soviet Union into Persia. He especially wanted to make sure every Polish child was taken to freedom, to be given a chance at life. He even sent soldiers out to orphanages all over the Soviet Union looking for orphaned Polish children. Many of the littlest ones had forgotten how to speak Polish, but if they could make the Sign of the Cross or could say some of the Our Father, they were brought to the Polish army base.

As soon as it was possible, we were told, we too would cross the Caspian sea with the Polish soldiers into Persia. But for the time being, our poor mother was in a hut with a resentful woman, who was not at all happy about having to share with a foreigner. Mama found out later to her horror, that a small black poisonous snake had been living under her bed, and a whole family of scorpions breeding under the torn half blanket she used for a pillow.

Tad and I were taken to stay in the children's camp, which was also a temporary orphanage as so many children had lost their parents. This camp was in a hot, humid, waterless valley called Kharkim Batash, which we soon found out means 'Valley of Death'.

Valley of death

It was so hot in children's camp, you felt you couldn't breathe. Sweat poured off us all the time. Water was scarce. There was just one very shallow, muddy stream a long walk away, which was murky and contaminated. Every drop of water from it had to be boiled, and even then, considering all the corpses and excrement and filth that went into that shallow steam, it was hardly drinkable.

There was a terrible smell everywhere from unwashed, soiled children suffering from dysentery. As everywhere in the Soviet Union, there were no toilets. Many of the children were too weak to get up off the floor to relieve themselves, so they lay in their own excrement, in the overwhelming stench, with flies swarming all over them.

Tad was given a blanket on the floor in the boys' outdoor dormitory and I was put with the girls. We had to sleep on the ground as there were no beds. At least this meant there were no bedbugs. We had unwelcome intruders each night nonetheless: spiders that bit viciously, and scorpions. Some children, in their weakened states, did not survive these nasty bites.

In the humid heat and dirty conditions, disease spread quickly. As we were arriving, there were corpses of emaciated children being taken away in a cart. We soon realised that the cart came every day, sometimes more than once. You went to sleep at night with your friend lying next to you, and in the morning she was no longer alive; you were lying next to a corpse. This, then, was our freedom.

We were free to come and go, and were told we could go and visit our mother in her tiny dark corner of the hut just outside the camp. But the first time we went to see her, we found her sitting on her torn blanket, her thin face swollen with crying.

'Mama! What's the matter?'

'What's happened?'

She explained to us that she had wanted to go to the army information office to make enquiries about where our father was. 'They would surely know by now, as all the prisoners of war have been released. Everyone receiving letters, but there was nothing from your Tata. I wanted to ask in the army office for news of him, so I asked Uncle Kazik to come with me.' She was unable to carry on speaking for a moment, then she continued quietly, 'He didn't want to come with me to enquire, because he already knew. He had known when he came to visit us in Siberia, but he hadn't wanted to tell us then as he'd thought it might have been too much to bear.'

Suddenly I remembered the dream I'd had on Easter Sunday.

'Tata's no longer on this earth is he?'

Mama looked at me, and nodded wearily.

'They shot all the police and army officers'.*

She looked so defeated.

'But not Uncle Kazik?'

She shook her head and shrugged. 'They lied to them as they were taking them away to the woods to be shot, telling them they were going to be released and sent back home. Uncle Kazik had heard something that made him suspicious.'

'Does Marianek know?'

Mama nodded. 'He knows. Uncle Kazik told him the truth when he came to us in Siberia.'

Our father would never again be with us. Nothing would ever be the same. Deep down, I had already known it, ever since the dream that had made me cry.

'At least he is truly free now,' Mama comforted us.

'But he came back so we'd be together, and after all that, in the end, he died alone.'

Mama hugged me close. 'Don't think that even for a moment, of course he didn't die alone. He had the whole company of heaven around him, his guardian angel and all the angels and saints! You can be sure Our Blessed Lady herself would have been there with him.'

'After all the Rosaries he prayed!' I nodded, smiling though my tears.

'We will all be together with him again one day, dear child, none of us are going to stay here in this valley of tears forever. We're all just passing through. It's life that is waiting for us beyond this world, child. Life – not death.' She was silent for a long moment, then continued, 'You know, I once heard a priest say that death is like a candle being snuffed out because a dark night has ended and bright new morning has come.'

The three of us sat close together on that small wooden bed, and prayed together for our poor Tata with all our hearts. '*Holy Mary, Mother of God, pray for us sinners now and at the hour of our death Amen.'* As I prayed the old familiar words, I felt suddenly surrounded by a great peace and such a presence of love, and I knew that it was true, what Tata used to tell us, that our prayers join our hearts to eternity, and bring us close to those we pray for.

We later learnt that when General Anders was forming the Polish army, and deportees and prisoners were streaming in, he noticed the absence of thousands of Polish army officers and began to make enquiries. It was later discovered that they had been shot by the Soviets. Made to kneel with their hands tied behind their backs they had been executed without trial, and buried in mass graves in the Katyn forest area. Saplings had been planted on top of the graves to hide the atrocities.

Burnt black toast

Tad came to me a few mornings later, his eyes red with crying, his face pale.

'If I die, at least I'll be with Tata, won't I?'

'Tad, are you sick?' I looked at him in dismay. My heart pounded in fear as he nodded and told me that there was blood pouring out when he needed the toilet, and he needed to go all the time. We both knew what that meant. Everyone knew. The corpses of children were taken away by the cartload each day.

I left him lying on the floor on my blanket and hurried to the big outdoor kitchen to ask for some boiled water for him to drink. All other water was contaminated and the main cause of the dysentery epidemic. The cook in charge that day saw me and said in concern, 'Why are you crying, child?'

'My brother's going to die. He has blood pouring out of him.'

'Ah! All right!' This kind woman nodded and told me to wait. She left her cooking and took some bread and put it over the open flames of the stove fire. She held it there, toasting it and toasting it till there was smoke coming from it and it was burnt, and still she continued to toast it. She didn't stop until all there was left of it was what looked like a piece of black coal. She handed this to me with a cup of boiled water. Give him this water. It's been boiled a long time. Give him this burnt bread to eat. If he drinks the water with it, he'll get it down, but he must eat it all! You'll see, it will stop it.'

Tad, already feeling literally sick to death, didn't want to eat it. He took a sip of water, but couldn't eat the coal-black bread. It made him retch. It was truly like eating coal. He was crying and choking over it, and shaking his head.

But there was no way I was going to let him leave it. I wasn't going to let my brother die. He was going to get it down even if it killed him! 'You have to eat it Tad. You can't just give up and die! Think what it would do to Mama!'

It was the only medicine we had; his only chance.

Bit by bit, slowly, with sips of water, he forced it all in, weeping and choking, every last coal-black crumb. May God reward that woman, though she will no doubt be in eternity now, and give all her descendants health, because she saved my brother's life. While hundreds of children in Kharkim Batash died from dysentery, my little brother recovered, thanks to the folk medicine of one kind and compassionate cook. I had the feeling we were being protected and cared for in some mysterious way, and was comforted to think it might be our dear father praying for us from heaven.

That evening one of the older girls who helped look after the younger ones, sang to us as we were going off to sleep. She sang beautiful Polish folk songs, including, 'Goralu' ('Man of the mountains')*:

'Man of the mountains you're leaving, the land that you've always known.

How your heart must be grieving, for the land that once was your home

The forests, flowers and streams, the mountains are now in your dreams

The land that you've loved and known, the mountains are calling you home.'

This was later to become the favourite Polish folk song of the Blessed Pope John Paul II. But at the time, although its beautiful haunting melody soothed us, it left me wondering if we would ever go back to Poland now. Would we ever see our forests and fishing lakes and streams again? Even if we were ever able to return, we would now never be able to go back to our little police house in Ros.

* *translated from the Polish by the author*

Terrible journey to freedom

Eventually, all the children were taken away from Karkim Batash, and after much more travelling and ~~several long nights~~ we were finally transported to the port of Krasnovodsk.

General Anders' urgent orders were for all children to be put on the transport ships as quickly as possible. He was determined to help as many Polish soldiers and civilians to escape as possible, but priority was given to the children.

We were taken to our ship by a smaller tender boat, and it was a shock to find nothing on the ship except floors thick with oily filth and tar, the spilt remains of the ship's normal cargo. This was soon added to by children sick with dysentery soiling themselves. Too weak to make it to the toilets, they had no choice but to relieve themselves where they lay, they cried from the shame and smell and degradation. Conditions were indescribably foul. The heat, humidity and stench were unbearable. Flies buzzed everywhere, getting in our eyes and mouths. There was nothing to hold on to for steadying yourself.

We were packed in as tight as herrings for the whole journey, sitting on towels we were given by way of a blanket. Many fainted even before we set sail. It was so crowded that many couldn't sit but had to stand. It was impossible to move.

The ship was dangerously low in the water. Those ancient rusty tubs were overloaded in a desperate attempt to help as many to freedom as possible. General Anders had to order everyone to throw all belongings overboard, no matter how precious. People, he explained, were more precious than any possessions.

We weren't allowed to keep anything. That was when I stopped feeling regret for my precious friendship album. Even if I had managed to bring it with me this far, I would now have had to have thrown it overboard. Much better that it had brought us some food when we had most needed it. Moments of peace come to us so unexpectedly at times.

Since the war was going on all round us, there was danger of the ships being bombed; out at sea we would be a vulnerable target. Tad and I sat squeezed together. We understood the ship might not make it and we were scared. We had been separated from our mother, as most of the children were, since children had priority boarding. Sadly, some of the children on these ships never saw their mothers again.

We had thrown everything overboard. Our threadbare clothes were all we possessed in the world.

We were not bombed, but even so, many children on that journey lost their lives. They were emaciated, sick and weak; they died from disease and dehydration. The journey took two days. After the first night, the towels we'd been given to sit on were so soaked in tar and vomit and other bodily waste, we threw them overboard. Those who had died lay side by side with those still alive. All of us had lips that were badly cracked and parched with thirst. Most of us were terribly sea-sick.

We were on our way to freedom, yet my heart ached. We were leaving my father behind in an unmarked mass grave.

But I think he must have been looking out for us from heaven, because just before we reached the Persian port of Pahlevi, on that terribly crowded ship, we were reunited with our mother. Somehow, against all odds, she had managed to board that same ship and had found us. She told us she'd had to put up a real fight to get on board, and she had managed to somehow make her way through the crowd to us. She had even managed to beg a little cup of water from the sailors for us, though we each had just a sip, as the children around us were also overheated and dehydrated and equally in need.

At last, the tender boats brought us to the shores of Persia.

Even those of us who were not ill, were hardly able to stand. On the beach we stood swaying and dizzy from sea-sickness as if we were still on the ship.

It was such a relief to have survived the journey. But sadly, our debarkation to freedom was also, for the many children who had died during the crossing, a funeral procession.

We were transported by lorries to the army camp a little further along the beach, where rows of army tents were pitched on the beach, right next to the clear sparkling blue sea. I will never forget the sight of them – how beautiful and clean they looked against the blue sky.

We were given water and some food. The following day, we were told, we would be given showers and deloused. Hair would be cut short or heads shaved, depending on how bad the lice were. In my vanity I was dreading this. Mama had borrowed some scissors from one of the hair cutters to chop off my plaits. 'They will have to come off Alinka!' she insisted, as I backed away from her in protest. 'Your only chance of keeping any of your hair is to cut it short and then I will pick out every single louse.' She spent the whole evening picking out every single louse, and when the other girls had to have their heads shaved and hair burnt, I was allowed to keep my short wavy bob, as I was no longer infested.

Gogiel-mogiel and halva sandwiches

After a period of quarantine on the warm, white sandy beaches, there were more long and uncomfortable journeys by lorry, often along treacherous mountain roads. Many of the children suffered from car sickness and vomited in the backs of the lorries. But life was beginning to be better.

During a brief stay at Ahvaz, one of Persia's oldest towns, we were put up in stables. It's an extremely hot and humid place, with temperatures reaching 53 degrees in the shade. In Persian, the word Ahvaz means hell. But we were stronger now, and clean. There was no disease, and there was water! There was a river, the Karun, and cool showers. In the evenings we played volleyball.

As we waited to be transported to a more permanent places we had libraries, and they their rehearsals for Mass

It was during our temporary stay at Teheran that we had the most memorable, never-to-be-forgotten first taste of Gogiel Mogiel.

We children were given, each day, a cup with raw egg yolk in it together with a few spoonfuls of sugar. We would sit outside in the sunshine, stirring the egg and sugar till it was smooth, then take a little lick. I would close my eyes to savour it, and sigh with absolute contentment, then stir and stir again before taking another lick. Oh how heavenly and delicious it tasted!

In Teheran our mother was able to find some work doing sewing jobs, and earned a little money. She was professional and very hardworking and conscientious, and her customers always went away very happy. She bought me my first pair of pretty shoes. They fitted me perfectly and were white and red; beautiful open, dress shoes. I was quite overwhelmed.

Tad and I now were given a little pocket money at times, and although we spent ages going through all the things we might buy with it, in the end we always bought exactly the same: halva and lipioszki. Halva is a sweet crumbly bar made of very finely ground sesame seeds and sugar, and Lipioszki were the local flat round breads – a bit like pitta bread.. We used to put the Halva inside the flat bread and have halva sandwiches. I can't tell you how good this tasted to us. We simply couldn't imagine anything better!

The hospitable Shah of Persia welcomed Polish refugees to his country. In Isfahan, he made available to the Polish children one of his own mansion houses with grounds, plus various other halls and large buildings as temporary camps.

It was here we were given our first beds to sleep on since leaving Poland. Having slept for so long on bug-infested hard wood, or dirt floors or blankets on the ground, here we were amazed to find rows and rows of proper beds with a pillow and clean sheets and blankets all neatly tucked in. That first evening I just stood looking at my bed in awe. I wasn't even sure how to get in it!

Life began to be good.

The American Red Cross helped with provisions, as did the Catholic Church and the British Red Cross.

Two hundred of the boys stayed in a Catholic monastery and a hundred girls in a convent. Both of these were supported by the Vatican and nicknamed 'the Holy Father's Hundreds'.

There were twenty establishments altogether set up for the Polish refugees, including an infirmary and schools. The orphanages were not called orphanages but schools, so the children in them would not be constantly reminded of their loss. But even those who still had their mother, as we did, were separated from them again during this time. Since most of our fathers were no longer with us, and we were so often parted from our mothers, we were growing up without a normal, family life.

I was put into establishment number six, with three hundred other 'girl cadets' of a similar age. Tad was in number fifteen.

We were eventually given a school uniform – a grey dress with a white collar. We wore these dresses every day so they soon became crumpled, but we devised a way of 'ironing' them each night. We would fold them carefully and place them between the mattress and the undersheet of the beds. As long as we didn't toss and turn too much in the night, by morning the dresses would be smoothed out from the heat and weight of our bodies. Not that there was much weight on our bodies!

Eating enough for thirteen days!

For the meals of the Polish refugees, there were once again, outdoor kitchens, with all the women taking turns for the kitchen duties. We sat outside to eat. There was enough food now, and we were so thankful for every bit of it, but I still always wished there was a bit more! Our bodies were catching up on two years of starvation, and food was always on our minds. In my diary at the time I wrote:

'In the morning a bell woke us up, and we washed and had breakfast. The tables for breakfast were under the trees. We had bread, jam and cocoa. After breakfast we went round and looked at the whole school. In the second courtyard there was a church and when I went in, I thought I was back in Poland. It was so very beautiful, in all designs.

The lunch they gave us was like the lunches I ate in Poland. There was sour cabbage soup, and for the main dish we had a meat burger and a full dish of potatoes and gravy and for desert there were grapes and pomegranates. This was really living, with food like that!

After lunch we played ball and the priest joined in. He is so kind and cheerful. In the evening we had supper and went to bed. In the morning it was the same. But the lunches are always different. Sometimes it's galabki, (Polish dish of cabbage leaves stuffed with meat and rice) sometimes goulash and cabbage, just as we used to have at home.'

When Christmas came, my thoughts kept returning to our father and the way he had died, and to our previous Christmas Eve, when things could not have been worse, with our mother lost in the blizzard, and wolves prowling on our straw roof. But this time there were proper Christmas celebrations, and good food to eat, and Midnight Mass to look forward to.

Heartfelt prayers were prayed for the souls of those who were no longer with us.

The staff went out of their way to show us kindness and even bought us little presents - some chalks or a handkerchief, a few walnuts or hazelnuts or dates. We were really touched by these gifts.

After we had our presents, we went into the dining room for Christmas Eve Wigilia supper. I was on duty for my table so I had to bring the food from the kitchen. There was potato salad, beetroot soup, rice with raisins and stewed fruit. There was plenty of everything.

After supper we sang carols and then went to sleep. I didn't even undress, because we were going to Midnight Mass. The church was so beautiful – lit up with candles and the altar all decorated and there was a crib in the side chapel.

On Boxing Day in the evening, there was a nativity play for the girl cadets, and at three o'clock for the other schools. Then we put on a special Polish national dance performance for the Armenians. On this occasion we danced three times, because the Armenians asked us to, and they applauded so loudly that our ears were bursting!'

After Christmas, unfortunately, for some reason, the food situation deteriorated. It was just bread and thin soup for lunch and dinner.

'Today is 24th January 1943, Sunday, and I am sitting and thinking about lunch because my stomach is rumbling. The girls who are on duty at the tables can eat plenty and I am waiting for my turn, because then I shall eat enough for thirteen days, enough to last me until my next turn on duty. Now I don't feel like studying because all we can think of is food – whether we will get an extra helping of soup or a little bit of something extra.'

After the Christmas holidays, school started again. We all took our school work very seriously and enthusiastically. We were keen to catch up on missed years of normal schooling, but it was hard at first to concentrate on what was being taught. Lessons were always outdoors, and at first I used to spend more time gazing up at the apples in the trees above our heads than listening to the lessons.

The teachers were themselves recovering from grief, deprivation and trauma, but they did their best for us, and were so generous with their time and totally dedicated. They introduced games and songs to make things easier for us and to help us to get to know each other.

After school there were scout and guide activities organised, games and songs, and cubs and Brownies, and we all joined these eagerly. Proudly and wholeheartedly we made our solemn promises to serve God and Poland and to help others. Our grey school uniforms were quickly changed into guide uniforms by adding a red and white cotton neckerchief.

I especially loved the huge camp fires, with sparks flying high into the dark sky, the heat of the fire on our faces, the cool of the night on our backs. I loved singing Polish songs again.

Slowly the hearts of all of us began to heal.

Five little visitors

It was no longer forbidden to go to church. Each day started with prayers and a hymn, which I loved, followed by a sermon caring first for the soul and then the body. There were also occasionally Litany prayers and Rosary as well as Mass. I used to watch some of the other girls running off up the hills to meet up with the boys instead of going to church, but not me. I must have taken after my father. We had received no religious formation of any kind for a long time, other than communist propaganda teaching us that Stalin was now our god, yet I was very much drawn to prayer. Perhaps it was because it made me feel closer to my father. Perhaps because I needed to hear the words of the priest explaining to us that God never promised us a life on this earth without suffering, that God himself sweated blood from anguish, that men tortured him, spat in his face and hammered nails in his hands and feet and killed him. But then came his glorious resurrection, opening wide the gates of heaven for all who follow him.

This same good, cheerful priest who played volleyball with us, and sang songs around the campfire with us, seemed to know the questions we had in our hearts and answered them all.

'But this isn't the only life he promised us. So lift up your hearts to him and offer him your tears; he will transform them into seeds of joy.'

He explained that God had given us freedom, because

without freedom there could be no love. 'It wasn't God who brought death into the world but man, in his freedom, rebelling against his creator. God is Life and when men rejected God they rejected Life. God is Love and he created us in his image – in the image of Love. When men rejected God they rejected love.'

I began at that time to pray in earnest for the souls in purgatory. I believed my father was already in heaven, but I prayed for those who were still in the place of purification. My heart was touched with compassion especially for those who had died all around us. I often prayed for them. Our priest read to us from the Bible that to pray for the souls of the dead was a great act of love, and this love helped to lift them into the brightness of heaven.

One morning, at dawn, as I woke - I do not think it was a dream because I was awake and didn't wake up again after it, five young girls came and stood by my bed, smiling to me with such love in their eyes. I looked at them in astonishment. Why were they up already; it was so early? They looked just like ordinary girls except for the radiance and gratitude in their eyes. For some reason, even though I wanted to ask them who they were, I stayed silent (not like me at all!) I just lay there looking at them and they stood there smiling at me, and then, all I can say is, they were gone. They just vanished. I leapt out of bed to see where they had gone to, but they had simply disappeared.

I couldn't stop thinking about them, and when I told the priest about it later, he asked if I'd been praying for the souls in purgatory. On hearing that I prayed every day, he said he thought they may have been the grateful souls of children whom I had helped into heaven with my prayers, coming to thank me. This frightened me and I stopped praying for the souls in purgatory for a while, but I have never forgotten it: even today I can remember them as clearly as if it had been this morning.

I wrote in my diary at that time:

'Today is Sunday, so we are going to church after breakfast. There will be green beans and schnitzels for lunch, and a nice soup.

News has come that that we are to leave Isfahan before the end of February, so in a few days, the transports start to leave for Africa. On Friday, the first convoy is to go with the orphans, and then we are to go - we are not absolutely sure, but it is probable.

I am worried because I have had no news from Mama and there is typhus in Camp Number One in Teheran – Mama is there. But on Wednesday there will be a transport from Tehran and perhaps she will be on it.'

Green tomato jam

To my great relief, we were reunited once again with our mother before the long journey to Africa.

All the older children had been transported with the Polish youth cadets to Palestine. I had so desperately wanted to go with them, since all my closest friends were amongst the Palestine-bound group. I had wept and begged, but hadn't been allowed to join them, as I was just under the age of the older groups. So I was now one of the eldest of the children who came to Africa.

What an experience it was, seeing our first black African people.

Now, the Kazak people in the Soviet Union had been strange enough to us who had never seen such foreign looking people before, with their yellow-brown skins and slanting eyes, but the shock of seeing our first native Africans was even greater, especially the ones that clustered around the train on the platforms when we first arrived.

The African huts that we were to live in were very simple, small mud huts with straw roofs and just a hole for a window; no glass was needed as it was so warm outside. Inside, just a bench and a table and a place to sleep. It was a tiny living space, but we couldn't have been more grateful if we had been given a palace to live in.

As in our camps in Persia, in Africa all the cooking was done in a huge outdoor communal kitchen which wasn't far away from our little mud hut. We went there three times a day, and everyone took their own aluminium army camping tins to eat out of. Everyone washed his or her own utensils and tins.

For breakfast it was always the same, day after day: a slice of bread with green tomato jam, and tea. For lunch we had potatoes or buckwheat or rice with some vegetable stew which sometimes had some meat in it.

Our mother had some work sewing again. Whenever people earned a little money, they saved it up until they had enough to buy a few chickens or ducks and kept these for eggs. Everyone's chickens would wander freely in the daytime but somehow knew which hut they belonged to and always came back in the evening. No one stole anyone else's chickens. Mama would occasionally kill one to make chicken soup for a special treat. That was so amazingly good.

We were getting older now, and life began to be fun. When we'd first arrived at the refugee camp (just outside Lusaka, which was just a very small town in those days), having been transported there from the station by lorries, the young people who had already been living in the camp some time gathered around to welcome us. With any new arrivals, in those days, there was always the hope of seeing again someone that you used to know.

As we were helped off the lorry, I looked round with interest at the crowd around us, and noticed a tall, fair-haired boy standing at the back of a group of boys. He stood out because he was the tallest, and like me, he must have been one of the eldest left behind when the older groups were moved to Palestine. I gave him a sympathetic smile as we were led away to our new quarters.

Beyond the refugee camp was the African bush.

There was a school already organised, mostly outdoors, and here I really began to enjoy my lessons and worked hard. I was able to learn quickly now, and we were taught all the subjects we would have been in Poland. There were very few books, but the teachers did their best from memory. We were given homework too – and here there were no indulgent young police officers to do it for me!

The 'Tree of Life'

One hot sunny afternoon, my friend Jadzia and I went beyond the camp to do some revising together. We sat in the shade, under a huge Baobab tree. These African trees are so enormous that even six grown men holding hands wouldn't be able to circle one. I loved those giants of Africa; it was just so good to see trees again of any kind, after the flat emptiness of the Steppes, but these were surely the most impressive I have ever seen. They are precious to that land as they store huge amounts of water inside their trunks. We were told that thirsty elephants occasionally ripped them apart to get to the water. It was because of this water storing capacity that the Africans call the Baobab the 'tree of life'.

So there we were, Jadzia and I, under a huge shady Baobab, revising for our matriculation exams, when two boys approached. One of them I recognised as the tall blond boy I'd seen when we'd first arrived at the camp, the other was dark haired. Of course, I immediately liked the look of the dark-haired boy, because, as I'd told my father years before, if I was going to marry, it was a dark-haired husband I wanted and dark haired children.

It was a shy 'Hi, what are you doing?' from the boys, and an equally scintillating 'Hello!' and 'We're revising,' from us girls.

They introduced themselves, and Ludwig, the dark haired one, seemed to be as taken with me as I was with him. The fair-haired one, however, not knowing he didn't stand a chance, kept managing to get into the conversation. His name was Witek. Witek Gryg. They stood around, chatting to us. There was no more revision done that day.

We agreed to meet up with them later that evening at the youth club barn, and that, although I didn't know it then, was the start of the rest of my life.

Many people, when they first meet the one they marry, remember a special song that was playing at the time, and that becomes their special song, or they have a special place, or a special date. But we had a special tree!

We met up that evening at the barn, all of us together; that's how things were done in those days. My friend Hela came along too. Although I liked Ludwig best at first, and although he was a really nice young man, the blond Witek was winning my attention more and more. He was so very determined and, for a quiet, shy boy, quite bold about asking if he could walk me home after the youth club meetings. He lived right across the other side of the camp so it was a long walk back for him in the dark afterwards. He soon began to ask if he could come over to see me in the day as well; eventually I agreed.

Before long he was coming over every single day, even if just for a brief hello. Come pouring rain or thunder and lightning, he always had to come and see me, and we began to get to know each other. The more I got to know him, the more I liked him. There was such a good-heartedness and gentleness about him which was winning my heart.

When we went walking out together in a group, the boys would often sing to us girls; songs like 'Szla Dzieweczka' (A girl walked to the woods) and other Polish folk and army songs. It wasn't at all like the intense romances today that grow too quickly and very often end equally quickly. When we went out it was always with a group, and it was a great thing because it gave us a chance to get to know each other well. There was always a lot of laughing and singing, we sometimes played cards or went for walks, or just sat around chatting.

Once there was a wedding in the town. One of the older Polish helpers was marrying a local white African. It was maybe two kilometres away from the camp and we all walked there, past the camp and the cemetery. For the first time in our lives, we tasted an alcoholic drink: sweet liqueurs, which tasted so delicious. We had no idea though how strong they were! The food was wonderful too; even to this day I remember it all. But my word, after those drinks, how we all sang and giggled and stumbled all the way back to the camp that night!

As silly as girls of fifteen often are!

For my birthday, Witek bought me a brooch from the one shop in the town that sold such things. He must have saved up a long time for it. I was the first girl in the camp to receive a bit of jewellery. It was beautiful and had little sparkly pink glass 'diamonds' in it. Now I had the problem of what to buy him for his birthday in April.

I wondered and agonised about it for a long time, as girls do about such things. Not that there was a lot of choice. It's hard to know what to buy for a boy. In the end I bought him a tie. He was the first of the boys in the camp to have one. Normally, in Africa, all the men and boys wore shorts as it was so hot, with short sleeved, open necked shirts, but whenever Witek came to visit me, he always put on his long trousers, and, once he'd received it, his tie. I always wore my brooch.

The younger boys would tease him when they saw him setting off looking so smart. 'There goes Gryg to see his Alinka!' they teased. And if they saw us together they would tease me by calling out 'Alinka Gryg! Alinka Gryg! Gryg, Gryg, Gryg!'

So, even though the African sun had bleached his hair even fairer and my olive skin grew darker, and even though in some ways we were very different, I slowly came round to the idea that maybe a boy as fair as a Polish summer corn field was not going to be such a bad thing after all.

My mother agreed. She said it wouldn't matter even if he had purple hair, as long as he had a good kind heart and would cherish me, that's what mattered. It was what my father had said to me all that time ago in Poland when we'd been sitting by the stream at the bottom of Aunty Anna's garden.

Ludwig, I was told, was heartbroken for a while, which I was truly sorry about, but he was good-natured and remained a close friend. There were other girls in the camp but he never really went out with any of them.

So there we were, growing up, and old enough to start romantic friendships, but we were still as silly as girls of fifteen often are. For instance, the toilets were not far from our little mud hut, whereas my best friend Hela lived quite a way in the opposite direction, yet in order to go to the toilets, I would often call on Hela first! I'd say, 'Hela come with me to the toilets!'

'Alinka, I've just been!'

'Hela! Come on, come with me!'

So Hela would come with me, and on the way there we'd exchange confidences and dreams, and on the way back, Hela would say, 'Come over to mine for a while.' And I always very gladly agreed. Compared to the rest of us, Hela was quite well off, as her father was still alive and still with her. This was a very rare thing in those days. It was because he had a limp and therefore hadn't been able to join the army, and was now earning regular money. Hela would talk and dream about Janek whom she really liked; he was very good-natured and very good looking

340

and danced really well, and all the girls really liked him. And I would talk about Witek.

And we would have a slice of bread with butter and mustard, which to me, brought up on a more frugal diet, tasted simply out of this world

Very sadly, Hela's handsome Janek was involved in a shooting accident. No one was quite sure what happened. He had gone over to a farm out in the bush, a place we all used to visit occasionally, as the farmer was known to us. This particular day, Janek had called round to our hut briefly, but wouldn't stay. He said he was off to the farm.

'Oh why go there Janek? Stay here with us!' I'd pleaded with him. He was always great company, and used to make us laugh. 'Hela will be coming over soon, and the others. Stay with us.'

Next thing we knew, he was in hospital, in a coma, with a gunshot wound to the head. We all went to visit him in hospital. His head was all wrapped in bandages, and he was still in the coma, from which, sadly, he never recovered. Although we were all accustomed to death in those days, and bereavement, Janek's death shocked us all. No one ever really knew what happened, and we never found out, but some suspected the farmer of foul play.

Hela never really recovered from it.

Strangers once again
in a foreign land

When the war ended, the other allied nations were celebrating being back home at last in their own lands. Poland, however, was still under the same regime that for the first two years of the war had been allied with Hitler.

It was therefore impossible for us to return home and live normal, peaceful lives. Our brave Polish soldiers had gained a reputation for the courage they had consistently shown while fighting against the Nazis for the freedom of Europe, yet, in the end, their own country was badly let down by the very allies they had so bravely helped.

Stalin was allowed to keep the land he had acquired by mass murder, brutality and debauchery.

Many countries throughout the world, however, filled with compassion at the betrayal and injustice the Poles had received, were opening their borders to Polish refugees: New Zealand, Australia, Canada, America, England. They were all just names on a map to us. We knew very little about them.

Then it was announced that those who had a brother or father in the Polish army now in England, could emigrate there. Since Witek and I both had a brother in the forces in England, it meant we could travel and stay together. We therefore agreed to emigrate to England.

We sailed away from the sunshine and warmth of Africa with an aching in our hearts. It was a wrench to leave the land that had welcomed us so generously and hospitably, that had warmed us and helped to heal so many wounds. The land where we had first met and fallen in love, and where we had spent the precious days of our youth - the land of our Baobab tree

We arrived in England on a cold grey drizzly day, without any warm or waterproof clothes, with no money, and unable to speak the language.

Once again we were penniless strangers in a foreign land. But we were no strangers to poverty, hardship and hard work. We were alive; so many were not. And we had each other.

A year later Witek and I were married in the Polish church in Manchester, and that was the start of yet another of life's greatest adventures.

Epilogue

Witek's younger brother Antony, emigrated from England to Canada, where he found a warm welcome and a home for his adventurous heart. He became an artist and presented Witek and Alinka with a huge painting of their Baobab tree as their wedding gift. Sixty-three years later, it still hangs in pride of place in their front room.

Peter, the eldest of Witek's brothers, the strong and brave one, became one of the youngest of the soldiers in the Polish army that won worldwide renown for its courage. He was wounded at Monte Cassino.

Although he worked all his working life in the same factory as Witek, his passion for gardening in his free time kept the whole extended family in spinach, sorrel, lettuces, beetroot, fresh parsley, tomatoes, cucumbers dill, raspberries and gooseberries and all sorts of other good things. His allotment had a home-made greenhouse made from recycled scrap, amazing grafted apple trees, and roses grown from cuttings. It was one of the best kept allotments in Manchester, and reminiscent of their Gajowka garden in Poland.

He also taught himself to play the accordion by ear. The highlight and joy of every family celebration gathering was when he would take the precious battered old instrument out of its case and begin to play. He would play Polish folk songs and army songs, and polkas to dance to. We danced, we sang along; I could have listened to him all night.

Alinka and Witek have lived in England for over sixty years. God willing, they will soon be celebrating their sixty-third wedding anniversary. They had three children. I was their first daughter, their middle child.

They both worked in factories all their working lives, and none of us ever heard them complain.

Witek worked in an asbestos factory sweeping up the dust for three years, and after that as a stone grinder on piecework; noisy, dusty work that has left him a little deaf. I remember him setting off for work when it was still dark, on his old black bike, with his ex-army knapsack over his shoulder. Even in the pouring rain and sleet, he went out, with the sandwiches our mother had prepared for him the night before, with a cheerful goodbye to us.

He was loved and respected by friends, neighbours and co-workers in the factory, and everyone he came into contact with. He was always patient and willing to lend a hand to anyone in need.

Alinka worked first as a waitress in a miner's canteen, where she was often asked out on dates by the miners, until it was explained to them that she was already spoken for. She then worked long hours in a noisy, dusty cotton mill in Lancashire, getting up before 5am in order to make the two bus journeys to the mill.

Eventually, she was accepted for packing work at Kellogg's factory nearer home, where, in spite of language barriers, she soon became popular with everyone and was promoted from packer to quality control inspector. She tells how she came home in tears after being offered the promotion, because she couldn't write in English and was convinced she'd never learn how to fill in the quality control charts which the job entailed. She learned quickly though, and enjoyed the job, which was more leisurely than packing, so there was more time to chat to everyone around her!

Alinka's mother Maria lived with Alinka and Witek in their terraced house in Old Trafford, Manchester until she died. She was my grandmother. She was the one who introduced us to the delights of cucumber dipped in sugar, potato pancakes, home-made apple cake and brandy-butter-iced nut torte at Christmas.

She was the first to tell us of their lives in Poland and Siberia and Africa. She was a generous, grateful and good-hearted woman.

Witek's mother, Anna, a quiet, kind and gentle lady, lived with Peter and his wife, in their terraced house which was only a five minute walk away from Witek and Alina's house.

Witek still has his beloved Alinka, and, both retired now, they live a quiet peaceful life, tending their little front garden that is always full of flowers, going to Mass each morning, and praying together for all those suffering throughout the world. They help locally as much as they can, giving lifts or visiting the sick, the housebound, the hospitalised, and anyone in need, be they neighbours, friends or strangers.

Hospitality and generosity is their way of life. 'A guest

in the house, is God in the house!' is Alinka's constant refrain, and the very best of what they have is always offered to any visitor to eat. Everyone is treated with equal respect, irrespective of their beliefs or lifestyle, be it the parish priest, the two young men who live next door, a Hindu neighbour, a single mother in need, or the Muslims who pass by their house daily on the way to the mosque.

In their own small way, they have made this drizzly grey land a warmer, kinder place.

Happiness comes from love, as light comes from the sun.

Henryk Sienkiewicz. Nobel Prize for literature winner

Acknowledgements

My warmest thanks to:

My uncle Antek for his gift to me of three C90 cassette tapes on which he had recorded the story of their family's lives during the war years.

My daughter, Annie Latham, for an absolutely splendid job editing and proof reading.

My daughter-in-law, Emma Latham, for the beautiful cover design and professional formatting.

My sister Renia Williamson for her constant encouragement over the three years it has taken to write this book.

Leo Madigan for his professional help and encouragement.

And last, but not at all least, my husband Alan, for his patience and all his help and support throughout the writing of this book.

3657655R10193

Printed in Great Britain
by Amazon.co.uk, Ltd.,
Marston Gate.